THE AUTHOR   Stephen G. Haw read Chinese at the University of Oxford and has an MA degree from the University of London. He first visited China in 1980 and then lived there for two years as a student and teacher at the University of Shandong. Since returning to Britain he has made frequent visits to China, travelling extensively around the country. In 1994 he journeyed by road right across eastern Tibet, an area seen by very few foreigners, and later spent four weeks cruising the Yangtze River between Nanjing and Chongqing. Since then, he has made several more adventurous journeys in western China and Tibet. He is the author of numerous articles and of *The Lilies of China* and *China: A cultural history*.

SERIES EDITOR   Professor Denis Judd is a graduate of Oxford, a Fellow of the Royal Historical Society and Professor of History at the University of North London. He has published over 20 books including the biographies of Joseph Chamberlain, Prince Philip, George VI and Alison Uttley, historical and military subjects, stories for children and two novels. His most recent book is the highly praised *Empire: The British Imperial Experience from 1765 to the Present*.

Other Titles in the Series

A Traveller's History of Australia
A Traveller's History of Canada
A Traveller's History of The Caribbean
A Traveller's History of England
A Traveller's History of France
A Traveller's History of Greece
A Traveller's History of The Hundred Years War
A Traveller's History of India
A Traveller's History of Ireland
A Traveller's History of Italy
A Traveller's History of Japan
A Traveller's History of London
A Traveller's History of Mexico
A Traveller's History of North Africa
A Traveller's History of Oxford
A Traveller's History of Paris
A Traveller's History of Portugal
A Traveller's History of Scotland
A Traveller's History of South East Asia
A Traveller's History of Spain
A Traveller's History of Turkey
A Traveller's History of The USA

THE TRAVELLER'S HISTORY SERIES

'Ideal before-you-go reading' *The Daily Telegraph*

'An excellent series of brief histories' *New York Times*

'I want to compliment you . . . on the brilliantly concise contents of your books' *Shirley Conran*

Reviews of Individual Titles

A Traveller's History of China
'In order to make the most of a visit to China such portable pocket-size guides as this are most useful.'
The China Quarterly

A Traveller's History of Japan
'It succeeds admirably in its goal of making the present country comprehensible through a narrative of its past, with asides on everything from bonsai to *zazen*, in a brisk, highly readable style . . . you could easily read it on the flight over, if you skip the movie.' *The Washington Post*

A Traveller's History of France
'Undoubtedly the best way to prepare for a trip to France is to bone up on some history. *The Travellers' History of France* by Robert Cole is concise and gives the essential facts in a very readable form.'
The Independent

A Traveller's History of India
'For anyone . . . planning a trip to India, the latest in the excellent Traveller's History series . . . provides a useful grounding for those whose curiosity exceeds the time available for research.' *The London Evening Standard*

A Traveller's History of China

Author's acknowledgements

Many people have assisted me to further my understanding of China. I would particularly like to mention Mr Raymond Dawson, my tutor at the University of Oxford, and all my other teachers, there and at the University of Shandong. The British Council awarded me the scholarship which enabled me to study in China. Finally I must acknowledge my great debt to the people of China, and particularly to my close friends there, who have played the major role in enlarging my comprehension.

Publisher's Note

Parts of this book originally appeared in Stephen G. Haw's previous book *China: A Cultural History* which is now out of print.

A Traveller's History of China

THIRD EDITION

STEPHEN G. HAW

Series Editor   DENIS JUDD

CASSELL
A WINDRUSH PRESS BOOK

First published in the United Kingdom in 1995 by The Windrush Press.
This edition reprinted in association with Weidenfeld & Nicolson, 2002

ISBN 0-304-36470-3

Typeset by Archetype IT Ltd, Cheltenham
Printed and bound in Great Britain by Mackays of Chatham

Cassell Reference
Wellington House
125 Strand
London WC2R 0BB

The Windrush Press
Windrush House, Adlestrop
Moreton-in-Marsh
Gloucestershire GL56 0YN
Telephone: 01608 658758
Fax: 01608 659345

Contents

Preface   ix

CHAPTER ONE: **Introduction**   1

CHAPTER TWO: **Geographical Perspectives**   11

CHAPTER THREE: **The Origins of Chinese Civilization,**
Prehistory to 771 BC   34

CHAPTER FOUR: **The Formation of China,** *771–221 BC*   57

CHAPTER FIVE: **Confucianism and Religion,**
221 BC–AD 589   75

CHAPTER SIX: **China and the Outside World,** *589–1279*   96

CHAPTER SEVEN: **China under Foreign Domination,**
1279–1842   121

CHAPTER EIGHT: **The Collapse of Empire,** *1842–1911*   154

CHAPTER NINE: **Chinese Revolutions,** *1911–98*   178

CHAPTER TEN: **Life in China Today**   201

CHAPTER ELEVEN: **The Minority Races**   220

CHAPTER TWELVE: **Hong Kong, Taiwan and the**
Future   235

The Chinese Language and Chinese Characters   251

Chronology of Major Events   257

List of Dynasties and Selected Rulers   263

Further Reading   269

Historical Gazetteer   273

Index   303

MAPS   **China: physical**   12

China in *c.* **560 BC**   60

China in *c.* **300 BC**   74

China in *c.* **210 BC**   76

China in *c.* **AD 1050**   112

Provinces and regions of China today   202

Preface

China remains one of the most self-contained and hence inscrutable countries in the world. One major obstacle to understanding China and the Chinese better is, of course, the language, in both its written and spoken form. The complexity of a language based upon individual symbols rather than upon an alphabet is, comfortingly perhaps, also a problem for the Chinese themselves. As Stephen Haw says in this outstandingly clear and comprehensive book ' . . . in order to become literate in Chinese, it is necessary not just to learn a couple of dozen letters of the alphabet and the correct way to combine them, but to commit to memory many hundreds, and perhaps thousands of characters.' It is small wonder that the Chinese government has plans to introduce an alphabet.

Another difficulty in coming to terms with China is simply its size. It is the third largest country in the world, with 9000 miles of land frontier and contains a fifth of the human race. Tourists to China can only begin to explore this vast area, and often get no further than the major coastal conurbations, or well-known sites. Even if the visitor has the time to explore the country more fully, the result can often be confusion rather than enlightenment as the often striking differences between the different regions and people are absorbed.

Western perceptions of China are not always helpful either. The long history of Chinese civilisation is somewhat routinely accepted, and yet this contrasts with a host of more hostile perceptions which are frequently based upon the political imperatives of former European and United States' imperial ideologies as well as upon the propaganda battle-lines imposed by the Cold War. As a result, China is still associated, superficially at least, with an impoverished, toiling peasantry, with a tyrannical landlordism, and with a traditional and vindictive rejection of the foreigner and his 'barbaric' habits.

The flip side of this, however, was the tendency to mock and ridicule the supposed characteristics of the Chinese. Behind all of this, arguably, was, and is, a potent compound of fear and awe. After all, the Chinese not merely invented paper, gun powder and the compass, but also produced artistic works much desired in the West. But China also posed a threat. Anxiety at the prospect of the huge population somehow swamping less densely peopled lands was responsible for the widespread perception of the 'Yellow Peril' during the nineteenth and early twentieth centuries – that a Chinese diaspora did in fact take place was token of the danger lurking in the wings. Moreover, Chinese civilisation seemed bafflingly impervious to European imperialism. Western military and technical superiority was eventually able to force open the door to trade with China and even to acquire territory in the shape of 'treaty ports' – like Hong Kong – but Christian missionaries made comparatively little headway against long-established philosophies.

The Communist Revolution seemed to throw down a further challenge to the capitalist West, especially when the entry of Chinese troops into the Korean War looked likely, for a while, to affect the outcome, and when the 'new' China not merely energetically set about raising the living standards of its own people but also declared its active support for the anti-imperialist struggle on a global scale.

As Stephen Haw so effectively demonstrates in this remarkably illuminating study, we have certainly moved on from there. There has been *rapprochement* with the West, which now sees China as a lucrative market and place of investment rather than the homeland of an aggressive and doctrinaire 'red peril'. Hong Kong is in the process of being restored to Chinese control. The Chinese government is experimenting with a variety of economic forms. Above all, the foreign visitor is positively welcomed. He or she should equip themselves with this invaluable guide before they depart.

Denis Judd, London, 1995

CHAPTER ONE

Introduction

China is a great nation. It has an ancient culture of major historical importance, and is now emerging as one of the foremost powers of the modern world. It is the third largest country in the world and the most populous, with about one-fifth of the world's total population. It dominates the Pacific coastline of the continent of Asia, and shares 9,000 miles of land frontier with more than a dozen other states, including India, Pakistan and Russia. Modern communications make it as easy to reach Beijing or Shanghai from London or New York as it is to get to Singapore, Sydney or Nairobi. Yet China remains little known and poorly understood; few foreigners learn its language or study its history and culture. Although foreign trade and tourism have increased dramatically during the last decade or so, they are only very slowly leading to any changes in foreign perceptions of China. Barriers of ignorance and misconception are not easily overcome.

WESTERN VIEWS OF CHINA
The history of Western conceptions of China is an interesting study in itself. Seven centuries ago, Marco Polo returned from several years of service with the Mongol conqueror, Khubilai Khan, to give an account of the magnificence and wealth of China which severely taxed the credulity of his medieval European contemporaries. During the eighteenth century, the wisdom of Confucius and Chinese methods of government were extolled by the philosophers of the Enlightenment, who perceived a Chinese model for their theories of 'benevolent despotism'. Things Chinese were in great vogue in the latter half of the eighteenth century, and the fashion for *chinoiserie* left a lingering

1

impression on European design ('willow pattern' porcelain being perhaps the most lasting relic of this taste).

But by the late nineteenth century Western ideas of China had changed remarkably. It was now seen as a land of poverty, of teeming masses labouring under the yoke of corrupt and tyrannical rulers, and in a benighted state of heathenism. This was largely based on the views of Protestant missionaries, who entered China in large numbers after the Treaties of Nanjing (1842) and Tianjin (1858, ratified in 1860). This drastic change in Western attitudes occurred despite the widely-held (though erroneous) opinion that China was unchanging, and had been so since ancient times. Oliver Goldsmith, in *The Citizen of the World*, wrote of China as 'an Empire which has continued thus invariably the same for such a long succession of ages', and Hegel declared that China had 'no history', to the extent that it was 'a state which exists today as we know it to have been in ancient times'. Even those who had lived for many years in China and knew it well were of this opinion. The missionary Medhurst stated that 'her language and her customs remain unaltered, and the genius and spirit of the people are the same as they were in the patriarchal age'. Such a view was much fostered by the Chinese themselves, who were always anxious to find ancient authority for their institutions.

Even in very recent times there have been drastic changes in views of China. Especially remarkable was the reversal of official United States policy towards the People's Republic of China during the 1970s. From being a 'red menace', fought against bitterly during the Korean War two decades previously, unrecognized and under a trade embargo, the People's Republic suddenly became a friend and potential ally. Official visits at the highest level were exchanged, and US opposition to the replacement of the Nationalists of Taiwan with the Communists of the mainland in the United Nations was precipitately withdrawn. The most astonishing aspect of this about-turn was its suddenness, the complete process requiring less than ten years.

Though it could be argued that changing Western views of China have had some basis in reality, there is no doubt that they have generally been seriously flawed by their lack of balance and completeness. 'Nothing could be more fallacious than to judge of China by any

European standard', as Lord Macartney, first British ambassador to China, wrote in 1794. The extreme complexity of Chinese culture and society have made it very difficult for foreigners to achieve a sound understanding of the country. Perhaps the most common popular vision of China among Westerners is of a land of peasants wearing round, conical hats, working their flooded rice-fields with the aid of water-buffaloes. This cannot be said to be a totally inaccurate vision, for it is true of *part* of China (it is, in fact, largely based on the coastal province of Fujian, the ports of which were for many years the main centres of the China tea trade). But it is so incomplete as to be seriously misleading. This is *not* what most of China is like, and it is not a sound foundation on which to build a fuller understanding of the Chinese nation and its people.

Even those who have been to China are rarely able to achieve an adequate understanding of what they have seen and experienced. The impressions formed by visitors are not simple responses to objective facts. They are coloured by all kinds of preconceptions, by comparisons and contrasts between conditions in China and in the visitors' own countries, and by the way in which the Chinese present their country to foreigners (and many Chinese themselves have a very narrow view of China, restricted by their own limited experience of the country beyond their native area and by the prejudices of national pride). It is often the case that the longer foreign visitors remain, the harder it is for them to feel certain of their impressions. There is a saying that someone who visits China for a week will go home and write a book about it, someone who spends a month there will write no more than an article, and someone who remains for a year or more will be unable to write anything. There is certainly no lack of books written by people with no more than a very limited experience of China and no real understanding of the country at all. These of course merely add to the already considerable quantity of misinformation about China.

My own excuse for producing yet another book about China is that, despite the fact that I once lived there for as long as two years, and have made many shorter visits over a period of twenty years, I feel able to rationalize my often conflicting impressions and reactions, to produce a view of China, her people and her culture that has some genuine value.

It is my greatest hope that readers of this book will obtain from it at least a slightly less defective view of China than they had previously. I do not flatter myself that I can realistically expect to achieve much more than this.

It is important to achieve a better understanding of China for several reasons. Perhaps the most prominent of these is that China is well on the way to becoming a world superpower, with influence which is already very significant. China's past contributions to world development have also been substantial, and may only be ignored at the risk of seriously detracting from our understanding of historical processes. Comparative studies of Chinese and Western development can be very instructive. We would, moreover, be missing an immense opportunity to enrich our lives, were we not to attempt to gain insight into the varied and ancient culture of this great Far Eastern civilization. As Lord Curzon, Viceroy of India from 1898 until 1905, once declared:

> The East is a University in which the scholar never takes his degree. It is a temple where the suppliant adores but never catches sight of the object of his devotion. It is a journey the goal of which is always in sight but is never attained.

This is rather fancifully worded, but otherwise expresses very well my own feelings about China. The study of its history and culture is fascinating, and even in a lifetime it is scarcely possible to do more than scratch the surface.

The Chinese Language

One of the greatest barriers to improving comprehension of China is the difficulty of attaining fluency in the language. Chinese is rather simple in its grammatical structure, but contains certain sounds, and a system of tones, which are not easy for most foreigners to master. To speakers of European (and, indeed, the great majority even of Asian) languages, it is unfamiliar in almost every respect; there are no similarities of vocabulary such as those which assist speakers of English in learning French or German. Yet it is not learning to *speak* Chinese which is the real problem. It is learning to read and write it which is the most formidable task. Even the Chinese find this hard: it takes years longer for children in Chinese schools to become adequately literate than it does for children learning a language written with an alphabetic script.

WRITING

Chinese is not written with an alphabet. Instead it uses characters, individual symbols which fundamentally each represent a complete word. Thus, in order to become literate in Chinese, it is necessary not just to learn a couple of dozen letters of the alphabet and the correct ways to combine them, but to commit to memory many hundreds, and preferably several thousands, of characters. An unfamiliar word written alphabetically can often be read and pronounced more or less correctly, even if not understood. Perhaps it will be recognized as a word known in speech though never seen written down before. But an unfamiliar Chinese character contains little or no clue to its pronunciation. The word may be familiar in speech but unrecognizable when written. Although almost all Chinese characters originally contained pictorial elements, and the majority also included phonetic elements which gave some idea of pronunciation, they have changed so much since their origins in the distant past that these elements are now of very limited use. The great Chinese writer of the twentieth century, Lu Xun, called Chinese writing 'a fearful legacy left us by our forebears'.

The problems of writing with characters are so great that the Chinese government has decided that they should eventually be replaced by an alphabetic system. This, however, is a proposal for the long-term future, one which seems to become ever more remote. Chinese will continue to be written with characters for many years to come. For those interested to know more about this subject, an essay on the Chinese language and Chinese characters appears on p. 251–6.

TRANSLITERATION OF CHINESE

Readers will probably be glad to know that no Chinese characters will appear in the main text. But although this solves one problem, it creates another. Since it is impossible to write a book about China without referring at least to a few places and people with Chinese names, these names will have to be somehow transposed from their original characters into the Roman alphabet. This would be a simple enough procedure if there were only one way to transliterate Chinese, and if the resulting transliterations were reasonably easy for those not familiar with them to read and pronounce. But since there are several sounds in Chinese which do not occur in Western languages, there have naturally been many differing attempts to represent them in Roman characters, none of which have in the end made it easy for the untrained reader to arrive at pronunciations close to the original Chinese. So at this stage I shall set out the transliteration system which will be used throughout this book, and try to explain its pronunciation.

The system I shall use is called 'Pinyin'. It was devised in the People's Republic of China, and may eventually be used to replace characters entirely. It is arguably not the best system ever devised for the transliteration of Chinese, but is very little worse than any other and has distinct advantages over most. It is now widely recognized and has become more or less standard, so the use of any other system would only increase confusion.

The pronunciation of Modern Standard Chinese in Pinyin transliteration

Modern Standard Chinese (*putonghua*) is the national language of China, taught in schools throughout the country. It is largely based on the Mandarin dialect as spoken today in Beijing.

Each syllable of Modern Standard Chinese consists of one or more of the following elements:

1) An initial consonant (e.g. *p, t, g, sh*).
2) A semi-vowel (*i* or *u*, written *y* and *w* as initials).
3) A final vowel (which may include the nasal sounds *n* or *ng*), or a diphthong (e.g. *a, e, o, an, in, eng, ai, ou*).

A vowel or diphthong may occur alone (e.g. *e, an, ai*), with an initial consonant only (e.g. *ba, pi, dan, lai*), with an initial semi-vowel only (e.g. *yang, wang*) or with both initial consonant and semi-vowel (e.g. *biao, dian, xue, shuang*). In addition, each syllable has a tone, which may be indicated in Pinyin by a tone-mark over the vowel. Tones will be ignored here.

Most of the letters used in the Pinyin system are pronounced more or less as they usually are in English, and should present no great difficulties. Some, however, are pronounced in a way which is not obvious, and a few represent sounds for which there simply is no near equivalent in English or any other European language.

The letters most likely to cause problems are:

c	pronounced like *ts*;
zh	pronounced like *dj*;
q	pronounced like *ch*, but lighter and more aspirated;
x	pronounced like *sh*, but lighter and more aspirated.

If these four are remembered, most Chinese names should be pronounced more or less correctly.

For those who wish to come closer to the original Chinese sounds, a more complete table of pronunciations follows. It must be remembered, however, that in many cases only a rough indication of pronunciation can be given.

a	as in *father*
e	usually like *a* in *ago*; except in the combination *ye*, which is pronounced like *yeah*, and after the semi-vowels *i* and *u*, when it is pronounced like *e* in *pen*
i	like *ee* in *bee*; *except* after *z, c, s, sh, zh, ch, r*, when it is pronounced somewhat like *r* (a sound not found in English)
o	like *au* in *author*
u	like *oo* in *too*; *except* after *y, j, q, x* and when written with an umlaut (*ü*), when it is pronounced like French *u* or German *ü*
ai	like *ie* in *pie*
ei	like *ay* in *day*
ao	like *ow* in *how*
ou	like *ow* in *low*
an	usually as in *ran* (with a northern English accent); *except* after *y* and *i*, when it is more like *en* in *hen*
ong	like *ung* in *dung* (with a northern English accent)
ui	like *way*

z   like *dz*
j   like *j*, but lighter (pronounced further forward in the mouth)
r   like a combination of French *j* as in *je* with English *r* as in *root*

Names of people in Chinese commonly consist of two or three characters, the first of which is the family name and the other one or two the personal name (there are a very few two-character family names). These are written in Pinyin with a space only between the family name and the personal name (e.g. *Wang Wei, Mao Zedong*). No gap is left in the transliteration of a two-character personal name. Similarly, names of places consisting of two or more characters are often written with no space in transliteration (e.g. *Nanjing, Shijiazhuang*). Occasionally this could lead to confusion – for example, *xi* and *an* are two separate syllables, but when written together without a space they become indistinguishable from the syllable *xian*. Similarly, is *jinan* a combination of *ji* and *nan* or *jin* and *an*? To overcome difficulties of this kind, an apostrophe is placed to mark the division, as in *xi'an* and *ji'nan*.

A number of Chinese place-names have become widely familiar in transliterations different from those of the Pinyin system. Peking is the most obvious example; in Pinyin it is written Beijing. Some of the differences between the two spellings arise from different means of representing the same sound – the 'P' of Peking and the 'B' of Beijing are an example; but many of the differences result from the fact that the older transliterations actually represent an old pronunciation which is no longer current in standard Chinese. Thus the sound represented by the 'k' in Peking has now softened to the 'j' of Beijing. Some of the old forms were based on Chinese dialect pronunciations; this is particularly true of the names of places in south-east China. It is also the case that many of these old transcriptions are now pronounced in a way never originally intended – 'Peking' was not supposed to be pronounced 'Pee-king'. For all these reasons, and in the interests of standardization, all place names will be written in their Pinyin transliterations in this book.

The names of Chinese provinces are particularly liable to cause confusion, as the Pinyin versions are sometimes not very easily recognized by those familiar with their old 'post office' forms. Here is a complete table of equivalents.

Old form	Pinyin	Old form	Pinyin
Heilungkiang	Heilongjiang	Sinkiang	Xinjiang
Kirin	Jilin	Tsinghai	Qinghai
Liaoning	Liaoning	Szechwan	Sichuan
Hopei	Hebei	Yunnan	Yunnan
Shantung	Shandong	Kweichow	Guizhou
Honan	Henan	Kwangsi	Guangxi
Kiangsu	Jiangsu	Kwangtung	Guangdong
Anhwei	Anhui	Fukien	Fujian
Hupei	Hubei	Chekiang	Zhejiang
Shansi	Shanxi	Kiangsi	Jiangxi
Shensi	Shaanxi	Hunan	Hunan
Kansu	Gansu	Taiwan	Taiwan
Ningsia	Ningxia		

I shall, however, continue to use the familiar names Tibet and Inner Mongolia, which are long established in English usage, and are in any case not romanizations of Chinese names. Manchuria is occasionally used in this book as a name for the whole of the extreme north-east of China, comprising the three provinces of Heilongjiang, Jilin and Liaoning. The term Chinese Turkestan indicates a region more or less identical with Xinjiang, which already formed part of the Turkic Uighur empire as early as the eighth century AD.

The words 'China' and 'Chinese' are themselves ambiguous, insofar as they may be used either of the whole of what is now politically China and its population, or of the area in which Chinese culture is predominant and of people of Chinese race. Thus Tibet is politically part of China but is culturally distinct. The Tibetan people are Chinese in the sense that they are citizens of China, but are not ethnically Chinese. Equally, many British and US citizens are ethnic Chinese but are not citizens of China.

The Chinese race is referred to in China as Han. Thus, where it is necessary to avoid confusion I shall refer to people of Chinese race as Han or Han Chinese. The area culturally and politically dominated by the Han has altered considerably within historical times, but for about the last 2,000 years has included more or less all of what is now China, with the exception of Tibet, Qinghai, Xinjiang, Inner Mongolia, Taiwan and most of Manchuria. Parts of other provinces in the south and south-west, especially mountainous areas of Sichuan and Yunnan, have also been outside the main area of Chinese culture. This core area of Han settlement will occasionally be designated in this book by the term 'China Proper'.

CHAPTER TWO

Geographical Perspectives

It is impossible to achieve any very sound understanding of China's history and culture without a knowledge of their geographical framework. The climate and physical structure of China have had a decisive influence on the development of the Chinese people and their civilization, and continue to be of fundamental importance.

China is very large. It is rather bigger than the United States of America, and almost as large as the whole of Europe (including European Russia). A country of such size would be expected to be diverse, but China's climate and physical geography must be the most varied of any country in the world. Northern Manchuria extends to roughly 54° N latitude and has a climate similar to that of neighbouring Siberia, while substantial parts of Guangdong, Guangxi, Yunnan and Taiwan lie within the tropics. In the west are vast deserts and towering mountains. The northern slopes of the great Himalayan range edge the high plateau of Tibet, the 'roof of the world'; the summit of the world's highest mountain, Mt Qomolangma (Everest), stands on the border between Nepal and Chinese Tibet. Beyond the northern edge of the plateau lie the Tarim Basin, filled largely by the Taklimakan Desert, and the Turpan Depression, 150 metres below sea level. Great rivers rise on the plateau of Tibet and Qinghai, flowing eastwards through the fertile and populous lowlands of China to the sea.

China extends across some 60 degrees of longitude. Xinjiang shares common borders with Afghanistan and Pakistan, at around 74° E; Manchuria has a long border with Korea, and stretches beyond this towards the Russian city of Khabarovsk, to almost 135° E. The sun rises more than two hours later in Xinjiang than it does in Heilongjiang.

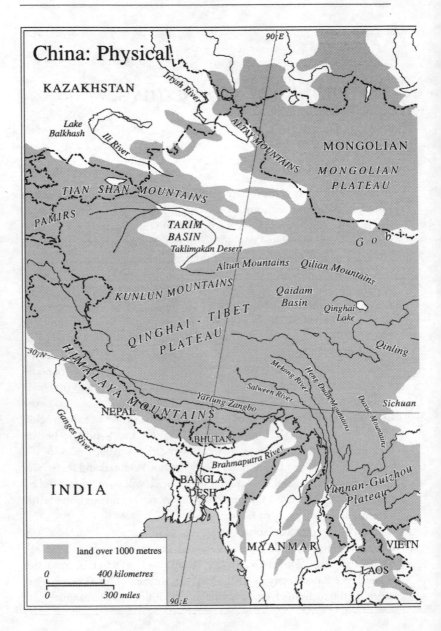

China: Physical

KAZAKHSTAN

MONGOLIAN

*MONGOLIAN
PLATEAU*

90°E

Irtysh River

ALTAY MOUNTAINS

*Lake
Balkhash*

Ili River

TIAN SHAN MOUNTAINS

PAMIRS

*TARIM
BASIN*

Taklimakan Desert

Altun Mountains   *Qilian Mountains*

G o b i

KUNLUN MOUNTAINS

*Qaidam
Basin*

*Qinghai
Lake*

*QINGHAI - TIBET
PLATEAU*

Qinling

30°N

HIMALAYA MOUNTAINS

Mekong River

Heng Duan Mountains

Daxue Mountains

Sichuan

Salween River

Yarlung Zangbo

NEPAL

Ganges River

BHUTAN

Brahmaputra River

*BANGLA
DESH*

*Yunnan-Guizhou
Plateau*

INDIA

MYANMAR

VIETN

LAOS

land over 1000 metres

0   400 kilometres

0   300 miles

90°E

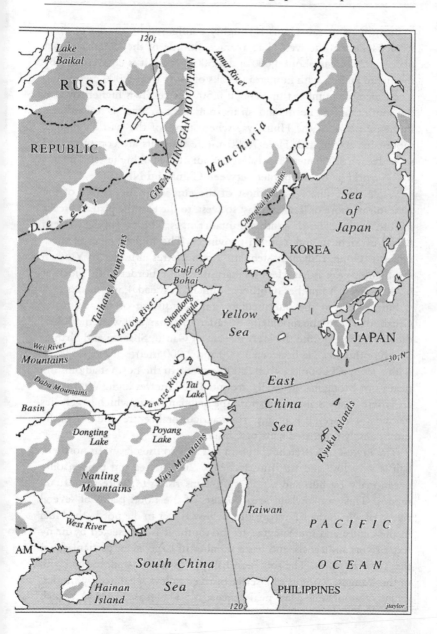

From west to east China is roughly configured in a series of three steps, highest in the west. The average altitude of the Qinghai–Tibet plateau is between about 3,000 and 4,500 metres. It is criss-crossed by mountain ranges, with numerous peaks of more than 5,000 metres and a considerable number rising above 6,500 metres. It is higher towards the south than the north, and on its southern rim ascends towards the immense peaks of the Himalaya, where most of the world's highest mountains are located. Here 7,000-metre summits are common, and several reach 8,000 metres and above. Four of the ten highest mountains in the world lie on the border between China and Nepal.

While the Himalaya and most of the ranges on the surface of the plateau run more or less from east to west, to the east the plateau breaks up into a series of north–south mountain ranges. These form the western halves of Sichuan and Yunnan provinces. The highest peak of these ranges is Gongga Shan in Sichuan, 7,556 metres altitude. In Yunnan the highest peak is Mt Meili (Kakarpo), on the border with Tibet, at 6,740 metres. A number of other mountains exceed 4,500 metres.

Further east is the intermediate step, consisting of the Yunnan–Guizhou plateau, the mountains of eastern Sichuan and western Hubei, the Qinling range and the loess plateau of Gansu, Shaanxi and Shanxi. Much of this area lies between 1,000 and 2,000 metres above sea level, with a few peaks of more than 3,000 metres. In the north it adjoins the plateau of Mongolia, generally around 1,000 metres high. Within this area there is one major depression, the Sichuan Basin, which largely lies below 500 metres. It is an important agricultural centre, and one of the most densely populated parts of China.

The lowest step stretches beyond this area to the ocean. Its northern half is very low and flat, mostly below 200 metres and broken only occasionally by hills and a few mountains rising to more than 1,000 metres. This vast lowland area consists of the flood plains of several rivers, of which the largest are the Yellow River in the north, the Huai in the centre and the Yangtze to the south. It is intersected by many lesser rivers and canals, and has a number of large lakes, particularly in the Yangtze valley. The southern half of this lowest step, to the south of the Yangtze, consists of a series of river valleys separated by modest ranges of mountains; a few peaks exceed 1,500 metres. Flat land is much less extensive than in the north, but there are some large lowland areas, particularly near Guangzhou (the Pearl River delta) and just south of the Yangtze around the rivers draining into the Poyang and Dongting Lakes.

River Systems

YELLOW RIVER

The main river systems of China follow the general land conformation, flowing from the high plateaux in the west eastwards to the sea. The great river of north China is the Yellow River, which rises on the northern slopes of the Bayan Har Mountains of Qinghai, and winds eastwards across the plateau into southern Gansu. It is already a considerable river when it reaches Lanzhou, provincial capital of Gansu. From here it turns away to the north, flowing up into Inner Mongolia, where it again turns to the east and then back towards the south. It thus encloses on three sides a large area of desert and semi-desert known as Ordos. As it flows back southward it forms the border between the provinces of Shaanxi and Shanxi, finally turning sharply to the east and flowing through Henan and Shandong provinces to the Gulf of Bohai, north of the Shandong peninsula. Its course in this lower stretch has varied considerably in historical times, and for a long period it reached the sea to the south of the peninsula. These changes of course often had drastic consequences for the people of the regions affected.

The quantity of water in the Yellow River varies enormously from season to season, and also from year to year. At times it is a huge river, prevented from flooding over the surrounding land only by the high dykes with which it is enclosed all along its lower reaches. But sometimes its waters sink so low that there is no more than a shallow trickle at the centre of the riverbed. In the early summer of 1981 it was possible to cross from one bank to another on bicycles at Ji'nan in Shandong. These great fluctuations in flow reflect the strongly seasonal rainfall of north China, where three-quarters of the annual precipitation occurs in the three summer months from June to August. With snow-melt in the mountains of Qinghai occurring as late as early June, and thus augmenting the rainfall in areas downstream, the river is usually at its highest between June and September. Its lower reaches are considerably affected by losses upstream through evaporation and use for irrigation, and it is not uncommon for the river to have a smaller volume of flow near the sea in Shandong than it has in its higher reaches.

The Yellow River (*Huang He* in Chinese) is so called because its waters are frequently so laden with silt, at least in the lower half of its length, that they really are of a muddy yellow colour. The thick deposits of fine, wind-blown soil (loess) of Gansu, Shaanxi and Shanxi, through which the Yellow River and many of its major tributaries flow, readily wash into the river-waters, and settle out only very slowly. This loess is of a pale ochre colour called *huang* in Chinese (translated as 'yellow'), the typical colour of north China. For thousands of years it has been blown out of the deserts of Central Asia to form deposits of great thickness in the western half of north China, and has then been washed by rivers across the North China Plain to the east. It gradually extends the delta of the Yellow River ever further into the Gulf of Bohai, and colours the sea-water for miles (thus giving rise to the name 'Yellow Sea'). This is a process which is still continuing. Vast dense clouds of dust blowing eastwards still darken the sky from time to time in places such as Lanzhou, where I have personally witnessed the phenomenon, and revised editions of the map of Shandong show the coast constantly extending north-eastwards where the Yellow River reaches the sea.

Of the tributaries of the Yellow River, it is necessary to mention only the Wei here. This flows from west to east across Gansu and Shaanxi provinces, joining the Yellow River at the point where it turns eastwards again after flowing south from its northward excursion into Inner Mongolia. The valley of the Wei is extremely important historically, as a major centre of settlement in early times, and as the major route westward from north China towards Central Asia.

Neither the Yellow River itself nor any of its tributaries are very important as waterways. This may seem surprising in view of the size of this river system, but the heavy burden of silt in the water and the large fluctuations in flow make navigation on the river so difficult throughout most of its length that it has rarely been worthwhile or even possible for boats of more than the shallowest draught to use it. Even at Ji'nan in Shandong, less than 300 miles from the river's mouth, the water usually exceeds six feet in depth only in a narrow central channel. The constant deposition of silt and the impossibility of charting the many shoals which shift with each change in the volume of flow make navigation hazardous even for small craft, which not uncommonly find themselves grounded. Moreover, winters in north China are so cold that long stretches of the river freeze during the winter months. Most of the boats on the Yellow River are used only for ferrying from bank to bank. There is some traffic up and down river within Shandong and for a short distance below the confluence with the Wei. The Wei itself is navigable for moderate-sized craft roughly as far upstream as Xi'an.

HUAI RIVER

To the south of the Yellow River is the Huai river system. This is a much smaller system, flowing from the low mountains to the west and south-west of the North China Plain. It is, however, more important for navigation than the Yellow River, and is linked by canals to the Yangtze. Formerly the Grand Canal also linked it to the Yellow River, and to smaller rivers near Tianjin and Beijing, but since the last great change of course of the Yellow River there has been little or no water in the northern sections of the Canal. Before 1855 the Yellow River reached the sea south of the Shandong Peninsula, linking with the Huai in Jiangsu province. After disastrous flooding during the summer of that year, it entirely changed the course of its lower reaches, ending a period of more than 700 years during which it had flowed to the sea via the Huai. This change of course had a considerable effect on all the waterways of the area and virtually emptied long stretches of the Grand Canal.

This was not the first time that such a drastic change of course had occurred. Until the fourth century BC the lower reaches of the Yellow River had flowed in various, often divided, channels. These frequently altered their courses, but all reached the sea well to the north of the present river mouth. Then the main channel was fixed by the construction of dykes, which prevented the regular flooding of the river. Unfortunately, though the dykes reduced the frequency of floods, they increased their severity; this was because the river bed between the dykes quite rapidly built up through deposition of silt until the river flowed

Boatmen propel their craft in traditional manner on the Daning River
in eastern Sichuan, a tributary of the Yangtze

above the level of the plain beyond the dykes. When floodwaters burst
the dykes, the resulting inundations were appalling and the river often
failed to return to its old bed. In 3,000 years of recorded history, the
Yellow River has flooded along its lower reaches more than 1,500 times.
In 1128 the main branch of the river first began to flow south-eastwards
into the Huai, only returning to its old north-easterly direction after the
great flood of 1855.

YANGTZE RIVER

The Yangtze River is the world's third longest, almost 4,000 miles from
its source to the sea. It is also the third largest river in volume of flow.
It is a major waterway for shipping, large enough for ocean-going vessels
to sail several hundred miles upstream. It and its tributaries form a
network of waterways allowing easy communication between most of
the provinces of central and south China, from Sichuan eastwards to
the coast.

Like the Yellow River, the Yangtze rises on the high plateau of

Qinghai, but somewhat further west and south. Their courses soon diverge, however, the Yangtze turning to flow almost due south, in a valley between two of the north–south mountain ranges at the eastern edge of the Tibetan plateau. Where it runs from Tibet into north-west Yunnan, it is one of three rivers flowing in parallel valleys within a distance of only about fifty miles. The others are the Lancang Jiang (Mekong) and Nu Jiang (Salween). While they continue southwards into South-east Asia, the Yangtze (here known as the *Jin Sha Jiang*, the River of Golden Sand, or probably more correctly the River of Gold Dust) performs some extraordinary contortions to find its way through the mountain ranges of Yunnan and flow away to the east. But even after leaving behind the mountains of Yunnan it still has further obstacles to overcome, for having broken through to the southern edge of the Sichuan Basin it then finds more mountains standing before it in eastern Sichuan and western Hubei. Through these it has carved the spectacular and famous Yangtze Gorges. Passing through the gorges it finally reaches the plains, and meanders for many hundreds of miles across lush and fertile lowlands studded with innumerable lakes and ponds. The largest of these are the huge Dongting and Poyang Lakes, respectively almost 1,100 and 1,400 square miles in surface area.

The Yangtze has several Chinese names, applied to different stretches (the name 'River of Golden Sand' has already been mentioned). The usual name for the whole river is *Chang Jiang*, the Long River. In early times it was just called *Jiang*, *the* River (similarly, the Yellow River was called *He*). 'Yangtze' is an Anglicized version of a very local name used for the river not far above its estuary. As it has become commonly accepted in the English language and is not derived from the usual Chinese name, it is used in this book without any alteration of spelling.

CANALS

Canals have played an important role in China for many centuries. They commonly had a dual purpose, as a means both of communication and of irrigation. There are extensive canal systems in the east of the Yangtze and Huai flood plains, linking these two river systems to each other and also to the Qiantang River at Hangzhou. Several of these canals date from the seventh century AD or before. Formerly the Grand Canal also extended water communications northwards to the Yellow River, Tianjin and Beijing. This northern section of the canal was constructed during the reign of the Mongol conqueror, Khubilai Khan, in the late 1280s; it was in almost continuous use from that time until its disruption in 1855. The first British embassy from Britain to China, under Lord Macartney in 1793–4, returned from Beijing to Macao by way of the Grand Canal and various rivers. In all that long journey of some 2,000 miles (which took just over three months), there were only two short overland stages totalling about 55 miles, each travelled in a single day.

Earlier, during the Tang dynasty (618–907), there had been a different northern canal route linking the capital of the period, Chang'an (modern Xi'an), to the Huai and Yangtze. These canals were designed to overcome the difficulty of feeding the large populations of the capital cities, swelled by government officials with their families and servants to beyond what local agricultural production could support. The lower Yangtze region normally produced a large surplus of rice, sufficient to make good deficiencies if it could be safely transported to the north. Thus, while rivers provided easy means of east–west communication, canals allowed transport from south to north.

OTHER RIVER SYSTEMS

The most southerly of the great river systems of China is that flowing into the Pearl River delta near Guangzhou. Three major rivers come from different directions to unite in this delta area. The largest is the West River, which with its tributaries allows water-borne communication between the two provinces of Guangdong and Guangxi. The North and East Rivers provide transport only within the province of Guangdong. The main sources of the West River rise on the Yunnan–Guizhou Plateau. Though it is considerably shorter than the Yangtze, it is still a large river, with a flow of great volume.

Outside the area of China Proper, with its series of parallel river systems each draining from west to east, are several other important rivers. Manchuria, for example, has two major systems, that of the Liao, running southwards into the Gulf of Bohai, and that of the

Sungari, which flows north-eastwards into the Amur. The Amur itself, with its tributary the Ussuri, forms the north-eastern boundary of Manchuria before flowing through Russian territory into the Sea of Okhotsk.

Tibet has only one great river. Though several others have their sources on the plateau, only the Yarlung Zangbo becomes a really large river within the boundaries of Tibet. A considerable stretch of it is navigable to small craft. It is a curious river, flowing eastwards between the great Himalayan range and roughly parallel mountain ridges on the plateau surface to the north, until it suddenly turns southwards and pours its waters into deep gorges through the Himalaya. On the plains of Assam it becomes the Brahmaputra, flowing into Bangladesh to the great delta area which it shares with the Ganges. It was only quite recently that the Brahmaputra and Yarlung Zangbo were shown to be sections of the same river (until the 1920s it was thought that the Brahmaputra rose on the southern slopes of the Himalaya). Originally they were not. The Yarlung Zangbo probably began by flowing from east to west, discharging its waters into a land-locked lake on the plateau surface, as many of Tibet's smaller rivers still do. But the Brahmaputra eroded its way northwards into the Himalaya, eventually cutting through into the valley of the Yarlung Zangbo. The Tibetan river reversed its direction of flow and united with the Brahmaputra.

The remaining great rivers of China lie to the north of Tibet, in the basins and valleys of Xinjiang. This is a region of desert and semi-desert, surrounded and divided by high mountain ranges. To the south are the Kunlun and Altun mountains, at the northern rim of the Qinghai–Tibet plateau. These are linked to the Karakoram and Pamirs in the west, with the long Tian Shan range running from just north of the Pamirs eastwards towards Mongolia. The western Tian Shan lie mainly within Kyrgyzstan, but in the east the range separates the Tarim and Junggarian Basins, both within the borders of China. To the north-east of Junggaria are the Altay Mountains, on the border between China and the Mongolian Republic.

Many small rivers flow down from the mountains into the basins, but lose themselves in the sand and stones of the deserts. These rivers usually have great variation in seasonal flow, swelling when the snows on the mountain peaks melt in summer but drying up, often almost entirely, in winter. Occasional summer downpours in the mountains may swell their waters to several times their normal level for a few hours or a couple of days, and they may then flow much further out into the desert than usual before drying up. Frequently there is some flow of water below the stones of the river-beds even when the surface is dry. Most of the oasis settlements around the edges of the basins rely on this underground water for their existence. A few of the rivers gather sufficient water to be able to maintain a permanent flow. The largest of these is the Tarim River, flowing at the foot of the Tian Shan along the northern edge of the Tarim Basin. Eventually its waters lose themselves in the Taklimakan desert.

Flowing north-westwards out of Xinjiang are the headwaters of two considerable Asian rivers. The lesser of these is the Ili, rising on the north side of the Chinese Tian Shan and flowing through a comparatively well-watered valley, one of the most pleasant areas of Xinjiang. Crossing into Kazakhstan, it finally runs into the land-locked Lake Balkhash. North of the Junggarian Basin, the Irtysh rises on the southern slopes of the Altay range and flows away to the north-west and north until it eventually joins the Ob, emptying into the Arctic Ocean.

Climate

China in general has a monsoon climate, with a long dry season throughout most of autumn, winter and spring, and rainfall concentrated in the summer. There is a decrease in both rainfall and average temperature from south to north. The great landmass of the Eurasian continent is the predominant influence on the climate, particularly in the north and west. In winter a large area of high pressure develops, centred on Mongolia; cold, dry winds blow outwards from this area, keeping much of China cold and dry. By about May the pressure has fallen and wind directions change. Low pressure develops over northern India and winds shift to become southerly to easterly, bringing warm, moist air from the Pacific Ocean. Most of China receives at least half its annual rainfall during June, July and August. In some areas the proportion is in excess of 90 per cent.

THE NORTH

Northern China and Tibet have extreme climates, with warm or hot summers and cold or very cold winters. Changes of season are rapid, with only short spring and autumn seasons. In north China rainfall is not only low but also uncertain, with large annual variations and high risk of drought. The climate of southern China is more moderate, with hot summers and cool winters. Annual rainfall is considerably higher, and although much of it still falls in summer, winters are moister than in the north and far west. In the south drought is almost unknown.

China has several distinct climatic regions. China Proper may be divided roughly into two halves, north and south China. The dividing line runs along the Qinling Mountains in the west and then along the River Huai to the coast. North of this line summers are hot, averaging about 25° C in July, with occasional maximums in the 40s. Winters are long and cold, with January averages a few degrees below freezing and occasional frosts down to −20° or −25° C. Spring comes in April, and by early May temperatures are already reaching the 30s. Northerly winds are common in spring, bringing with them dust from the Mongolian Gobi. Autumn is the most pleasant season, being dry, warm and less dusty, but it lasts only from late September until the end of October. November is already cold. There is little snow in winter, however, because there is hardly any precipitation. The low rainfall of this region falls almost entirely between late June and mid-September, and does not exceed 40 inches per annum. Throughout much of the region it is less than 30 inches, decreasing towards the north and north-west until it falls below 15 inches a year near the border with Inner Mongolia.

AGRICULTURE IN THE NORTH

There is little rice grown in north China. Summers are usually hot enough but it is hard to provide sufficient water; the climate is much more suited to the cultivation of wheat, barley and millets. Winter wheat is now the most important grain crop of north China, usually sown in October and reaped the following June. A second crop can then be grown after the wheat has been harvested. In some areas cotton now follows the wheat, though it is necessary to sow the cotton just before the wheat is actually harvested. Other major crops are maize (corn), sorghum, panicle and foxtail millets, sweet potatoes and water melons. Irrigation is usually necessary during the dry season. There is considerable production of vegetables, particularly Chinese cabbage, leeks, Chinese radishes, turnips, celery, aubergines, tomatoes and peppers. These vegetables are strictly seasonal, being grown when temperatures are suitable. There is thus, for example, a time of year when aubergines are available in plenty, and can be seen in piles at every market, though a few weeks later there are none to be had at all. Several kinds of bean are also extensively cultivated. Recently polythene sheeting has begun to be used to extend the vegetable season, reducing the winter period during which only stored cabbages, leeks and onions, and dried beans and peppers, are available.

Chinese cooking commonly involves frying, and cooking oil is an important commodity. In north China most edible oil is derived from peanuts, soya beans, sesame, sunflower, safflower and rape. Tobacco is an important cash crop in parts of Shanxi, Henan and Shandong. Silk production, and therefore the cultivation of mulberry trees to feed the silkworms, is important in Shandong and Henan. Orchards are often planted on land unsuitable for tilling, producing mainly apples, pears, persimmons, peaches, apricots and pomegranates.

The most common domestic animal is the pig, as it is in all China. Virtually every country household keeps one or more, often in a sty in the courtyard of the house. North Chinese houses were traditionally built with a walled courtyard on to which all the windows opened, so that only blank walls and wooden doors were presented to the outside. Large houses had several courtyards, with living quarters along one or more sides of each. Although this traditional style of building is no longer universal, it is still common in the countryside, even for new houses. In most country homes there is a pigsty in one corner of the courtyard. Chickens are also commonly kept, and ducks where there is any water. Sheep and goats are raised in some numbers in the hillier areas around the edge of the North China Plain and in Shandong. Cattle are not very common, but are increasing in numbers as milk consumption in China rises. Traditionally, the Han Chinese did not drink milk at all.

A water buffalo pulls a plough across a rice paddy near Dazu in central Sichuan

THE SOUTH

South China has similar summer temperatures to the north, with July averages between 25° and 30° C. Winters are much warmer, however, with January averages above freezing point and frosts rarely as low as −10° C. In the extreme south and south-east there is a narrow coastal strip where frosts never occur; in a large part of this region they occur only occasionally. Rainfall is between 40 and 100 inches per annum, and although summer is still the wettest season, there is a more even spread of precipitation throughout the year than in the north. About a quarter of the year's rain falls in the six cooler months from November to April. In summer, coastal areas are afflicted with typhoons blowing in from the ocean.

AGRICULTURE IN THE SOUTH

The most important crop throughout south China is rice. Except for a few of the winter months, most of the fields of the region are flooded to provide wet paddy-fields for the rice crop. In more southerly areas two or even three crops of rice are harvested per year. Where only one harvest is possible, other crops are sown after the rice has been reaped. In some areas, particularly in the north of the region, winter wheat is alternated with rice, as it ripens as early as May, allowing time for a crop of rice to be grown on the same land during the summer. Cotton is also important in the north of the region along the Yangtze valley. Silk is produced mainly around the lower Yangtze, in Sichuan and in Guangdong. On the hill slopes of south-east China there are extensive tea plantations. The steeper slopes are forested. In the warmer south of the region sugar cane is widely grown, providing most of the sugar for all China (sugar beet is grown in quantity only in small areas of the north, mainly in Manchuria). In certain areas there are extensive orchards, mainly producing various citrus fruits. In the extreme south many different tropical fruits are grown, including bananas, pineapples, lychees, longans, mangoes and loquats. There are also plantations of various camellia species, grown for the oil which is pressed from their seeds. Other southern oil crops include soya beans and rape. Vegetables are grown all the year round in most of the south, in greater variety than in north China.

The typical domestic animal of the south is the water buffalo. Its main use, however, is as a draught animal in the fields rather than for its meat or milk. As in north China, the pig provides the greater part of the meat diet (the Chinese word for meat is assumed to mean pork unless otherwise specified), but in the wet south various kinds of fish assume a prominent position on the table. Fish farming is widely practised – sometimes fish are reared in the paddy among the rice, but more frequently they are kept in special fish ponds. Various species of the carp family, especially the grass-carp, are the most commonly eaten fish. Rivers and ponds also provide terrapins and freshwater shrimps, and water weeds for animal fodder. Ducks and geese are kept everywhere in the south, and are taken to feed along canals and rivers, and in the paddy-fields before the young rice is transplanted. They are useful consumers of paddy-field pests.

The courtyard is a less prominent feature of southern architecture, and in this region it is much more common for ordinary homes to have more than one storey (a feature rare in the north except in grand or modern buildings). The upturned eaves and ornamented roofs which are so much associated with Chinese architecture had their origins mainly in the south, and were always more widespread there on ordinary buildings.

OUTLYING REGIONS

These two regions, north and south China, constitute the heartlands of the Chinese culture area, but form well under half the total area of the People's Republic of China. To the north and west they are enclosed by an extensive territory in which the terrain and climate are much less congenial, and the intensive agriculture typical of north and south China is only rarely possible. Most of the inhabitants of this large area were originally not Han Chinese, though some parts were settled by Han at quite an early date. It can be divided on the basis of climate and physical geography into four major regions, the two plateaux of Yunnan–Guizhou and Tibet–Qinghai in the south-west and west, the arid region of Inner Mongolia and Xinjiang in the north and north-west, and the mountains and valleys of Manchuria in the north-east.

YUNNAN–GUIZHOU PLATEAU

In the far south-west of China the land rises abruptly to altitudes in excess of 1,000 metres. This is the Yunnan–Guizhou Plateau, covering the greater part of the two provinces after which it is named. In the south and east it is lower than in the north and west, where it averages almost 2,000 metres altitude. In the north-west it adjoins the mountains which rim the Tibetan plateau, which commonly rise above 4,000 metres. The surface of the plateau is by no means level, but is heavily dissected by river valleys and broken by occasional upthrust ridges. There are a number of large natural lakes in depressions on the plateau surface. Major tributaries of both the Yangtze and West Rivers rise on the plateau, as do the Red River of Vietnam and other rivers flowing into South-east Asia. The elevation of the plateau and its southerly location (only just to the north of the tropics) combine to ensure summers which are not too hot and winters which are rarely very cold – a land of eternal spring to Chinese accustomed to the less equitable climates of China Proper. This region undoubtedly has the most pleasant climate in China. July average temperatures are generally between 20°

The Li River and karst limestone pinnacles near
Guilin in Guangxi Autonomous Region

and 25° C, with only occasional maximums above 30°; averages in
January lie in the range between 5° and 10° C. Frosts occur regularly
in winter but are never extreme, temperatures below −5° C being very
uncommon. Winters are moderately dry, especially on the western half
of the plateau; there are only occasional snowfalls, which usually soon
melt. Summers are quite wet, with more than 80 per cent of an annual
average precipitation of around 50 inches falling during the period from
May to October.

More mountainous parts of the plateau are forested, and there are
considerable areas of upland grazing, used for raising sheep and goats.
Valleys and basins are cultivated for field crops, with both rice and winter
wheat important crops. Less fertile fields are used to grow maize. Beans,
including soya beans, are widely cultivated. Broad beans are a very useful
winter crop, ready for harvesting early in spring. Rape is also grown on
a large scale during winter and spring, flowering as early as January.

To the south, the plateau falls away to the less elevated uplands of
Laos and Vietnam. There is a small lower-altitude zone close to the
border with a hotter and wetter climate, where large rubber plantations
have recently been established. Bananas and sugar cane are also grown

here. In contrast, the western and northern edges of the plateau rise up to high mountain ranges, which in the west form the border with Burma and in the north mark the transition towards the much higher plateau of Tibet and Qinghai.

QINGHAI–TIBET PLATEAU

The average altitude of the Qinghai–Tibet Plateau is in excess of 4,000 metres. It is easily the largest region of such great elevation anywhere in the world. Because of the altitude of the plateau and its isolation from oceanic influences by the Himalaya, the climate is extremely severe, being both cold and dry. Annual average temperatures in some parts of the region are below freezing point, and over the whole region are generally no higher than 7° or 8° C. January averages are very low, around −10° to −15°; minimums below −40° sometimes occur. July average temperatures range between 5° and 15° C; only in valleys below the level of the plateau surface do temperatures ever rise above 30°. The frost-free period is very short, exceeding three months only in a few favoured areas; over most of the plateau it is less than one month, and in large areas there is always the possibility of frost at night even in midsummer. Rainfall is also small, generally below 20 inches per annum and in many areas below 10 inches. It falls almost entirely in the summer months from June to September, mainly on the mountain ranges which rise up from the plateau; much of the plateau surface is watered largely by the streams running down from the mountains. This gives rise to some remarkable landscapes, as lower areas through which rivulets run may be lush and green, while adjacent, slightly higher land remains unwatered. Such landscapes can be seen around Qinghai Lake (Koko Nor), where there are areas of sandy desert immediately adjacent to green marshlands, the transition occurring within a couple of feet. Many of the smaller rivers and streams of the plateau are unable to find any outlet except into land-locked lakes in depressions on the plateau surface. These lakes are often brackish or salty through accumulation of dissolved minerals in the water, which are concentrated by evaporation. Qinghai Lake, the largest lake in China, with a surface area of almost 1,600 square miles, has brackish waters. Other lakes are so salty that crusts of crystalline deposits form around their shores. In the north of the plateau is the Qaidam Depression, at an elevation of about 2,600 to 3,100 metres, a large area of salt marsh and desert.

Very little of this region is suitable for growing crops. It is generally only in the lower river valleys that any large areas of land are under cultivation. The most important crop is a hardy kind of barley with a short growing period, but spring wheat and millet, and even some winter wheat, are also grown, as well as peas and beans, potatoes and rape. Animal husbandry is much more important, however, as vast areas of the plateau surface are suitable for grazing, at least during the short summer. The yak is the major Tibetan domestic animal, providing milk and meat for food and yak-hair for coarse cloth. Hybrids between yak and ordinary cattle, and sheep and goats, are also important, and in some northern parts of the plateau horses, donkeys and Bactrian camels are herded. There are, however, large areas, especially in the north-west, which are more or less desert, and unsuitable even for grazing yak. Though Tibet and Qinghai are of vast extent, equivalent to several European countries, their population is tiny, totalling only about six million people.

MONGOLIA AND XINJIANG

The northern edge of the Qinghai–Tibet Plateau is rimmed with high mountains, the Kunlun, Altun and Qilian ranges. Though they are not so immense as the Himalaya to the south, they include many peaks of 5,000 to 6,000 metres and higher. Beyond these ranges the land falls away sharply to below 2,000 metres, to the arid region of Mongolia and Xinjiang. Between them, Inner Mongolia and Xinjiang constitute almost 30 per cent of the total land area of the People's Republic of China, but most of this large portion of the country is desert or semi-desert. There are large stretches of grazing land in the east of Inner Mongolia and around the mountains of Xinjiang, but cultivation is possible only in a few districts where underground water or rivers allow irrigation. The Great Hinggan Mountains in the extreme north-east of Inner Mongolia are extensively forested. There are also large forests in the Tian Shan and Altay ranges.

Rainfall throughout this region is low. In almost all of Xinjiang and the western third of Inner Mongolia average annual precipitation totals less than 10 inches. Further east it rises gradually, but only exceeds 20 inches per annum on east-facing mountain slopes in the extreme eastern portion of Inner Mongolia. Such rainfall as there is falls mainly in summer. Temperature ranges are extreme. January average temperatures are generally below −10° C, with occasional falls to as low as −49°. In July, however, averages are generally between 20° and 25° C, with occasional maximums in the 40s. In the Turpan Depression summer temperatures are particularly high and regularly reach 45° C. There is often very considerable difference between the maximum and minimum temperatures of one day, sometimes as great as 16°.

In Xinjiang the large mountain ranges have considerable local effect on water supply. Precipitation is usually much higher on the mountains than on surrounding lowlands, and the mountain slopes are generally comparatively well watered except at the lowest levels. There are forests and good summer pastures on the middle levels. Around the bases of the mountain ranges the rivers and streams flowing down from above water the valleys of the dry foothills and allow oasis cultivation at the edges of the surrounding deserts. Sheep, goats, cattle and horses are moved up and down the valleys according to the season, grazing the highest pastures during the summer when they are clear of snow. Bactrian camels are herded in semi-arid areas. The growing season in the oases is reasonably long, especially in the south of the region. Spring wheat is the principal crop, but maize and sorghum and even a little rice are also grown. Cotton and rape are other important crops.

There are very extensive pasture-lands in the moister eastern half of Inner Mongolia. Sheep and goats are the main domestic animals here, along with cattle and horses. The drier west is the main camel-raising area of China. Cultivation is concentrated mainly in the area around the Yellow River where it flows through this region, and in the south-eastern lowlands adjacent to Manchuria. Major crops include spring wheat, oats, millets and potatoes. Sugar beet cultivation has been greatly developed in recent years.

MANCHURIA

Manchuria is divided into the three provinces of Heilongjiang, Jilin and Liaoning. The whole region consists of an extensive lowland area stretching northwards from the Gulf of Bohai, surrounded on three sides by mountains. To the west lie the Great Hinggan Mountains of Inner Mongolia, to the north-east the Lesser Hinggan, and to the south-east a series of ranges rising up to the Changbai Shan on the Korean border. Summers in this region are warm, with July averages generally around 20° C. Winters are very cold; Heilongjiang in particular has winters of a severity comparable with those of neighbouring Siberia, with January average temperatures as low as −30° C, and occasionally dropping below −50°. The south of the region is less cold, January averages in the Liaodong peninsula being between −5° and −10° C. Rainfall is moderately low, generally averaging around 30 inches per annum, and tends to be variable from year to year, as in adjacent north China.

There are large forests in the mountainous areas; Manchuria has some of the most extensive forests still remaining in China and is the main source of timber for the country. The Manchurian Plain is the most northerly major area of cultivation in China, with a rather short growing period. Winter wheat can, however, be grown in the southern half of the plain, though it is replaced by spring wheat in the north. Millet, sorghum, maize and soybeans are other important crops. Tobacco and cotton are grown in Liaoning, and the central and southern part of the plain produces most of China's sugar beet.

MINERAL RESOURCES

China has important mineral resources. The largest oilfields are at Daqing in Heilongjiang and the Victory field on the Yellow River delta in Shandong. There are also large fields in northern Xinjiang, Qinghai, Gansu and Sichuan, as well as offshore in the South China Sea and the Gulf of Bohai. There are huge reserves of coal; the largest centres of coal mining are in Shanxi and Manchuria, but there are mines in many other parts of the country. Several other minerals, including iron ore, are mined, and prospecting for new reserves is still in progress, especially on the Qinghai–Tibet Plateau. China is a major world producer of tungsten, antimony and tin. There are good prospects for the development of hydro-electric power, and already several large schemes and numerous lesser ones are in operation. The Gezhouba Dam on the Yangtze at Yichang includes hydro-electric generators. There is still a lack of generating capacity throughout most of China, however, with insufficient supply to meet industrial requirements. New power stations of all kinds continue to be built, therefore, including a small number of nuclear power stations.

INDUSTRIALIZATION

China is attempting to industrialize as rapidly as possible. Factories of all kinds have sprung up throughout the country since the foundation of the People's Republic in 1949. Manchuria, under Japanese domination from 1931 until 1945, was the most heavily industrialized area prior to this, and is still an important centre of heavy industry. Shenyang in Liaoning is the largest industrial city in the region, a centre of the aircraft, automobile and machine-building industries. Shanghai, as well as being China's major centre of water communications, is also heavily industrialized. Historically it was China's main textile-producing centre, but more recently it has diversified, especially into chemical production, shipbuilding and other engineering. Tianjin, Wuhan and Guangzhou are also very large centres of industry and communications.

But although there are several huge cities which are very heavily industrialized, China remains predominantly rural. Eighty per cent of its population still lives in the countryside, engaged mainly in agricultural pursuits, though small-scale industry is increasingly appearing in rural China. For many Chinese, the way of life has not changed fundamentally from what it was several centuries ago, and despite great progress in raising living standards, most Chinese are very poor by western standards. The huge increase in population during the present century has caused tremendous problems, straining all China's resources. The population has trebled since 1900 and is now estimated at more than 1,200 million; it is not without difficulty that this huge number of people is fed. Overpopulation is the main problem facing China in its bid to modernize and raise the general standard of living of its people.

CHAPTER THREE

The Origins of Chinese Civilization,
Prehistory to 771 BC

Chinese civilization is indisputably ancient, with arguably the longest *continuous* history of development of any civilization in the world. Compared with ancient Egypt and Mesopotamia, however, China remained at a primitive stage of development until rather late. Current evidence suggests, for example, that metallurgy began in China no earlier than 2500 BC, at least 1,000 years later than in Mesopotamia. The earliest organized Chinese state is unlikely to have come into existence much before 2000 BC, when Chaldaea and the other Mesopotamian city-states were already ancient and several dynasties had risen and fallen in Egypt. The development of Chinese civilization in fact shows some remarkable chronological parallels with that in Europe. The first period of strength and unity in China under the Empires of the Qin and Han dynasties, for example, was roughly contemporaneous with the domination of Europe by the Roman Empire.

Chinese history begins with the period of the Shang dynasty, in about 1600 BC. Later tradition puts the Xia dynasty before the Shang, and various rulers of a legendary character before that. To date the existence of the Xia dynasty remains unproven, though many Chinese scholars now seem inclined to accept it. Even the precise dating of the Shang dynasty has not been satisfactorily determined. The earliest positively-dated event in Chinese history occurred in 841 BC, at least two centuries after the downfall of the Shang. Current knowledge of the early history and prehistory of China is still very incomplete, despite vast additions to available evidence and data within the last few decades. A hundred years ago China had virtually no known prehistory, and all that was recorded of her early history was unreliable, as it had been set down long after the event and lacked the support of contemporary evidence. As recently as 1912, Berthold Laufer was forced to conclude that 'as far as the present state of our archaeological knowledge and the literary records point out, the Chinese have never passed through an epoch which for other cultures has been designated as a stone age'.

This lack of knowledge of Chinese prehistory and early history led many Westerners to the conclusion that Chinese civilization was founded, not upon indigenous development, but upon transmissions from the Near and Middle East. At first, various attempts were made to link the early Chinese with the Egyptians (as, for example, by de Guignes in 1759). Later, even after the excavation of Chinese Neolithic sites during the 1920s, a strong case was made for close connections with Mesopotamia and the Near East. As recently as the 1950s it was still commonly considered that 'many of the fundamental elements of Chinese culture had their origin in the countries near the Mediterranean sea'. It is in fact only during the last two or three decades that it has become at all widely accepted that there was a spontaneous development of a distinct culture within the area of China without the stimulus of outside influences.

This change of view has come about through the discovery of new evidence. Archaeology is a young science in China, but has developed

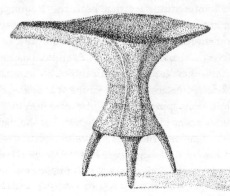

An early Shang or late Xia bronze vessel for pouring wine, *c.* 1700 BC

very rapidly. It was only in the 1920s that significant archaeological work began within the area of China Proper, and then under the direction of Westerners. But despite the upheavals caused by the wars of the 1930s and 1940s, and by the Cultural Revolution, the Chinese have successfully undertaken a massive programme of archaeological excavation. Evidence of the early stages of development of the people of China has gradually accumulated, so that it is now possible at least to draw tentative conclusions about the origins of Chinese civilization. It must be stressed, however, that in many respects knowledge is still incomplete.

Early Man

There are a few indications that China was already occupied by humans (or hominids) during the early Pleistocene period, roughly two million years ago. The evidence is at present only fragmentary, however. Considerably more is known of man in China during the middle Pleistocene, the period to which the famous Beijing Man fossils are assigned. Early human remains have also been discovered more recently at Lantian in Shaanxi, Yuanmou in Yunnan and other locations. These are of an earlier stage of evolution than modern man, *Homo sapiens*, and are assignable to the *Homo erectus* group. These Palaeolithic humans were makers of primitive stone tools, generally of rather crude and unspecialized type. It is an interesting fact that both the Beijing and Lantian remains have certain morphological features in common with modern Mongoloid populations. This has led some authorities to suggest continuity between these ancient populations and the modern Chinese, but there is as yet insufficient evidence for this to be generally accepted.

Humans of modern type appeared in China at least as early as the late Pleistocene period, very approximately in the region of 80,000 years ago. There is some recent evidence to suggest that the date may have been much earlier. The pace of human development increased rapidly thereafter, and stone tools became ever more specialized and sophisticated. Limited skeletal evidence suggests that the population of the Far East during the latter part of the Palaeolithic Age was of a generalized Mongoloid type. The date of the appearance of a distinct Mongoloid race cannot yet be exactly determined, but must have been before about

40,000 years ago for it was at about that time that the Mongoloid ancestors of the American Indians began to colonize the Americas. The early Mongoloids were probably closer in appearance to American Indians than to modern Chinese. Most recent analyses of the Upper Cave remains from Zhoukoudian, which date from about 17,000 years ago, place them closest to American Indians.

It is still not known when and where people of recognizably Chinese type first appeared. It has been suggested that the flattish face, low nose and particular eyelid shape of the Chinese evolved as adaptations to extreme cold, probably during the last period of glaciation some 20,000 years ago. There is little hard evidence to support this, however. But it is certain that by about 7,000 years ago the inhabitants of north China at least were more or less indistinguishable from the modern Chinese population.

Neolithic Cultures

At some time probably about 9,000 years ago the people of China ceased to rely solely on hunting and gathering for their food supplies, and began the domestication of animals and cultivation of plants. This must have been a long and gradual process, but it was a crucial turning-point in human development, allowing a more settled way of life and the growth of more complex cultures. It was from this period that a distinctly Chinese cultural assemblage began to emerge.

From the evidence available now, it is clear that agriculture not only began in China independently of developments in western Asia, but also that it had independent beginnings in more than one area of China. During the earlier part of the Neolithic period there were, in fact, at least three contemporary but distinct cultural regions within the area of China Proper, each of which played a part in the later development of Chinese civilization. They were centred respectively in the middle Yellow River and Wei valleys of north China, in the lower Yangtze valley and adjacent coastal plains, and along the coast of south-east China. Each of these Neolithic cultural regions had its own distinctive characteristics.

Evidence of the earliest stages of agriculture in China has only recently begun to come to light, so that it is not yet possible to make firm statements about the exact time and place of agricultural origins.

Recent archaeological work has, however, thrown much light upon the beginnings of rice cultivation and a number of other issues. Knowledge of the Chinese Neolithic in many areas has been extended back to about 7,000 BC or even earlier. Though there is still much work to be done interpreting all the data, it is possible to give at least a rough sketch of the general outline of the Chinese Neolithic period.

SOUTH-EASTERN CULTURE

In south-eastern China (roughly the area of the modern provinces of Fujian, Guangdong and Guangxi, and probably including Taiwan), a number of sites have been found which date from as early as 9000 BC. They are characterized by brown, cord-marked and incised pottery, chipped-pebble choppers and flakes, polished stone discs, points and chisels, and bone points and harpoons. Shells and animal bones indicate a considerable reliance on hunting and fishing, but there are also indications that some plants may have been cultivated for food. In this region the main domestic food plants would probably have been tubers such as taro and yams. There were almost undoubtedly strong affinities between this south-east Chinese culture and Neolithic cultures further south in the area of modern Vietnam, particularly the Bacson culture of about 9000–6000 BC. This link with Indochina persisted well into historical times. The south-eastern coastal area of China was known as *Yue*; 'southern *Yue*', at one time part of the Chinese Empire, covered the northern part of Vietnam. Influences from South-east Asia certainly entered China at a very early date, and remained important for many centuries.

LONGSHAN

Recent discoveries in the Yangtze and Huai River valleys in central China have considerably extended knowledge of early rice cultivation. At the Yuchanyan site near the Dongting Lake in Hunan, evidence of the cultivation of rice some 10,000 years ago has been excavated. Other nearby sites, such as Pengtoushan, show that rice was cultivated on a large scale about 8,000 years ago. At the Jiahu site in central Henan, in the Huai River drainage area, rice was also cultivated some 7,000 to 8,000 years ago. Stone and bone ploughshares have been excavated at this site, along with many other implements used in tilling the ground, harvesting and processing grain. Arrow heads, darts and stone balls, together with numerous bones of wild animals and fish and shells of molluscs and terrapins, show that hunting remained an important means of obtaining food at this period, alongside the cultivation of grain. The Jiahu site has also yielded one of the most remarkable finds of recent Chinese archaeology, some 30 flutes made from crane bones, a few still in playable condition.

At Hemudu on the southern side of Hangzhou Bay, northern Zhejiang province, remains of rice up to half a metre thick have been excavated, including grains, husks, straw and leaves. This site dates to about 5,000–4,500 BC and shows that, by that period, rice cultivation at quite an advanced level had spread down the Yangtze valley and along the East China coast. Dogs (which in early China were an important food animal), pigs and probably also water-buffalo had been domesticated at Hemudu, but remains of fruits and nuts, probably collected from the wild, and bones of deer, turtles, rhinoceroses and elephants, show a continued partial reliance on hunting and gathering.

Artefacts at Hemudu include bone, wood and stone implements and pottery. Stone implements are rather few, mainly axes, adzes and chisels; bone implements predominate. In addition to the hoe blades, there are also chisels, awls, needles, spatulas, weaving shuttles, saw blades and arrowheads, and other items. The pottery is handmade and thick, and fired at low temperature. The clay was tempered with large amounts of grass, straw, grain husks and similar organic materials, which carbonized during firing, imparting a blackish colour to the pottery. The vessel types include round-bottomed pots decorated with cord-marks and incised designs, plain or cord-marked flat-bottomed jars with one or two handles, basins and bowls. Three pieces with painted designs were found at the oldest level. They have dark brown designs over a layer of clay wash, and are also cord-marked. Remains of elaborate wooden structures were excavated, which were almost certainly huts and possibly pile-dwellings. There are certain similarities between the pottery of this site and of the more southerly sites of the *Yue* region, but the exact relationship between the early cultures of these two regions is unclear.

At a rather later date the cultural assemblage of this area showed very distinct characteristics of its own. A series of related cultures has been identified in the east coastal area of China from Hangzhou Bay northward to Shandong province, including the lower reaches of the Yangtze and Huai Rivers. These were probably all rice-growing cultures related to the earlier culture of Hemudu, and can all be placed within the same cultural tradition. This tradition is called Longshan, after the site in Shandong at which the first remains assignable to this group were discovered.

The Longshan tradition has often been identified with black pottery, and has even been called the Black Pottery culture. One of the most distinctive types of artefact of the original Longshan site is indeed a fine kind of black pottery, often highly polished. However, this kind of pottery is not the predominant type at any site of the Longshan tradition and is primarily a late development. It is not the essential indication of Longshan affinities; the Longshan cultural tradition is characterized by certain distinctive types of pottery vessels, which are raised either on a circular foot or on tripod legs. Most Longshan pottery is unpainted, and only rarely cord- or basket-marked. Decoration usually consists of either raised ridges or incised designs.

YANGSHAO

The third major Neolithic culture complex developed in the area known as Zhong Yuan, or the Central Plains. This is a slightly misleading name, as the area in question lies not in central China but in the central part of north China. It comprises the valley of the Wei River in Shaanxi and adjacent parts of the Yellow River valley and flood plain in southern Shanxi, northern Henan, southern Hebei and western Shandong. It is an area of loess soils, with primary wind-blown deposits in the west and secondary river-borne deposits to the east. There is still much argument about the climatic conditions and natural vegetation of this area during the Neolithic period, but it is likely to have been somewhat warmer and moister than today (though still much cooler and drier than south China, either at the time or now), and to have been largely covered with deciduous woodland. The crops cultivated here were quite different from those grown further south. Early agriculture in north China was based on millets. Current evidence suggests that the fox-tail millet (*Setaria italica*) was the predominant crop in Neolithic times, but broomcorn millet (*Panicum miliaceum*) may also have been grown and was undoubtedly a major crop during early historic times. Both these millets are highly drought–resistant, and must have been particularly suited to the north Chinese climate, especially in the period before irrigation became common.

The first Neolithic site excavated in this area was at the village of Yangshao in Henan province, discovered in 1920. The most distinctive artefacts were red pottery painted with decorative designs in black, so that this Yangshao Neolithic culture is often called the Painted Pottery culture. Many other sites clearly belonging to the same cultural horizon have been excavated since this first epoch–making discovery, which provided the first definite evidence of a Neolithic culture in China Proper. One large and important site has been preserved as excavated in a museum at Banpo on the outskirts of Xi'an.

Artefacts from Yangshao sites always include many agricultural implements, such as chipped or polished stone hoes, spades and harvesting knives. Stones for grinding grain have been found. Bone and stone arrowheads, as well as bones of non–domestic animals, show that hunting continued to be important. There are also numerous bones of domestic pigs and dogs. Many Yangshao settlement sites were on loess terraces on river banks, and it is clear from bone fish-hooks and stone net-sinkers that fishing was also carried on. Other tools include stone

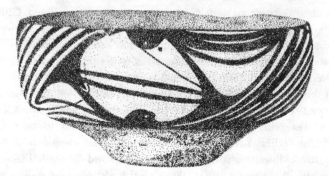

A Neolithic pottery bowl of the Yangshao culture, with painted design

axes and adzes, chisels and spindle whorls. Needles, awls, spearheads and other small implements are commonly made of bone or antler. The pottery is varied, including many simple utensils of red or greyish-brown paste, frequently decorated with cord, mat or basket impressions. At several sites some of the pots have incised signs or symbols that may be early forms of writing, or at least related to writing. At all but the earliest stages of this culture, there is also a proportion of very striking pottery pieces with painted decoration. There is some variation in styles and techniques according to place and period, but commonly the basic red or brownish pottery was polished or burnished and then painted with designs in black pigment. Red pigment was less frequently used. Sometimes white slips were applied before painting. Designs seem usually to have been based on animal or plant shapes – fishes, birds, flowers and so on – but became more and more stylized and abstract, as spirals and geometric patterns. Much of this painted ware is very beautiful and impressive.

Because the culture of this area was the first Neolithic culture to be identified in China, and because it was in this area that the earliest civilized Chinese state arose, the culture of the Central Plains was for long regarded by many scholars to be China's primary Neolithic culture and the direct (and even the sole) predecessor of the later historical Chinese civilization of the region. Other cultures were thought to be secondary and to a greater or lesser extent derivative from it. New evidence has changed this view: the Yangshao culture can no longer be considered the only ancestor from which later Chinese culture descended. Chinese civilization had diverse origins, and throughout its long history has continued to be more diverse than has often been appreciated.

After the excavation of the Longshan type site in the late 1920s, a problem arose in deciding the relationship between the Yangshao and Longshan cultures. Evidence was at first scanty, and in some cases appeared to be conflicting. New sites were excavated in the Central Plains area where Longshan-type artefacts appeared in later levels overlying earlier Yangshao cultural strata. This suggested that the Longshan culture might have been later than and descended from the Yangshao. But then at other places in the east sites were discovered where the early levels seemed to be very much of Longshan affinity,

A Neolithic painted pottery urn of the Gansu phase
of the Yangshao culture, from Banshan

but some painted pottery of Yangshao type occurred in later layers. The evidence was confusing. Only the excavation of a greater number of sites, and the establishment of some absolute dates using carbon-14 and other dating techniques, has enabled a clearer picture to emerge. It is now evident that the Yangshao and Longshan cultural horizons were at first contemporary and distinct, but at a later period came more and more closely into contact, with many mutual borrowings and transmissions. After about 3200 BC transformations occurred throughout China, which resulted in the appearance of broadly similar cultures in all the three previously distinct cultural regions. Painted pottery, for so long characteristic of the cultures of the Central Plains, entirely disappeared; the Longshan pottery tradition became dominant everywhere. Although many elements of the previous Central Plains and south-eastern cultures persisted, they were assimilated into a cultural complex which generally resembled the east coast Longshan assemblage.

This late Neolithic Longshanoid horizon must have been the result of increased contact between the inhabitants of the various cultural areas. This explains the appearance of Yangshao-type artefacts at some fundamentally Longshan sites in the eastern coastal region, as well as the occurrence of items of Longshan affinity at Yangshao sites in the Central

Plains. It seems likely that the Longshan potters were more highly skilled at the period when contacts intensified (the use of the potter's wheel probably began in China in the east coast region), and that their more advanced techniques therefore displaced those of other regions. The black pottery characteristic of the late Longshan tradition, as well as other Longshan elements, thus spread to areas well beyond the original area of Longshan development. But this was not a case of complete replacement of earlier cultural identities by an intrusive external culture. The late Neolithic Longshan of the Central Plains maintained many aspects of the preceding Yangshao culture, such as vessel types, and remained distinguishable from the late east coast Longshan though clearly heavily influenced by it. Interestingly, Yangshao cultural elements do not seem to have had any persistent influence on the east coast Longshan; the cultural transmissions were almost entirely one-way.

The Chinese Bronze Age

By about 2000 BC major new developments were occurring in northern China. Societal organisation was becoming more complex; settlements were becoming larger and were often walled; divisions of class (or at least of wealth and possessions) had arisen. Among the artefacts of stone, bone and clay appeared some of a new material, metal. The Stone Age in China was coming to a close, the first civilized Chinese state was about to be formed, and the development of writing was laying the foundations of China's history. From this period onwards the evidence of archaeology is increasingly supplemented by written records.

Unfortunately, though not surprisingly, the early history of China is very obscure. Written accounts include much that is clearly legendary, and were susceptible to errors, omissions and corruptions during the course of copying and transmission. The vast majority of early written documents have certainly not survived at all, and the authenticity of some that appear to have survived is dubious. In the absence of other supporting evidence, records for the early period of Chinese history have to be treated with great caution.

Traditional accounts of the beginnings of Chinese civilization commence with stories of various legendary figures who clearly never existed as historical personages. Thus there are, for example, Shen Nong, the Divine Husbandman, credited with originating agriculture and ascertaining the uses of medicinal herbs, and Yu the Great, who is said to have controlled and channelled China's watercourses and relieved a great flood. The Yellow Emperor, Yao and Shun are other divine rulers of this kind. The stories about them contain much that is of interest from various points of view but cannot be considered factual. The first recorded Chinese dynasty is called Xia, followed by the Shang and Zhou dynasties. The annals of these three dynasties constitute the earliest Chinese records with a strong claim to be regarded as historical, though there remain many doubts as to their accuracy.

HISTORICAL SOURCES

The earliest Chinese historical sources are of several kinds and of varying value. They fall into two fundamental groups, those transmitted continuously over many centuries, and those long buried in the ground and recovered recently in the course of archaeological investigations. The second group are generally more reliable, having been set down at or near the time of the events recorded and remaining unaltered since, but are often fragmentary and difficult to interpret. The first group includes much longer texts which are usually more easily understood, but having often been written down long after the period recorded, and copied and recopied over a long period, they cannot be considered entirely reliable.

It is generally accepted now that no surviving continuously transmitted document was originally written down in its current form before the early years of the Zhou dynasty. No Xia or Shang documents were preserved, copied and handed down to the present time; records of those dynasties were written down long after the period to which they relate. A number of genuine Zhou documents have been transmitted, but many even of these have to a greater or lesser extent become corrupt during the transmission process. The earliest complete history of China was not compiled until about the turn of the first century BC, some 150 years after the death of the last Zhou ruler and many centuries after the Xia and Shang periods. Nevertheless it is one of the most comprehensive sources of historical information about the Xia and

Shang dynasties. There is still no certainty that the Xia dynasty ever existed, but since later records relating to the Shang dynasty have been proved by archaeology to be at least partly accurate (see below), it seems unreasonable to reject completely later accounts of the Xia. Excavations in the area where these accounts suggest that the Xia dynasty was centred have uncovered sites that, from their period and level of culture, could well be remains of Xia cities. The Erlitou site, near Yanshi in northern Henan province, was once generally thought to be early Shang. Now it is often considered to be late Xia, possibly the site of the last Xia capital city. A site at Taosi in Shanxi may be an early Xia capital. A major Chinese project of the late 1990s aimed to establish clearer dates for the three earliest Chinese dynasties. It concluded that the Xia was founded between about 2,100 and 2,000 BC and overthrown by the Shang between about 1,600 and 1,500 BC. It also concluded that the Zhou dynasty replaced the Shang in 1050–1020 BC. The methods used to establish these dates have already begun to be questioned, however, and they cannot be considered absolute. The dates for the beginning and end of the Shang dynasty seem unlikely to be far wrong, but the Xia dynasty is supposed to have been founded by the semi-legendary Yu the Great and its origins can probably never be completely unshrouded from the mists of antiquity.

The Shang Dynasty

Doubts about the existence of the Shang dynasty were dispelled by the recognition of inscriptions on pieces of bone from the vicinity of Anyang in Henan province as writings of Shang date.

Archaeological excavations from the 1920s onwards have now provided large quantities of inscribed Shang bones, which have not only proved the existence of the Shang dynasty and at least partly confirmed the accuracy of the transmitted accounts, but have also provided valuable additional information about this early period in the history of China. These inscriptions on bone (and also on turtle shells) date from the later half of the Shang dynastic period, and were made as part of a process of divination. Heat was applied to the bones and the resulting cracks interpreted as favourable or unfavourable answers to questions asked. Oracle bones of this sort have been found at

Neolithic sites also, but without inscriptions. The writing on them recorded the questions asked and the answers given, and sometimes also the subsequent outcomes of the events concerned. Many questions relate to sacrifices to Shang royal ancestors, enabling the names and relationships of the kings to be confirmed; they conform closely to the transmitted records. Other questions relate to activities of the king, such as hunting or visits to various parts of his domains, to whether harvests would be good and other agricultural problems, or to what should be done about attacks on the Shang lands.

This inscriptional evidence, together with other archaeological data and later recorded traditions, has allowed some idea of the China of the Shang dynasty to be formed. The Shang kings held authority over an area roughly covering most of the Yellow River plain in western Shandong, Hebei and Henan, and a considerable part of Shanxi and the eastern Wei River valley in Shaanxi. Some other areas, particularly to the south-east towards the River Huai in northern Anhui, were probably also under their domination. The exact borders, and the extent of Shang authority, must have varied from time to time. Archaeological evidence indicates that the influence of the Shang state was felt far beyond the areas directly under its control.

The Shang kings were regarded as more or less divine, absolute rulers on earth during their lives and influential in heaven after their deaths. The early Chinese had clearly believed in an after-life at least since early Neolithic times, as they commonly buried offerings in the graves of their dead. Shang kings were buried in most elaborate tombs, with extensive offerings to accompany them, including large numbers of sacrificial victims. Most of these were probably slaves or enslaved war captives, others may have been expected to follow their king in death by committing suicide. Certainly some of those who accompanied the dead king were given honourable burial, while others were beheaded and simply thrown into pits, the heads sometimes buried separately from the bodies. The dead king was also given a military guard, complete war chariots with horses and drivers being interred with him. The Shang believed in a supreme deity, Di or Shang Di, and the oracle inscriptions make it clear that the dead kings were influential with Di in shaping the destinies of their successors.

ZHENGZHOU

Excavations have revealed the sites of several large settlements of the Shang period. These include the great ceremonial and ritual centre where eleven of the later Shang kings were buried, near Anyang in Henan, and a large walled city at Zhengzhou in the same province. Several important features characterize these Shang sites. One is the extensive use of compressed earth for building; important buildings were raised on earth platforms, and vast defensive walls were constructed of this material. The city walls at the Zhengzhou site, which was probably a capital city, enclose a roughly rectangular area of more than three square kilometres and were originally more than nine metres high and as much as 36 metres wide at the base. It has been estimated that it would have required the labour of 10,000 workers over a period of some eighteen years to construct such a wall. This enormous effort is particularly striking when it is considered that the Shang rulers spent much of their time moving from place to place (perhaps partly to maximize their personal influence, partly to spread the burden of feeding the large royal retinue), and that they are supposed to have changed the site of their capital city some seven times.

BRONZE

The use of bronze is another major feature of the Shang period. It is very likely that metallurgy was first discovered in China during, or slightly prior to, the period of the Xia dynasty, but early evidence is very fragmentary. There is solid evidence for a developed bronze-casting technique being in use by the early period of the Shang dynasty, however, and Chinese techniques are so distinctive that they are likely to have been of independent local origin. Chinese workers in bronze did not work the metal with hammer and anvil; they used a sophisticated and unique technique of casting in pottery moulds. A model of the piece to be cast was first made in clay, around a clay core, and then sheathed in a clay outer mould. This was then cut into segments, so that it could be taken apart and the model removed. When reassembled, a gap was left between the outer mould and the core, of the exact shape of the model. Into this gap molten bronze was poured, thus forming the final bronze object. For simple pieces such as knives and axes only a single or two-piece mould was necessary, but the Shang bronze-founders were quite capable of making large and complex vessels, requiring comparably complex moulds in several sections. One large square vessel with four legs (of the type known as *ding*) found at Anyang is 137 cm. tall, 110 cm. long and 77 cm. wide, and weighs some 700 kg.

Several Shang bronze foundries have been excavated, and it seems that the workers in bronze were privileged people, with much better housing and higher status than average. The various kinds of handicrafts, including the making of pottery and implements or ornaments of bone and stone as well as bronze-casting, were specialized activities by this period, and seem generally to have conferred high status on the artisans who carried them out. It is possible that the special technical knowledge involved was handed down within families. The degree of specialization was such that particular kinds of pottery were produced at different workshops.

Although some Shang bronze pieces are more or less utilitarian, the use of bronze was largely confined to the upper strata of Shang society and was strongly associated with ritual and ceremony. The most ornate bronzes are the various kinds of vessels used during sacrifices to gods and ancestors. Many of these are superb works of art, beautifully formed and with extensive surface decoration, mainly of animal-based motifs. Several types of vessel were used for preparing offerings of wine, others for sacrificial meat or other food. They were commonly buried among the grave goods of their noble owners.

Although the Shang civilization was undoubtedly sustained primarily by agriculture, there is comparatively little information about the large mass of people engaged in tilling the land. It is possible that many of them were slaves or of a status little better than slavery, but even this is uncertain. They continued to work the land with very much the same tools as their Neolithic ancestors, and the necessity to support the Shang royalty and nobility must have imposed an additional burden on their already hard lives.

ETHNIC GROUPS IN EARLY CHINA

According to tradition, the first king of the Shang dynasty overthrew the Xia in about 1750 BC. The traditional view assumes the temporal succession of the dynasties, but there can be little doubt that the Shang rulers had been chiefs exercising power within at least a limited local area for some time before their challenge to the Xia. Similarly, there must have been many less powerful chiefdoms, no doubt largely at a less advanced stage of development, around the periphery of the Shang domain throughout the period of the Shang dynasty. Several external groups are mentioned on oracle bones as enemies of the Shang, either attacking areas under their control or being attacked. Whether these groups can be called 'tribes' or 'states' is unclear. Some may have been ethnically identical with the people under Shang rule but at a lower level of development, others are likely to have differed in language and race. The ethnic and linguistic situation in China at this period is obscure, but it is probable that there were many different peoples in contact with the Shang state. It may even be that the Shang rulers held sway over people of varied race and language. There are strong indications that the origins of the Shang royal house itself lay on the east coast of China (probably in Shandong, perhaps with an early connection with Liaoning across the Gulf of Bohai), and it may be that the Shang and the Xia were ethnically distinct. There is no doubt that at a slightly later period peoples speaking different languages existed around (and even within) the main Chinese culture area of the north China plains, though it is not certain whether these languages were Chinese dialects (related in the way Cantonese is to Mandarin), or whether they may have been related to Tibetan or Mongolian or the languages of the other minority peoples found within the borders of China today. The likelihood is that in this early period Chinese was the language of a rather small area of north China, and that it spread with the expansion of Chinese civilization, replacing or displacing other tongues. The development of a system of writing for Chinese at a time when no other tradition of literacy existed in East Asia no doubt assisted this linguistic dominance.

The Expansion of the Chinese Culture Area

As Shang influence spread, the culture of the Central Plains diffused to regions beyond its area of origin. Major sites of Shang civilization extend from northern Shanxi southward into central Jiangxi and Hunan provinces. At least some of the more southerly sites were certainly outside the area of the Shang state. These sites must be remains of organized and civilized groups of people who shared Shang culture but were not under direct Shang political control.

THE ZHOU DYNASTY

One such group, which eventually became a powerful rival to the Shang state, was called the Zhou. The Zhou are mentioned in some of the earliest Shang oracle inscriptions, and were clearly at that time subordinate to the Shang. The area occupied by the Zhou was in the Wei River valley, west of the modern city of Xi'an, and near the western limits of Shang power. In fact, it is likely that at certain times the Zhou were completely independent of the Shang. Further west still lay lands occupied by 'barbarian' peoples outside the main area of Chinese culture. It is quite probable that the Zhou may have derived from one such 'barbarian' group, the Qiang, a people of Tibetan affinities. By the period when there is good historical evidence about the Zhou, however, they were undoubtedly more or less thoroughly sinicized.

Finally the Zhou state became sufficiently powerful to challenge the Shang. This challenge may have begun some three or four generations before the Shang were finally overthrown. Certainly tradition has it that the 'Mandate of Heaven' to destroy the Shang was given to King Wen of Zhou, although the conquest was not completed until the reign of his son, King Wu. Whatever the exact facts, there is no doubt that in the end the Zhou overthrew the Shang by force of arms and became the new rulers of the Chinese culture area, which was much enlarged during the period of the Zhou dynasty.

The date at which the conquest of Shang by Zhou took place is the most disputed in all Chinese history. Traditionally it was placed in 1122 BC, but this was long ago shown to be unreliable. Many other dates have been proposed, most of them later, and in some cases as much as 150 years or more later. Recently it has been argued that the battle of Muye, in which the Zhou overthrew the Shang, took place on 15 January 1045 BC, but this can still not be considered an absolute date. It is reasonable to suppose, however, that the conquest must have occurred within a few decades either side of 1050 BC.

The state which the Zhou rulers acquired had been much enlarged during the last few years of the Shang dynasty. It was at least partly because of the difficulties of maintaining authority over this enlarged area that the Shang fell from power. The Zhou conquerors solved the problem by establishing a feudal system in which relatives of the Zhou king and other loyal associates were installed as lords over various subordinate states. They held their power as vassals of the king, and owed unquestioning allegiance to him. Rulers of states which had been partly subservient to Shang or independent were also often enfeoffed by the Zhou ruler if they submitted voluntarily. Thus the early Zhou state consisted of an area around the capital city (near modern Xi'an) directly ruled by the Zhou king, and of a number of subordinate states ruled by lords who acknowledged the Zhou king as their overlord, and could be called upon to serve him in various ways and to pay him tribute or taxes. In theory, all land belonged to the king and was held by others only as a gift from him and for as long as the holder retained the king's favour. Such a system had probably partially evolved before the period of Zhou rule, but had not previously been so fully organized.

The system worked well for so long as the Zhou kings ruled firmly and energetically and ensured that the feudal lords knew their place. The position of the kings as 'Sons of Heaven', virtual deities, greatly strengthened their authority, so long as their divine rights remained unquestioned. But within such a system lay the seeds of its undoing, for if the feudal lords became too powerful they could throw off central control. This indeed was the situation throughout the second half of the Zhou dynastic period. It was indicative of the religious importance of the Zhou kings that they retained at least symbolic status for hundreds of years after they had lost actual power.

The culture of China under the Zhou differed little from that of the period of Shang rule. There was, however, much less interest in divination by oracle bones, and the bones virtually ceased to be inscribed. But ritual vessels of bronze continued to be cast, and it is on these that inscriptions of the Zhou period often appear. While during the Shang period inscriptions on bronze were much less common and always very short, during the Zhou dynastic period they became more usual and sometimes rather lengthy. They often record the special occasions for which the bronze vessels were cast, such as the bestowal

A three-legged bronze sacrificial vessel of the
early Zhou period (late 10th century BC)

of a fief or other royal favour, or success in battle. Though there are
many problems with their interpretation and use, they are important
sources of information, especially for the early part of the Zhou dynasty.
In addition, this period is documented by several major contemporary
or near-contemporary writings which have been transmitted down to
the present day. With the Zhou dynasty, Chinese history begins to
emerge from obscurity.

ZHOU EXPANSION

After King Wu had overthrown the last Shang ruler, who was killed,
he enfeoffed his son with a state, for he had no desire to incur the wrath
of the former Shang kings by leaving them with no one to offer them
sacrifices. A Shang successor state in fact continued to exist for several
centuries. But the loyalty of the newly-conquered people was in some

doubt, so King Wu appointed some of his brothers to act as 'Inspectors' and keep watch over the Shang heir. Unfortunately, King Wu died soon after the conquest and was succeeded by his young son, who became King Cheng. Real power was held for some time by one of King Wu's brothers, the Duke of Zhou. The Duke seems to have been an energetic and capable ruler, and was in later times given much credit for the establishment of Zhou power. But there may well have been jealousies between him and some of his other brothers, for the Inspectors allied themselves with their Shang ward and rose in rebellion. The Duke of Zhou reacted strongly, defeating the rebels in battle and executing the Shang heir and the eldest of the Inspectors, who was his own elder brother. Firm measures were taken to ensure that there was no more trouble with the former Shang royal family. They were forcibly moved away from their old centres of power and settled where they could be closely supervised. The Duke extended Zhou conquests far to the east, perhaps as far as the coast. A subsidiary capital city was built close to the centre of the area under Zhou control, near the modern city of Luoyang, though the old western capital near Xi'an continued to be the principal one for several centuries.

The exact area under Zhou control is uncertain, and it is in any case quite likely that the authority of the Zhou king became gradually weaker with distance from the royal capitals. Outlying 'barbarian' states may have acknowledged Zhou dominance when it suited them to do so, but not when it did not. The extent to which the central Zhou government actually influenced what happened in outlying states, beyond occasionally demanding certain goods or services, was probably small. Nevertheless, there were often strong ties, of loyalty and often also of blood-relationship, between the Zhou kings and their vassals. Thus, the important outlying state of Yan, with a capital which lay some 60 miles east of modern Beijing, and thus more than 400 miles from the subsidiary eastern capital of Zhou, was bestowed upon the Duke of Shao. This Duke was a major figure in early Zhou government, second in importance only to the Duke of Zhou, and responsible for major military conquests which much enlarged the Zhou state. He was probably a royal relative. So important was he at the royal court of King Cheng that he may never have ruled Yan personally, sending his eldest son in his stead. This close connection between the ruler of Yan and the royal court must have assisted greatly in ensuring the sway of Zhou authority in a region which was a bastion of Chinese civilization against the barbarians of the north-east.

The rule of Zhou in the early part of the dynasty was strong in the areas around the two capitals, near Xi'an and Luoyang, and in the valley of the Yellow River between the two. It extended northwards through much of what is now northern Shaanxi and considerable parts of Shanxi and Hebei. In the east it covered at least the western half of Shandong. Its western limit was in the Wei valley somewhere near the present border between Shaanxi and Gansu. To the south limits are much less certain; it is possible that it reached to the Yangtze valley, but was probably never very strong there. Within the area of the Zhou state there were many mountainous or otherwise marginal districts inhabited by peoples regarded as barbarians, who were more or less outside the Chinese government system.

The Zhou sovereigns maintained their prestige by frequent visits to various parts of their realm and by military expeditions, usually aimed at punishing barbarians on the borders or rebellious vassals. These two groups increased their effectiveness by acting in combination. Indeed, various barbarian groups are said to have assisted the Zhou in their conquest of Shang. The Zhou armies were splendid enough to impress all on the route of their marches who saw them, and were frequently victorious. Thus they overawed the vassals whose lands they crossed, and increased Zhou prestige even among the peoples beyond the boundaries of Zhou rule. The achievements of the Zhou kings assured their dominance for several centuries.

THE DECLINE OF ZHOU POWER

But after the first couple of centuries of the dynasty, Zhou royal power began to decline. The kings took less interest in maintaining strong central government, and their vassals became increasingly disaffected. Pressure from barbarians, particularly in the west, also seems to have increased. This may have been associated with the development of pastoral nomadism on the steppes, which probably emerged fully by about 900 BC. Horse-nomads armed with bows formed formidable and highly mobile fighting forces, and from the ninth century BC onward there was considerable upheaval on the steppes of central Asia. In the west this resulted in the incursions of several waves of invaders from the steppes, beginning with the Cimmerians and Scythians, and there must also have been similar movements in the east. The peoples on the north-western borders of the Zhou state may have been impelled south-eastwards by pressure from the steppe nomads, thus bringing them into conflict with Zhou.

Whatever the precise causes, a major attack was mounted on the Zhou royal domain in the Xi'an area in 771 BC (dates are now firmly established). The attacking forces included both disaffected vassals and barbarians, and the fighting seems to have resulted in the loss of large areas in the west to the latter. The Zhou king, You, was killed, and the feudal lords set up one of his sons as King Ping in the eastern capital. The western lands were reconquered by one of the feudal lords, from the state of Qin (of which more will be heard later), but were simply incorporated into that state. From this time onward, the Zhou kings held only nominal authority over their vassals. The various feudal states became independent entities, vying with each other for power and frequently fighting among themselves. Gradually the smaller and weaker states were conquered and absorbed by the stronger ones, so that eventually only a few large states were left to struggle for ascendency.

CHAPTER FOUR

The Formation of China, 771–221 BC

The collapse of central power in the Zhou state in 771 BC was the beginning of a long period during which the Chinese culture area was politically divided. This was a time of much strife, with frequent warfare between the states, and also a time of social and intellectual turmoil. After the rather slow development of a distinct Chinese civilization with its own individual culture, which had taken place over thousands of years during the Stone Age and the early historic period, changes occurred much more rapidly during the next six or seven centuries. These changes brought about the emergence of a single Chinese state, for the first time including large areas south of the Yangtze, in which almost all the essential features of later China were already present, if only in embryo. In many respects these few centuries are the most interesting and important in the whole of the long history of China.

The Zhou dynasty, though deprived of most of its power, continued to exist for another 500 years. This second part of the dynasty, during which the Zhou kings resided in the formerly subsidiary eastern capital, is usually referred to as Eastern Zhou (the first part thus being Western Zhou). It is normal to divide the history of Eastern Zhou into two sections, called the Spring and Autumn and the Warring States periods. There is really no developmental reason for this division; it is based simply on the fact that for the first part the main historical source is a book called the *Spring and Autumn Annals* and its commentaries, while for the second it is a book known as *The Strategies of the Warring States*. These two periods may conveniently be taken to run from 770 to 464 BC and from 463 to 222 BC. The Zhou dynasty was finally extinguished just before the end of the Warring States period, in 256 BC.

The Spring and Autumn Period

The Western Zhou state had established a form of government which was very much founded on a familial pattern and in which heredity was of fundamental importance. The rulers of subordinate states were commonly actual relatives of the Zhou king, and were treated very much like relatives even where there were no real ties of blood. The terms of address used by the king to his nobles and vice versa were those of the family. Thus, nobles having the same surname as the royal house were addressed as paternal uncles by the king, those with different surnames as maternal uncles. This was true even where no actual relationship was known to exist. The nobility thus deferred to the king not only as their sovereign but also as the head of the family to which they all were considered to belong. In addition the authority of the king was founded to a large extent upon relationships to illustrious ancestors. Dead rulers were revered as gods, and the living king was thought to hold power by virtue of the charisma passed on to him by his forebears. This charisma derived ultimately from the supreme god Di. The nobility, as royal relatives, also inherited it in lesser degree. Clearly within such a system relations between the rulers and the ruled were virtually immutable. The overthrow of a king or a member of the nobility could only be excused on the grounds that he had so offended his ancestors and Di that the 'Mandate of Heaven' had been taken from him. This was indeed the justification used by the Zhou rulers for their conquest of Shang, and by most other conquerors in later Chinese history.

Battle scenes from a Warring States period vessel
excavated in Henan, central China

During much of the Spring and Autumn period the heavenly authority of the Zhou kings remained unquestioned. Though they had little actual power over their former vassals, they retained their position as ritual heads of the Chinese culture area. Rulers of states deferred to their exalted status in matters of protocol, and required their approval for their acts. Thus, for example, in 632 BC the state of Jin defeated the state of Chu in a major battle. The Marquis of Jin afterwards presented 1,000 captured soldiers and 100 chariots to the Zhou king. The king gave a feast for the marquis, and gave him a written appointment as the chief of all the feudal lords, together with various presents of ritual significance. The appointment addressed the marquis as 'uncle', and instructed him to 'discharge the King's commands'. The marquis declined the honours offered three times, as etiquette demanded, before finally accepting.

Such ceremonious occasions were an integral part of the accepted system of government at this period. Although the king had no real power over the lords of the states, they could not treat him as what he actually had become: the ruler of nothing more than a small and weak state, much less powerful than many of his supposed subordinates. To do so would have challenged the whole basis of their own authority, for if the king had no divine authority to rule, then neither had they. The strength of the old ideas was such that it took centuries for them to change.

At the beginning of the Eastern Zhou period, there were some 170 states. Most were small, but a few, especially around the borders of the Chinese culture area, where there was room to expand at the expense of the barbarians, were large. Some formerly barbarian states, which had not been included in the old Western Zhou state, gradually absorbed Chinese culture and became accepted into the Chinese sphere. In all, there were about a dozen major states during the Spring and Autumn period, which vied with each other for supremacy and gradually conquered and absorbed the smaller and weaker states. Qi was in the east, covering a large area in what is now Shandong province. To the north lay Yan, including the sites of modern Beijing and Tianjin and extending to the Liaodong peninsula. West of this, centred on what is now southern Shanxi, was Jin. In the far west lay Qin, including the old Western Zhou capital and areas further west and south-west that

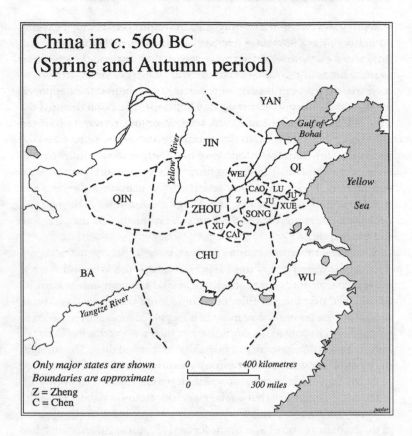

China in *c.* 560 BC
(Spring and Autumn period)

YAN

Gulf of Bohai

JIN

Yellow River

WEI

QI

Yellow Sea

CAO LU
Z JU
ZHOU SONG XUE
XU C
CAI

QIN

CHU

BA

WU

Yangtze River

Only major states are shown
Boundaries are approximate
Z = Zheng
C = Chen

0   400 kilometres
0   300 miles

had not long before been barbarian regions. South of Jin and between Qin in the west and Qi in the east lay (roughly from west to east) the Zhou royal domain, Zheng, Wei, Cai, Chen, Song, Cao and Lu. In the far south, covering a large part of the lower Yangtze valley, was Chu, originally a barbarian state but increasingly important within the Chinese sphere. From the early sixth century another state of barbarian origins, Wu, also entered the scene. Its territory was around the Yangtze estuary, including the site of modern Shanghai. Faced with aggression from partly sinicized states such as Chu and Wu, the states of the core Chinese culture area came to think of and refer to themselves as 'the

Central States'. In Chinese this is *Zhongguo*, which has become the common Chinese word for 'China'. As the Chinese language usually does not indicate plurality, this term later came to be interpreted to mean 'the Middle Kingdom', but this was not its original sense.

Warfare among the states was almost constant. It has been calculated that during the roughly 300 years of the Spring and Autumn period, less than fifty were entirely peaceful. Wars at this time were rarely very prolonged, however; usually one state or alliance of states would attack another and the outcome would be decided by a single major battle. The object of attacks was normally either to seize a part or the whole of the territory of the state attacked, or to force it to adhere to a particular alliance. Weak states were quickly dominated and extinguished by their larger neighbours.

This process of absorption of small states by more powerful ones led to the downfall of many noble families. Rulers of conquered states might, if they were lucky, be allowed to remain in their old territory as subordinates of their conquerors; at worst, they might be reduced to the status of slaves. Their fate was usually shared by their ministers and retainers. Obviously there was a great reduction in the number of noble families as a result of the extinction of states.

Another result of the frequent warfare was the converse process of the exaltation of successful warriors of humble origins. In 552 BC the ruler of Qi established a system of conferring honorific titles on those who were valorous in battle. Later, grants of land or official positions were given in Jin to good soldiers. The wars of this time therefore tended to break up the old social system; gradually the old nobility lost its prestige, and could no longer expect automatically to receive preference because of its hereditary status. Increasingly rulers came to appoint advisers, ministers and officials for their talents rather than their ancestry. The social and governmental system which had for centuries maintained order in China thus fell apart, and a great search began for a new system to replace it.

Confucius

Thus began the great age of social and political philosophy in China. Every state ruler wanted to know how to preserve and strengthen his position in the unstable world in which he found himself, and there were many who tried to advise him. At first such advice tended to be empirical and piecemeal, but as more and more thought was devoted to methods of government whole philosophical systems began to emerge. One of the first thinkers to elaborate such a complete philosophy, and certainly one of the most influential in the long term, was the man known to Westerners as Confucius.

Kong Qiu or Kong Zhongni was known to his disciples by the honorific term Kong Fuzi ('Master Kong'), whence the Latinized form 'Confucius' was derived. He was born in 552 or 551 BC in the state of Lu, the capital of which was Qufu in what is now Shandong province. Little or nothing is known about his parents, but various traditions state that he was descended from noble ancestors and this seems likely to be true. He was most probably from a class of growing size and importance which consisted of more or less impoverished descendants of nobility and former nobility, who may have owned little more than the mass of peasantry but retained a certain prestige that placed them between the nobility and the common people. Minor official positions were commonly filled from their ranks, and they increasingly aspired to advancement to the highest posts. Usually they had at least a modicum of learning, an important asset which the more ambitious of them strove to increase. Confucius himself had clearly acquired much knowledge during his earlier years, and had many disciples studying with him later, some of whom held high official positions.

Confucius would probably have thought of himself as essentially conservative, attempting to preserve old ways against the breakdown in society which he saw taking place all around him. He had much to say about 'the Way of the Former Kings', and emphasized the importance of adhering to tradition in etiquette and ritual. Yet in many ways his teachings were revolutionary, for he largely denied the validity of heredity in the determination of status, claiming that only adherence to a certain moral code could confer any right to respect and authority. Order in society, he considered, could only be maintained by government which accorded with this moral code. Moreover, the morality he taught extended to all levels of society and was designed to benefit everyone down to the lowest of the toiling masses. Although he did not advocate government *by* the people, he stated clearly that it should be *for* the people.

There is little in Confucius' teachings of a religious character. He certainly maintained that it was essential to perform all the traditional rites and sacrifices, and seems to have believed that his teachings accorded with the 'Decree of Heaven', yet said that it was wise 'to keep one's distance from the gods and spirits'. On being asked by one disciple how to serve the spirits of the dead and the gods he retorted: 'You are not able even to serve man. How can you serve the spirits?' When the disciple went on to ask about death, his reply was in similar vein: 'You do not understand even life. How can you understand death?'

The fundamental concept of Confucius' philosophy was benevolence: 'Do not impose on others what you yourself do not desire.' When this principle was adopted by the government of a state, then the whole population would be benefited and, influenced by the example of their leaders, would likewise behave correctly. In such a state, life for all would be comfortable, the people would be easily governed, and would be ready to fight courageously against attack from other states. The problem was that conforming to the strict moral code which Confucius advocated was far from easy. His teachings were not readily embraced by the opportunist and often self-seeking society of his day, and although he travelled to several major states in an attempt to win over their rulers he was never given high office. When he died in 479 BC he was no more than a junior counsellor in his native state of Lu.

Confucius had attracted a number of disciples, however, and they handed on his teachings to later generations. At first this transmission was more or less entirely oral, but within a couple of generations Confucius' words were set down in writing. The surviving collection of his sayings, the *Lun Yu* or *Analects*, has been transmitted for almost 2,500 years and still allows its readers to form a clear impression of the character and ideas of this remarkable man. Revered as a sage by the Chinese until recent times, he must surely have been one of the most influential philosophers of any nation and any period.

Other Philosophers

As far as we now know, Confucius was the earliest thinker to propose a more or less systematic philosophical approach to the problems of this troubled period of Chinese history. If he failed to make any really significant impact on the society of his own day, it was because he was ahead of his time. Old ways of thinking could not be changed in just a few decades. But as the ferment in Chinese society increased and intensified after his death, so it became ever more imperative for new ideas to be put forward to replace old ones which were rapidly becoming irrelevant. Many practical developments were occurring that were irrevocably altering Chinese society. Iron tools first began to be used at about the time of Confucius, and became widespread during the century after his death. Riding on horseback, and with it techniques of cavalry warfare, came into China from the steppes to the north by the end of the fourth century BC (previously the Chinese had used horses only for pulling carts and chariots). At about the same period the soybean began to be grown in rotation with cereals to improve fertility, and therefore increase agricultural yields (soybeans became commonly cultivated in China after the mid-seventh century BC). Money began to circulate widely, along with an expansion in inter-state trade and the growth of regional specializations in production. These and other developments swept away old life-styles, requiring new responses and the establishment of new forms of society. Faced with such a situation, numerous thinkers came forward with ideas and theories intended to solve the problems which a society in flux inevitably faces.

MO ZI

Born at about the time of Confucius' death, the rather enigmatic philosopher Mo Zi based his teachings on 'universal love'. This was really an extension of Confucian ideas, an enlargement of the principle of 'not imposing on others what you yourself do not desire'. The Confucians, however, were in complete agreement with the strong Chinese characteristic of according special devotion to parents and relatives, whereas Mo Zi saw the corrupt partiality and nepotism which often flowed from family loyalties and insisted that all should be loved equally.

This seems a thoroughly impractical theory, but Mo Zi was a highly practical man. His goal was to establish peace, order and prosperity, and he saw his ideas as providing the best means to do so. His 'universal love' was not conceived as emotional (Mo Zi in fact disapproved of emotion) but as purely mental, and he felt that it was by no means impossible to persuade people that it was in their own and everyone's interests to put his principles into practice. He advanced many arguments to prove his 'universal love' to be a good policy. All disorder stemmed from selfishness, he said. If universal love prevailed, there would be no disorder.

Unlike Confucius and his followers, Mo Zi had strong religious beliefs and considered that Heaven and the spirits played an active part in regulating the acts of living people. He related many stories of spirits avenging wrongs or rewarding virtue, and said that Heaven sent down retribution for improper acts. 'Even in deep gorges and great forests, where there is no man, one may not act improperly. There are ghosts and spirits who will see.' He clearly believed that his teachings accorded with the will of Heaven.

The practicality of Mo Zi was most clearly demonstrated by his mastery of the techniques of defensive warfare. This may seem odd in a philosopher, but it seems that his greatest abhorrence was for the terrible wars of his time, and in case persuasion failed he liked to have other means of dissuading one state from attacking another. On one occasion he heard that the large southern state of Chu was intending to use the advice and techniques of a strategist called Gongshu Pan in attacking the smaller state of Song. He at once hurried to Chu to try to dissuade its ruler. His verbal arguments lacked success, whereupon he challenged Gongshu Pan to a sort of war-game, repulsing his attacks nine times. Running out of stratagems, Gongshu Pan uttered a veiled threat to kill Mo Zi. The ruler of Chu did not understand, so Mo Zi explained:

> Gongshu Pan thinks that if I were murdered, then there would be no-one to defend Song . . . But in fact three hundred of my disciples . . . are at this moment waiting on the walls of Song . . . You may murder me, but you can't get rid of them.

The ruler of Chu agreed to abandon his planned attack on Song.

Mo Zi seems to have had many disciples in his own time, and his school of thought flourished for several centuries, from before 400 BC until about the turn of the Christian era. Thereafter it seems to have died out more or less completely. Little interest was shown in the surviving writings of the school of Mo Zi until the general revival of studies of the thought of this period in comparatively recent times.

MENCIUS

After about 400 BC philosophy became fashionable in China. The rulers of each of the various surviving states entertained philosophers at their courts and listened to their ideas, hoping to learn something of benefit. King Hui of the state of Liang, for example, invited a number of philosophers to his court, treating them with great respect and offering rich presents. Among those who accepted the invitation was Meng Ke, known in the west as Mencius (*c.* 372–*c.* 289 BC). He came from the small state of Zou, just south of Confucius' native state of Lu (both states lay within the boundaries of modern Shandong) and had studied under a disciple of a grandson of Confucius. He became the second great Confucian philosopher.

Like Confucius himself, Mencius insisted on moral principles. The virtues which he considered fundamental were benevolence and righteousness. When he first appeared before King Hui of Liang, the king remarked that since he had taken the trouble to come such a long distance, he must surely have to offer some means of profiting the king's state. Mencius replied that 'profit' should not be considered; what he had brought was benevolence and righteousness and nothing more.

The point which Mencius tried on many occasions to convey to the various rulers to whom he spoke was that considerations of profit would inevitably lead to strife. If a king wished to profit his state, the nobility would wish to profit their clan and the rest of the people would wish to profit themselves. Thus there would be contention for profit and the state would be endangered. On the other hand, if a king were to practise benevolent government, ensuring prosperity for the people, then he would win popular support and even those outside his state would turn towards him. He might thus win the allegiance of all the Chinese people, and conquer all the Chinese world without even having to fight for it.

Compared with Confucius, Mencius seems to have been rather arrogant and contentious. This was probably partly a real difference in personality, and partly due to the different conditions of the times when they lived. Mencius seems to have been more successful than Confucius in gaining audience with rulers, though like Confucius he failed ever to gain any high administrative office. But as we have seen, in the time of Mencius there were many philosophers with many different ideas, who were frequently admitted to audience with rulers. Mencius' success in this respect was not exceptional in his period; he had to contend with all these rival theories, and therefore developed a more argumentative style of discourse based on the assumption that the ideas of the Confucian school were right and superior to those of other schools. His recorded discourses rarely show the rather attractive humanity and humility often found in the words of Confucius.

YANG ZHU

The two major schools of thought against which Mencius had to contend were those of the followers of Mo Zi and of Yang Zhu. While we have considerable information about the ideas of Mo Zi, of Yang Zhu we know only very little, most of which is found in the writings of his opponents from other schools of thought. Mencius said, 'Master Yang chooses egoism. Though he might benefit the whole world by pulling out one hair he would not do it.' This may well be a distortion of Yang's teachings – it seems more likely from other evidence that in reality he taught that it was not worthwhile to forfeit one hair in exchange for rule over the whole world. His philosophy was one of self-preservation in a dangerous world. There was no point in striving to be good and noble, or to gain wealth or fame, for any results achieved would be no more than transitory and often illusory. The best way was to take life as it came, free from fear and worry.

Daoism

Yang Zhu seems to have developed many ideas which were later incorporated into the philosophy called Daoism (Taoism). The early history of Daoism is very obscure, and the traditional supposition that its first major exponent, Lao Zi, was an older contemporary of Confucius cannot be accepted. Indeed, there is no good evidence that he ever existed. The name could be translated 'Old Master', and may well have been applied to several people, both real and legendary. The book supposedly written by Lao Zi, known as the *Dao De Jing* ('The Book of the Way and its Virtue'), is certainly a composite work assembled from the writings of several different authors. Its date is unclear, and indeed different sections may be of different dates, but it is likely that it was compiled at some time around 300 BC. The other major early Daoist text, the *Zhuang Zi*, is of about the same date or even slightly earlier (though it includes much material added later).

There are differences between the ideas expressed in the *Zhuang Zi* and the *Dao De Jing*, and even between the ideas of different sections of the latter work, but they also have features in common. The Daoist ideal is to accord one's way of life with the operations of the *Dao*, the Way, which is a more or less mystical concept, an absolute embodying the principles by which all things in the universe operate. Any kind of strenuous human action is likely to run counter to the Way, so the Daoist embraced Inaction (*wu wei*). This did not mean literally doing nothing, but never acting unnecessarily and always harmoniously and naturally. 'The Way never acts yet nothing is left undone', and likewise 'the sage knows without moving, identifies without seeing and accomplishes without taking any action' (*Dao De Jing*).

> There are those who are lofty though without intense thoughts, who are cultivated though lacking benevolence and righteousness, who govern though without either achievements or fame, who find leisure though they do not withdraw to remote places, who live long though they do not indulge in esoteric practices. They divest themselves of everything, but lack nothing. . . . This is the Way of heaven and earth. (*Zhuang Zi*)

Unlike philosophers of other schools, Daoists did not strive to gain high office and govern states. 'It is always through not meddling that the empire is won', says the *Dao De Jing*, and a story in the *Zhuang Zi* tells how Zhuang Zhou refused an invitation to become chief minister of the state of Chu. He was fishing in a river when two high officials came to convey the message. Without bothering to put down his rod or turn round, he replied that he had heard that in Chu there was a sacred terrapin, already dead for 3,000 years, which the king kept in a place of honour in a temple. 'Do you think', he continued, 'it would rather be dead and have its bones kept and honoured thus, or rather be alive and dragging its tail in the mud?' The officials replied that it would rather be alive. 'Go away then!' said Zhuang. 'I am dragging my tail in the mud.'

But there was another side to Daoist thought. 'Heaven and earth are ruthless, and treat the myriad creatures like straw dogs; the sage is ruthless, and treats the people like straw dogs', says one passage in the *Dao De Jing* (straw dogs were used as offerings for the dead, treated with great care before the offering but discarded afterwards). There are, indeed, many passages in this text which deal with how a ruler should act, saying, for example, that the common people should be kept ignorant in order to make them easy to govern. This authoritarian streak in Daoism no doubt helped to recommend it to the rulers who patronized Daoist scholars. It was a strain of thought which became rather widely accepted in the later Warring States period in China, affecting other schools as well as Daoism.

There were in fact many schools of thought apart from those discussed above, but only fragmentary information has survived about most of them. Some of the scholars of the time specialized in argumentation, seeking to prove, for example, that 'a white horse is not a horse'. The fundamental proof of this is that 'a horse' is not limited by colour, so that a brown or a black horse can be accepted as 'a horse', but 'a white horse' carries an exclusion on colour grounds, so that a brown or black horse will not do. Thus, the terms 'a horse' and 'a white horse' are not the same. This kind of argument may seem specious, but it was an important step for the Chinese to examine their language and try to attain precision in its use.

LEGALISM

We do have considerable information about one other important philosophy of this period, however. It is called Legalism, because one of its characteristics was an insistence on the use of strict laws as a basis for keeping order in society. The aim of the Legalists was to ensure absolute power for the ruler of a state, and to achieve this they advocated a strongly centralized government with power embodied in fixed and rigid laws. Under strong central direction the state could be strengthened and prepared for the ultimate challenge, that of conquering all other Chinese states and unifying the empire.

Unlike the other major Chinese philosophies of this period, Legalism scarcely formed a school of thought. It had no recognized founder, and thus there were no coherent groups of disciples, as with the Confucians and Mohists. There were simply various thinkers and writers who shared similar ideas to a greater or lesser extent. Some of those later considered Legalists would not, during their lifetimes, have thought of themselves as such.

The State of Qin

Legalism in a developed form first emerged during the fourth century BC. One of the earliest Legalists about whom much information survives was Shang Yang, who died in 338 BC. Like other important Legalists he came from the ruling class, and early in his career served as an official in the state of Wei. Afterwards he went to Qin, where he soon found favour with the ruler and was given office. He proposed radical reforms, which were eventually adopted. These reforms strongly favoured agriculture and weaving as basic occupations, and gave rewards for military prowess. Ranks in society were clearly defined, and the quantities of servants, land and other possessions appropriate to each rank precisely stated. Severe punishments were specified for wrongdoings, and families were grouped together and made mutually responsible for the behaviour of everyone in the group. Anyone who did not denounce a malefactor was to be cruelly put to death. Moreover the laws were made to apply to everyone, whatever their rank, so that even the crown prince was not above punishment.

These reforms turned Qin into a well-organized, centralized state governed by a bureaucracy selected on the basis of merit. It was able to expand, at the expense of both the barbarians on its western borders and the Chinese states to the east. In 341 BC, Shang Yang led an army into Wei and seized lands disputed between the two states. His victory was ensured by a treacherous ambush which Shang Yang was easily able to set up because of his old acquaintance with the ruler of Wei. Shang Yang was not apparently a popular man even in Qin, and when the crown prince who had fallen foul of his regulations succeeded to the throne, Shang Yang had to flee. It is recorded that he came to a sticky end.

It was in the state of Qin that Legalism was most thoroughly put into practice. In other states Legalist thinkers were not paid so much attention. Han Fei Zi (died 233 BC) was actually a member of the ruling family of the state of Han but failed to persuade his relative the ruler to follow his advice. Frustrated, he put his ideas down in writing. Two of his essays were seen by the ruler of Qin, who expressed admiration and a desire to meet him. A meeting actually took place when Han Fei Zi was sent by his own state as an envoy to Qin. The ruler of Qin considered offering him high office in his government. Han Fei Zi had been a student of a Confucian philosopher, Xun Zi. A fellow student, Li Si, had taken office in Qin, where he had become a minister to the ruler. He seems to have realized that he was not as capable as Han Fei Zi, and probably feared him as a rival for high position in the government of Qin; he may also have felt that Han Fei Zi could not be expected to co-operate in the conquest of his own state. Through various machinations, Li Si managed to have Han Fei Zi thrown into prison and forced to commit suicide.

The Legalists considered that people could not be relied upon to act in the kind of moral and righteous way that the Confucians advocated. The only way to create order in society, they believed, was to impose it by the use of strict rewards and punishments. The ruler could only maintain his position by the use of force. While the Confucians talked of benevolence and righteousness, the Legalists stressed power, techniques of administration and law. Their ideas were in many respects much more practical than those of other schools of thought, and there can be no doubt that they were, at least initially, very successful. The state of Qin, from being a more or less barbarian state on the western periphery of the Chinese culture area, developed under the guidance of Legalist ministers into one of the most powerful of the Chinese states. Eventually it was to succeed in the conquest of all China.

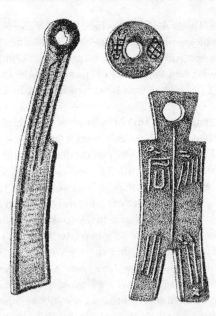

Bronze coins used in different states during the Warring States period

Qin had other advantages in addition to its government organization. It position on the north-western edge of the Chinese culture area not only gave it room for expansion at the expense of barbarian tribes less well organized than the Chinese states, but also placed it astride the trade routes between China and central Asia, which reached eventually to the Roman Empire and India. Trade became an important activity during the late Warring States period, and large fortunes were made by successful merchants. Lü Buwei, chief minister of Qin in about 240 BC, was originally a merchant who had clearly done very well for himself. The importance of the overland trade routes of central Asia at this period is evidenced by the fact that Qin became known in India under the Sanskrit name of Cinasthana. The name 'China' derives from this.

The only other Chinese state which had a more or less similarly favourable situation was Chu, on the southern edge of the Chinese culture area. In the east lay the sea, and northwards was largely desert where the agricultural Chinese way of life could not flourish. Chu's position in the Yangtze valley, a warm, fertile and well-watered region, gave it a rich home base and plenty of room for expansion southwards into similarly plenteous country. There were no southern trade routes to compare with those to the north-west, however.

The remaining Chinese states were either entirely surrounded by neighbouring states or had boundaries limited by the sea or the inhospitable regions to the north. The rise of horse-nomadism in the steppes had in fact resulted in the appearance on China's northern borders of warlike peoples of such military prowess that they had become formidable opponents for the Chinese, and elaborate defences were constructed against them. Thus the only real opportunities for these other states to expand their boundaries were by conquest of their Chinese neighbours, not an easy undertaking, especially in the face of complicated inter-state alliances. All the states wished to increase their own power and weaken or destroy their neighbours, but none wished to see any other state embark successfully upon a similar course, and would join alliances to prevent this happening. Thus there tended to be many conflicts between the states, without many really decisive conquests.

THE UNIFICATION OF CHINA

But by 318 BC Qin had become so powerful that it was strong enough to defeat an attack by Han, Wei, Zhao, Chu and Yan acting together. Two years later Qin absorbed Shu, a barbarian state in the area of modern Sichuan, and subjugated its neighbour, Ba. This left the fertile Sichuan Basin entirely under Qin control and greatly increased its power-base. In 312 Qin destroyed a large Chu army. From then on it was clearly the most powerful of the Chinese states, which the others were incapable of destroying. Gradually it came to dominate: in 293 Han and Wei were subjugated (though not yet annexed), and in 260 a similar fate befell Zhao. In 256 the Zhou royal domain was conquered, finally destroying even the pretence of Zhou royal authority. Qin was now poised for the final series of campaigns.

In 246 a new king, Zheng, acceded to the throne of Qin. This was the king under whom first Lü Buwei and then Li Si were chief ministers.

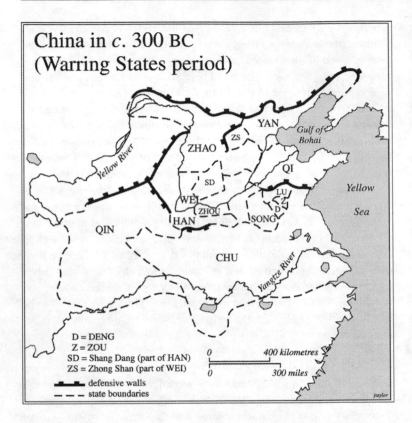

China in *c.* 300 BC
(Warring States period)

YAN

Gulf of Bohai

ZS

ZHAO

Yellow River

QI

SD

Yellow

WEI

ZHOU

LU

Sea

HAN

D

QIN

SONG

CHU

Yangtze River

D = DENG
Z = ZOU
SD = Shang Dang (part of HAN)
ZS = Zhong Shan (part of WEI)

0   400 kilometres
0   300 miles

■■■ defensive walls
— — — state boundaries

jtaylor

He was clearly a ruler of great ambition and continued the process of conquest. In 230 Han was finally annexed, followed in 228 by Zhao and in 226 by Qi. This enlarged the territory of Qin from its earlier western borders all the way to the sea in the east. Yan, north of Qi, was isolated and a large part of its territory seized. Wei was annexed in 225; Chu suffered severe defeats in 226 and 224, and was finally annexed in 223. With the annexation of the remainder of Yan in the following year, Qin completed the conquest of all its rivals, and in 221 BC King Zheng of Qin changed his title to Shi Huangdi, the First Emperor. For the first time an area approximating that of all China Proper was unified under one ruler.

CHAPTER FIVE

Confucianism and Religion, 221 BC–AD 589

The Qin Dynasty

Chinese history up to 221 BC had seen the emergence of a distinctive Chinese culture and of a Chinese cultural identity, the foundations upon which the Chinese nation were to be built. Under the Shang and early Zhou dynasties the people had thought of themselves as owing allegiance only to the dynasty, that is to the king and his successors. They were the people of Shang or Zhou. But by the Warring States period there was a strong sense of belonging to a cultural entity not limited by the borders of one state, of sharing the superior, Chinese culture of the 'Central States'. A sense of 'Chineseness' had emerged. But the China which Qin Shi Huangdi had conquered and brought under unified rule was by no means a homogeneous entity. Though the 'Central States' shared many common basic cultural elements, they still had their differences. Peripheral states such as Chu had cultures strongly influenced by that of the Central States but retaining much of their original 'barbarian' identity. There were language differences, and although they all used written Chinese there was no standardization of characters or styles of writing. Administration, currency, weights and measures and many other essentials varied from area to area. All these differences were inherited by the new Qin state, making its task of welding the fragments of China into a political unit very difficult. The First Emperor was not one to shrink from such a task, however, and threw himself into it with vigour.

First of all it was necessary to organize the newly-conquered areas into parts of the administrative system of the Qin state. A uniform system

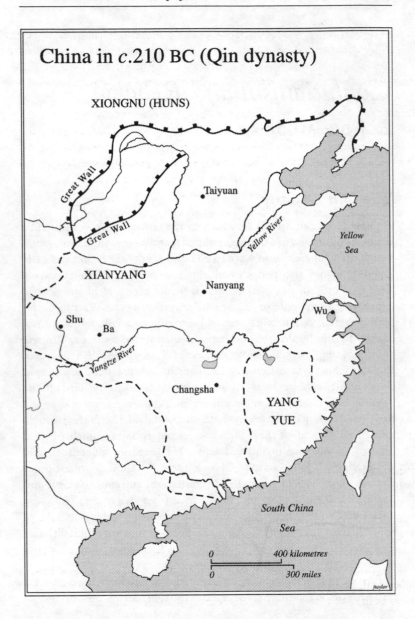

China in *c*.210 BC (Qin dynasty)

XIONGNU (HUNS)

Great Wall

Great Wall

Taiyuan

Yellow River

Yellow Sea

XIANYANG

Nanyang

Shu

Ba

Wu

Yangtze River

Changsha

YANG

YUE

South China

Sea

| 0 | 400 kilometres |
| 0 | 300 miles |

jtaylor

was applied throughout the empire. It was divided into provinces, each further divided into prefectures. A hierarchical structure of officials governed these units. All remnants of the former feudal administrations were swept away, the noble families of the conquered states being mostly removed from their home regions to the state capital at Xianyang (close to modern Xi'an). This administrative structure formed the basis of all subsequent Chinese governmental systems. Then, in order to make the collection of taxes easier, weights, measures and money were made uniform. To reduce the problems of officials posted from one region to another, the language was also standardized. Regional variations in styles of writing and usage of characters were officially abolished. Finally, it was decreed that all carts should have axles of the same length. This may seem a strange requirement, but in the conditions of the time it was eminently sensible. Roads were not well surfaced, and the wheels of the carts wore deep ruts in them. It was difficult, if not impossible, to haul carts over roads in which the ruts were not the same distance apart as the carts' wheels, for if the wheels on one side were in a rut, on the other they were not, so that the carts tipped over at alarming angles. In the unified state, where it was necessary, for example, to transport grain long distances to feed the population of the capital, this situation would clearly have caused great difficulties. All these reforms also encouraged trade between regions, thus increasing the prosperity of the state.

THE GREAT WALL

But the Qin empire also faced threats from outside its borders. The nomadic peoples of the steppes to the north of China had been pushed back from their best pastures by the expansion of the Chinese, losing, for example, the Ordos region within the great bend of the Yellow River. Probably under the influence of the organized Chinese states to their south, the nomads had begun to unite into large confederations, which began to have sufficient power to be a serious military threat to China. It had long been a practice of the Chinese to build large walls around their towns and cities. These were normally of rammed earth, soil compacted into surprisingly strong and durable structures. From about the middle of the fifth century, much longer walls had begun to be built, as barriers between the various Chinese states and between

Chinese states and barbarian regions. By about 290 BC an extensive system of walls existed, largely along the northern borders of the Chinese culture area. After the unification of China only the threat from the north remained, and intensified as the steppe peoples became increasingly organized. Qin Shi Huangdi therefore decided to link and extend the existing walls on the northern frontier, and thus created the first Great Wall of China, completed in 214. This wall was of rammed earth construction, built by the forced labour of many thousands of peasants.

THE DECLINE OF QIN

The First Emperor believed that he had founded a dynasty which would last for 10,000 generations. He himself died in 210 BC when he was only fifty. The strains of the centralized totalitarian system which had been established under his rule no doubt contributed to his early death. He intended his eldest son to succeed him, but Li Si and another minister, Zhao Gao, preferred one of his other sons (there were twenty in all). They concealed the emperor's death until they were able to ensure that their own candidate took the throne. But disputes over the succession and the widespread unrest caused by exactions of forced labour completely destabilized the empire, and within a few years the Qin dynasty had crumbled.

Despite all efforts to unite the empire, dissent had continued throughout the reign of Qin Shi Huangdi. Arguments about political philosophy had been so widespread that the First Emperor, at the suggestion of Li Si, had banned all such discussions and ordered the destruction of all books outside the imperial collection except for those on purely practical subjects, such as medicine and agriculture. Many scholars opposed to Legalist ideas were executed. But even these draconian measures, which earned the First Emperor the lasting opprobrium of the Confucian scholars, failed to extinguish dissent. After the downfall of the Qin dynasty, Legalism was thoroughly discredited.

Qin Shi Huangdi was given a burial in keeping with his exalted status. The historical sources record that his tomb was filled with rare and precious objects, that it had representations of the heavens on its ceiling and of the earth, with rivers and seas of mercury, on its floor, and that it was guarded by automatic crossbow mechanisms, set to shoot anyone who

The Terracotta Army: the head of an officer (Qin dynasty, *c.* 215 BC)

tried to break into it. The site of the tomb has always been known, but it was only recently that some of the grave goods were accidentally uncovered by peasants digging a well. Subsequent archaeological excavations revealed the now-famous Terracotta Army, an astonishing assemblage of life-size clay statues. Nothing else comparable of similar age is known from China, and their quality is outstanding by any standards. Thus, although Qin Shi Huangdi's dynasty only just outlasted his own life, two of China's most renowned historical remains, the Terracotta Army and the Great Wall, are monuments to his achievements.

The Han Dynasty

After a couple of years of confusion, with several different rebel groups contending against the Qin government and each other, the empire was finally brought together again under the leadership of one man. Liu

Bang was of humble origins, but became the first emperor of a new dynasty, the Han. Founded in 206 BC, this was to prove much more durable than its short-lived predecessor and must be considered one of the great dynasties of Chinese history.

THE CONFUCIAN TRIUMPH

The first Han emperor inherited a fundamentally sound administrative system from the preceding Qin dynasty, but the Legalist ideology that had created it had to be rejected. It was too unpopular. To some extent there was a return to old ways, with fiefs being conferred on some of the relatives and close adherents of Liu Bang, but much of the empire continued to be ruled by officials in the same way as under the Qin. This mixed administration persisted for about a century, but gradually the new class from which the administrative officials were almost exclusively drawn asserted itself, and the rights and powers of the feudatories were reduced to little more than nominal. The old feudal nobility disappeared, displaced by a class of gentry which maintained itself in power through land-ownership and the holding of government posts. This class was descended from the similar class which had evolved during the Eastern Zhou period from impoverished branches of noble families, the class to which Confucius had belonged. Its ideology was largely Confucian. Legalism necessarily remained influential, as many of the Legalist laws and practices continued in use from the Qin dynasty into the Han, but Legalism had become so unacceptable that it could not be openly advocated. Though in the process it absorbed many Legalist ideas which Confucius himself would never have countenanced, Confucianism was able to establish itself as the essential ideology of government in China. It was to maintain itself in this position more or less continuously until the downfall of the last imperial dynasty, a period of more than 2,000 years.

At first Liu Bang was not much inclined to accept Confucian ideas. His chamberlain Lu Jia is said often to have quoted to him the Books of Poetry and Documents, old texts important to the Confucians. 'I won the empire on horseback,' Liu Bang eventually exclaimed, 'what use are the Poetry and Documents?' Lu Jia answered that though the empire could be won on horseback, it could not be governed on horseback. Qin had conquered the empire, but had failed to hold it long because of the unpopularity of its government. Had Qin employed the Confucian principles of benevolence and righteousness, things would have been different. Liu Bang apparently had very little concept of how to govern his empire, and of necessity allowed scholars to instruct him.

In 141 BC a system of recommendation of talented persons for government posts by provincial administrators was begun. This is considered the beginnings of the later system of examination for official positions. Those who had principally studied writings of schools other than the Confucian were excluded from government, for knowledge of the Confucian texts was established as the prime requisite for appointment to government office. During the first century of the Han period, all the major schools of philosophy apart from Confucianism and Daoism faded into insignificance. Daoism probably survived because it did not compete with Confucianism as a philosophy of government.

CULTURAL CONTACTS

The period of the Han dynasty saw a gradual synthesis between the various parts of the empire. Regions in the south and west which had originally been outside the Chinese culture area were administered by Chinese officials, and many of the local people absorbed Chinese culture. There was also some settlement of Chinese in the south. But away from the major towns and the valleys where Chinese forms of agriculture could easily be practised, the inhabitants retained their distinct local cultures. Even today remnants of these indigenous peoples still live in mountainous areas as far north as Zhejiang and southern Anhui provinces (the She minority) and south-west Hubei province (the Tujia minority). During the Han dynastic period, much of China south of the Yangtze valley was only patchily assimilated into Chinese culture. Some of the more remote mountainous areas were not even under Han government control.

In this connection it is interesting to relate a story from the official history of the first half of the Han dynasty (compiled in about AD 100). It is recorded that in about 145 BC a man called Wen Weng was appointed governor of Shu (roughly within the area of modern Sichuan). He found the area to be uncivilized, with barbarian customs,

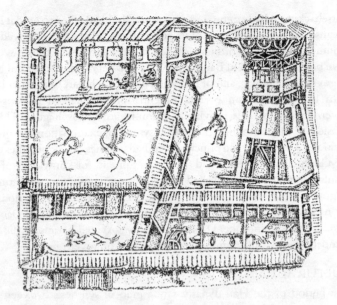

View of a dwelling, from a Han dynasty stone carving from west China

so he established an office of education at which boys from outlying districts were taught. They later became junior officials in the provincial administration. After some years Shu began to produce local scholars (versed in Chinese literature and culture) equal to the best from anywhere in China. Later a similar education system was set up throughout the Han empire. The process of acculturation of originally non-Chinese areas was thus intentionally encouraged by the central government.

Influences were not entirely one-sided. The peoples of south China had their own cultures, many elements of which became incorporated into the Chinese. Though it is difficult now to trace all these elements to their precise origins, there can be little doubt that Chinese art and architecture received many southern influences, and that it was in the south that various important developments first occurred. Water transport, for example, was highly developed in the wet south but little used in the north until major canals were dug there, as late as the sixth century AD. The characteristic half–cylindric roof tiles widely used on Chinese buildings may well have their origins in the use of split bamboo for roofing, which must have come from the south as bamboo with canes of large diameter does not grow in north China. Rice was certainly first cultivated in the Yangtze valley, and tea (which became widely used only after the Han dynasty) was most probably first drunk by native peoples in the far south-west. The downfall of the Qin dynasty can to some extent be considered the result of a reaction by the south against northern conquest. The first Han armies were called the 'Avenging Army of Chu'.

HAN EXPANSION

The Han empire also extended its territory well beyond traditional Chinese borders to the north-west. The borders of the Qin empire had roughly followed the Yellow River from its northernmost point south to the vicinity of modern Lanzhou, continuing more or less straight south where the river turned westwards towards its source on the high Tibetan plateau. During the first century of Han rule, much of what is now north-western Gansu was added to the empire. This long strip of territory, sandwiched between the Qilian Mountains edging the Tibetan plateau to the south-west and the Gobi Desert to the north-east, is known as the 'Gansu Corridor'. It is largely semi–desert itself, and of little value except as a route of communications, giving access to Central Asia and the countries beyond. At this period a considerable volume of trade developed along what is now usually called the 'Silk Road'.

At the beginning of the Han dynasty the area north of the Great Wall was inhabited by the Xiongnu (Huns). They had founded a state which, with the help of immigrants from China, threatened to become a rival to the Han dynasty itself. Liu Bang was in fact forced to conclude an agreement with the Xiongnu by which they were given food and goods from China in return for observing the peace; the treaty was sealed by the marriage of a Chinese princess to the Xiongnu chief. But neither side fully honoured the agreement and Xiongnu raids into China continued to occur from time to time. The Xiongnu also made war on their other neighbours, and in about 170 overcame a people known as the Yuezhi and drove them from their lands near the Qilian Mountains.

The Yuezhi are interesting because they can probably be identified with the Tokharians, who spoke an Indo-European language. The remnants of the Yuezhi moved west across Central Asia, settling in Bactria (within modern Afghanistan) in about 130 BC.

The resulting commotion in Central Asia was naturally very disruptive to trade, and the Chinese were less than happy to find the Xiongnu astride their major route to the Tarim Basin. The Han emperor Wu Di determined to act, and sought an alliance with the Yuezhi against their common enemy. An emissary, Zhang Qian, was sent out into Central Asia to find the Yuezhi and seek their assistance. After a long absence, during which he was twice imprisoned by the Xiongnu, he returned to China in 126; he had found the Yuezhi, but failed to interest them in joint action against the Xiongnu. He did, however, bring back a great quantity of information about the 'western regions' of Central Asia and beyond, and inspired further Chinese expeditions along the same route. These culminated in the large military expedition under General Li Guangli which reached Ferghana (within modern Kazakhstan) in 101 BC. All this activity resulted not only in the extension of Chinese rule over the area of the Gansu Corridor, but also brought many of the Central Asian states into tributary relations with the Han empire. The Great Wall was extended westwards to protect the route as it passed through the corridor. The Central Asian trade routes were thus made safe, and the first caravans made the through journey from China to Persia in about 106 BC. The Xiongnu declined in power, and were finally defeated by 58; denied access to China, and harried in their weakness by other steppe peoples, they moved away westwards to become known in Europe as the Huns.

The Silk Road, along which Chinese silks reached Rome, was the major channel of communication between the Far East and the West throughout the Han dynasty (though there were also sea routes from south China to India and the Persian Gulf). Along this road (or roads, for there were alternative routes across many of its sections) many things travelled both into and out of China. Zhang Qian had himself brought back the grape vine and alfalfa. Other important food plants to enter China by this route were chives, coriander, cucumber, fig, safflower and sesame. Among those which travelled westwards were day lily (which had medicinal uses), peach and apricot. Ideas and techniques were also transmitted.

Buddhism

One major transmission to China during this period was the Buddhist religion. This had, of course, originated in northern India, probably during the sixth century BC, and had gradually spread throughout south Asia. Southern branches of the Silk Road led from Khotan into Kashmir, and along these Buddhism spread to many of the Central Asian states. From there, once the western regions had been pacified, it was an easy journey to China. There are various legends about the introduction of the Buddhist religion, but the earliest indisputable evidence of Buddhism in China is a mention of a Buddhist community at Pengcheng (modern Xuzhou, Jiangsu province) in AD 65. These Buddhists are likely to have been foreigners. They were under the patronage of Liu Ying, Prince of Chu, who also patronized Daoists. At this early period of Chinese Buddhism it was not a popular religion, but largely restricted in its appeal to patrons from the higher strata of society. Like Liu Ying, many of these were not devotees of a single creed but interested in all mystical (and magical) practices.

Only towards the end of the Han dynasty (i.e. after about AD 200) did Buddhism begin to gain wide acceptance among the Chinese people. Until then it was mainly Chinese who had come into direct contact with foreign Buddhists, through trade or travel, who became converts. One of the earliest Buddhist writings by a Chinese, for example, probably dating from about AD 192, was composed by someone who had lived for a time in Indo-China. Yet already the text talks of a vast mass of sutras and other Buddhist literature. Large quantities of Buddhist writings reached China during the first few centuries after the introduction of the religion; they were mainly written in Sanskrit or Pali, and translating them required a considerable effort. Many of the earliest translations were undertaken by foreign monks, who lacked a thorough knowledge of the Chinese language; results were therefore often unsatisfactory, so that the same text had later to be translated again. The Chinese had many problems dealing with Indian texts, as they received them in a haphazard order and never knew which were earlier and which later, or the various different schools of Buddhist thought to which they belonged. They therefore developed their own classification of the Buddhist scriptures, based on the premise that the Buddha had preached his doctrines in several stages, not at first revealing the full truth.

Although Buddhist influences also reached China from the south, as has already been noted, it was from the north-west that the earliest Buddhist missionaries arrived. Among the first was An Qing, the Parthian, in AD 148. Zhi Chan, the Yuezhi, and Zhu Shuofo the Indian, came a couple of decades later. There were already native Chinese monks during the second century. Buddhism prospered in China during the few centuries after the downfall of the Han dynasty in 220, when the empire split apart and there was a succession of short-lived dynasties controlling only parts of China. The difficulties of life in those troubled times no doubt increased the attractions of a religion which preached escape from the sufferings of the world. By 315 there were 180 monasteries and 3,700 monks at Luoyang, capital of the Western Jin dynasty (AD 265–316). 'After this the Buddhist faith was widespread, reaching everywhere to the Four Seas', according to a later Chinese history.

The fortunes of Buddhism fluctuated. Sometimes it was persecuted, as under Emperor Tai Wu (424–52) of the Northern Wei dynasty, when monks were killed and monasteries destroyed. Other emperors were themselves adherents of the faith. Through all vicissitudes, Buddhism survived and established itself as a permanent part of the Chinese scene. The Chinese quickly began to adapt the foreign religion, developing purely Chinese Buddhist schools as early as the fourth century. One of the most important (and earliest) of these was the Pure Land sect, which taught that through various devotional practices it was possible to be reborn in a 'Pure Land' paradise somewhere in the far west, a stage closer to nirvana. The widespread Chinese practice of invoking the name of Amitabha Buddha originated with this sect, as also did the cult of the Bodhisattva Guanyin (Avalokitesvara). Originally male, this Bodhisattva underwent a gradual transition in China and eventually took on a female form, for reasons which are obscure. Some later images of the goddess are surprisingly reminiscent of the Virgin Mary (Guan Yin is sometimes depicted holding a child), and must have heightened the impression often gained by Christian missionaries in China that Buddhism was a debased form of Catholic Christianity. No possible influence can be traced, however.

Buddhism introduced many new ideas into China. While all the native Chinese philosophies had tended to concentrate on the affairs of this world, the principal objective of Buddhism was to throw off all worldly bonds and escape into nirvana. Some Buddhist sects even believed that the world was unreal, a fabrication of human imagination. One writer of the fifth century summed up the differences between Buddhism and the native philosophies thus: 'For Confucianism and Daoism the regulating of the world is basic, but for the Buddhists the object is to escape from the world.' The Buddhists had begun with the Indian idea of reincarnation; they believed that death was followed by rebirth, over and over again, so that there was no end to the sufferings of life. Only by achieving enlightenment was it possible to escape from the endless chain of existence, passing from the world into the state of nirvana.

Buddhism developed into several sects at a very early period. On many of the earliest little or no information has survived, but they all in common believed in the salvation of the individual through personal progress towards enlightenment. This later came to be known as the 'lesser career', Hinayana. A view which developed just before the entry of Buddhism into China was that such stress on individual enlightenment was wrong, that Buddha had worked for the salvation of all, and so all his followers should do so too. This way of the 'greater career', Mahayana, played down the idea of nirvana, and gave great prominence to the Bodhisattva, a being who had achieved enlightenment but voluntarily remained in the world to assist others. Self-culture, according to Mahayana beliefs, would not lead to the salvation of the self; only selfless devotion to assisting others could do so. Mahayana naturally tended, therefore, to be more evangelical than Hinayana in its outlook.

Mahayana Buddhism also developed the doctrine of the Void, claiming that the world of experience was no more than an illusion, and even denied the existence of a permanent self. Individual salvation was also, therefore, illusory. Nirvana could only be attained by mystical enlightenment, a sudden realization which could not be anticipated. This idea was taken to its logical extreme by the Chan school of Buddhism, developed in China in the late fifth century, and now better known by its Japanese name of Zen. Even the sacred sutras were rejected by Chan Buddhists, who relied entirely on mystical faith and sought enlightenment through prolonged meditation.

Daoism

At the time when Buddhism was just beginning to make its way into China, Daoism was also establishing itself as a popular religion. It had to undergo many changes for this to become possible. These had begun early, at least during the first century of the Han dynasty, and led to a major transformation of Daoist thought. The early Daoist philosophers would have had little in common with Daoists of the late Han dynasty and after. In the text of *Zhuang Zi*, there are many passages dealing with death, most of which emphasize that it is a natural occurrence which must be accepted calmly, and sometimes speculating that existence after death may be much happier than life. When Zhuang Zi's wife died, he was found by a friend who went to offer condolences drumming on a bowl and singing. The friend upbraided him for not mourning. Zhuang Zi replied that when she first died, he had of course been very upset. Then he had thought that at first there is no life, nor even any form or essence. Life evolves from emptiness. 'Now another change has brought death, just as the seasons follow one another. She has lain down and gone to sleep in the Great Chamber, and if I should follow making a terrible noise of wailing, then this would seem not to conform with fate. Therefore I stopped.'

The rational nature of early Daoist thought is well summed up in a quote from the book called *Huai Nan Zi*, written (by various authors) during the early part of the Han dynasty, in about 120 BC. 'Heaven and earth cannot terrify one who is intelligent in nature, strange phenomena cannot delude one who has judgement through experience. Therefore the wise man knows what is distant through what is near, regarding the myriad different things as elements of a fundamental unity.'

Later, the mystical aspects of Daoism became increasingly important, with Daoist adepts claiming supernatural powers. The acceptance of death as a natural occurrence, a normal part of the action of the Way, gave way to a desire to extend the normal span of life. The ultimate aim of the mystical Daoists was to achieve immortality. Thus the focus passed from attempting to accord with the natural way of the Dao, to being able to control at least some of its manifestations. Numerous spirits and immortals were assembled into a Daoist pantheon, and elixirs of life were concocted. The Daoist adept became a kind of magician or wizard.

An organized Daoist 'church' made its appearance during the second century AD. It is more than likely that this was at least in part a reaction to the arrival of Buddhism in China, the Daoists copying the Buddhists in establishing temples with images of deities and priests as counterparts of the Buddhist monks. But there had also, for a long period, been many links between Daoism and early Chinese primitive religion, which undoubtedly eased the transformation.

THE PERSISTENCE OF PRIMITIVE CHINESE BELIEFS

The earliest religion in China had been animistic, seeing gods and demons in mountains, rivers, winds and other natural phenomena. If there were floods, then the spirits of the waters had to be propitiated, or if crops were poor, the spirits of the earth were to be appeased. The souls of the dead joined this world of spirits, where they had some influence, hence the importance of sacrificing to dead ancestors. A complete calendar of sacrifices was developed at a very early period, designed to procure the good influences of all the most important spirits. There was no kind of human activity which was not subject to their intervention.

To some extent the philosophies which began to be worked out in China during the latter part of the Zhou dynasty accepted many aspects of the earlier Chinese beliefs. Confucius advocated the continuance of the old rituals, including most of the sacrifices. When one of his disciples proposed to abolish the sacrifice of a sheep at the announcement of the new moon, he protested, saying 'You love the sheep, I love the ceremony'. Yet equally there were aspects of the old beliefs which his humanity led him to condemn, such as the use of human sacrifices. There is also every reason to think that Confucius may have seen the old rituals as a necessary way to maintain the structure of society, without actually believing in their efficacy. He talked little about gods and spirits, generally presenting a rational point of view.

Later Confucians certainly tended towards rationalism, taking a sceptical view of animistic beliefs and superstitions. In about 415 BC one Ximen Bao, on taking up a new appointment as governor of a town in the state of Wei, put a stop to the practice of sacrificing girls as brides of the Yellow River. The great Confucian philosopher Xun Zi (third century BC) wrote:

> Whoever says that there are demons and spirits, must have made that judgement when they were suddenly startled, or at a time when they were not sure, or confused. This is thinking that something exists when it does not . . .
>
> Thus when a person, having got rheumatism from dampness, beats a drum and boils a sucking pig [as a sacrifice to the spirits], then there will necessarily be the waste resulting from a worn-out drum and a lost pig, but he will not have the happiness of recovering from the illness.

But interestingly Xun Zi also wrote about old customs being carried on even though they were not necessarily believed in:

> When [officials] 'save the sun and moon from being eaten' [during eclipses], or when they pray for rain during a drought, or when they decide an important affair only after divination, this is not because they think that in this way they will get what they want, but only because it is the thing to do. The prince regards it as convention, but the people regard it as supernatural.

Thus even the sceptical Confucians often accepted old practices and carried them on despite the lack of any real belief. Even within quite recent times the emperors of China were expected to plough ritual furrows, pray for good harvests and so on, in vestiges of ancient rites in which the great majority of the educated class certainly did not have any strong belief. Belief was not important in Confucianism, and no doubt some Confucians adhered more to old beliefs than others, but the continuation of the old practices *was* considered to be important. Many primitive religious rituals were therefore carefully preserved by the Confucian official class, and continued to be believed in at least by the mass of common people.

But it was the Daoist religion that absorbed the greater part of the original primitive religious practices of China. It was, in fact, largely because of this process of absorption that Daoism changed from its early, philosophical form to its later, theistic and superstitious form. The rejection by Daoism of the pursuit of worldly glory and even of altruistic (and, to the Daoists, misguided) attempts to regulate human affairs led many devotees of the Dao to withdraw entirely from public life, often to lead a secluded existence in remote areas. They naturally tended to be drawn into association with others who were similarly outside the normal network of society. In a world increasingly dominated by the Confucian scholar–official class, these soon came to include the various seers of the old religion, those who had interceded with the spirits to forecast the future, cure sickness, ensure good fortune and so on. These *Wu* (comparable to the shamans of the steppe peoples and the medicine-men of the American Indians) often came into conflict with Confucian officialdom, as in the case of the 'brides of the Yellow River' (see p. 90), in which *Wu* were heavily involved. They were thus natural allies and associates of the Daoists, the more mystically-inclined of whom easily accepted the magic and rituals of the *Wu*. After Daoism became an organized religion, its priests took on many of the former roles of the *Wu*, such as fortune-telling and the casting out of evil spirits.

Buddhism, as a foreign import which became widespread in China only after the establishment of Confucianism as state philosophy and the development of religious Daoism, was much less affected by primitive Chinese religious beliefs. It had in any case brought with it a whole pantheon of deities and demons largely acquired from Indian Hinduism. The whole concept of reincarnation, for example, which is central to Buddhist doctrines, was of Hindu origin. For many centuries, too, Buddhism was accorded a hostile reception by the native Chinese beliefs, and tended to have little amicable contact with them. This situation changed only slowly, and it was not until the Sui and Tang dynasties (late sixth century onwards) that the three creeds began to coexist more or less peaceably (though jealousies persisted for very much longer). Only in 694 did the Tang government cease to treat Buddhism as a foreign religion.

The isolation of Buddhism is well exemplified by the fact that it had to create its own sacred mountains in China. The two native creeds both took over primitive cults, and shared the sacred peaks of the five directions, east, south, west, north and centre. At some periods different mountains were honoured, but the generally recognized locations were at Tai Shan in Shandong in the east, Heng Shan in Hunan in the south, Hua Shan in Shaanxi in the west, Heng Shan (written with a different character from the 'Heng' of the southern peak) in northern Shanxi in the north, and Song Shan in Henan in the centre. Though Buddhist temples were eventually established on or near these mountains, the principal sacred peaks of the Buddhists were entirely distinct. Associating them with various legends about Bodhisattvas and so on, Chinese Buddhism took as its holy mountains Putuo Shan on an island off the Zhejiang coast in the east, Jiuhua Shan just south of the Yangtze in Anhui, Emei Shan in Sichuan in the west and Wutai Shan in Shanxi in the north. At the height of their prosperity, these mountains were the sites of dozens of Buddhist temples with many hundreds of monks (and nuns) resident in them, and received pilgrims from all over China and even from Buddhist regions beyond the borders.

The Collapse of the Han empire

The Han dynasty lasted, with a short break from AD 9 to 23 when the reforming Wang Mang established his ill-fated Xin (New) dynasty, from 206 BC until AD 220. It was thus among the longest-lasting Chinese dynasties. But for much of the second half of this long period central government was weak. The final extinction of the dynasty in 220 was no more than the culmination of a long process of decay. It was to be several centuries before China was again firmly united under strong central government. It is a tribute to the strength of the Chinese identity established under the Han that such reunification was a constant aim throughout the period of disunion. Throughout its long history, the vast area of China has been difficult to govern (particularly in the era before modern communications), and has shown a recurring tendency to split into smaller states, yet the ideal of a united China has never faded.

The break-up of the Han empire can at least partly be attributed to economic factors. At the end of the Warring States period, although the state of Chu with its rich lands in the Yangtze valley had been very powerful, it was unable to compete with the Qin state once the latter had conquered the whole area of the northern plains around the Yellow River and its major tributaries. The Yangtze region was simply not sufficiently well developed at that period, and could not provide comparable resources to those of the original heartland of Chinese culture. By the later part of the Han dynasty much had changed. Major irrigation works and a long period of stability had greatly improved the economic situation in the Yangtze valley, which had come to rival the northern plains. Control of the old northern Chinese culture area was no longer a guarantee of sufficient strength and resources to enable easy domination of the rest of China. Anyone who could succeed in usurping control of the Yangtze valley had the resources to challenge the central government in its northern base. Similar development had also taken place in the Sichuan basin, which had the added advantage of being surrounded by mountains and therefore easily defensible. For some sixty years after the downfall of Wang Mang it maintained its political independence, and was frequently able to do so again in later Chinese history.

DISUNITY

When a series of rebellions led to the final downfall of the Han dynasty, China split into three separate states, centred on each of the three key economic areas described above. In the north, the state of Wei controlled more or less all of China south of the Great Wall and north of the Yangtze, excluding what is now northern Sichuan. Wu held all of south-east China from just north of the Yangtze, including part of what is now Vietnam. Shu, also called Shu Han, as it claimed to be the legitimate successor to the Han dynasty, held the Sichuan basin together with much of what is now Guizhou and part of Yunnan. These three states were more or less continuously at war with one another, until

Heavenly musician, from a mural in a Buddhist cave
temple at Dunhuang in Gansu province, dating from
the Northern Wei dynasty (AD 386–534)

Shu was overcome by Wei in 264. Wu was then at a disadvantage, being
much smaller than Shu and Wei combined, and held out only until 280.
But the ruling house of Wei did not enjoy the victory, as one of its
generals took the throne, founding a new dynasty of Jin.

The reunification of China was short-lived, however. Internal
struggles continued, with some Chinese generals seeking the aid of the
peoples north of the Great Wall. First the Huns and then the Xianbi
were called upon, but the problem was that once south of the Wall these
peoples were reluctant to return to the steppes. The Jin state lost most
of its northern territories and was pushed back to the Yangtze valley.
No less than seventeen, mostly short-lived, dynasties ruled in the north
during the period from 304 to 535. All but three had ruling houses of
non-Chinese stock. Although all these foreign conquerors from the
north generally became very largely sinicized, their absorption into the

population of north China undoubtedly had some effect. Many of the northern peoples were either already Buddhist or quickly accepted Buddhism, and this period was a high tide for the Buddhist religion in China. One of the longest-lasting of these dynasties, the Northern Wei (386–534), was responsible for the creation of some of the finest Buddhist art in China. This includes some of the best of the fresco paintings in the cave temples near Dunhuang and the sculpture of the Yungang caves outside Datong, the site of their capital for almost a century from 398.

The south of China was slightly less unsettled than the north at this period, but also suffered a succession of dynasties, none of which endured for much more than fifty years. At last a general appeared who was able first to conquer all of north China, establishing the Sui dynasty in 581, and then to overrun the south. By 589 the new dynasty controlled most of China, and by 610 had even brought part of Vietnam and large areas in Central Asia under its rule. Never again was China to undergo such a long period of disunity and confusion.

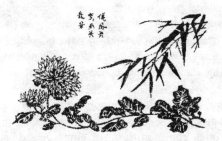

CHAPTER SIX

China and the Outside World, 589–1279

The Sui Dynasty

The founder of the Sui dynasty fixed his capital at the traditional site of Chang'an (modern Xi'an). This must have seemed an obvious choice, for Chang'an had been the preferred capital city ever since the founding of the Zhou dynasty, some sixteen centuries previously. The use of Luoyang further east during the latter halves of both the Zhou and Han dynasties had been forced by dynastic weaknesses. In all, Chang'an had been the capital of almost a dozen dynasties by the time the Sui dynasty established itself there. In the days when the plains of northern China had been the main economic and cultural centre of China, the siting of its political centre in this region had been entirely natural. Many changes had occurred since the fall of the Han, however, and the maintenance of the capital at Chang'an was to cause constant problems during the next few centuries, until it finally had to be abandoned.

The main problem was that of supplying the large population of the political and administrative centre of the Chinese empire with sufficient food, fuel and other commodities. The emperor and his court, and the many officials of the central administration, necessarily expected to be able to maintain a lavish standard of living. The immediate area of the capital was unable to supply all that was necessary, so that much had to be brought in from considerable distances. The lower Yangtze valley had by this time become the most productive region of China, but moving large quantities of grain and other commodities from there northwards was difficult. Boats could easily move up and down the rivers, but these generally flowed from west to east. Roads were inadequate for the large quantities of commodities involved. North of the Huai River problems were particularly severe, as the Yellow River was only navigable in rather short stretches. Some means of facilitating transport from the south to the north was essential to the maintenance of the political centre in the north.

The Sui emperors quickly took this problem in hand. First a canal was built to bypass the Wei River, which was treacherous because of sandbanks, and so link Chang'an directly with the Yellow River. An existing small canal connecting the Huai and Yangtze Rivers was greatly improved. A few years later Luoyang was rebuilt as a secondary capital, one more easily supplied should shortages arise at Chang'an. A third capital was planned at Yangzhou, on the north bank of the Yangtze. The essential project was the construction of a complete canal system from north to south. Luoyang and Yangzhou were linked in 605, and in 610 a southern extension was constructed as far as Hangzhou. Large granaries were established along the canals to allow storage of grain. This work formed the basis of the Grand Canal, which was maintained intermittently until the middle of the nineteenth century.

All this work was undertaken using forced labour, including in some areas all commoners between the ages of fifteen and fifty. A total of some 5.5 million people was forced to participate. At more or less the same time, another million were conscripted to restore the Great Wall. Though these projects were undoubtedly of great use, the suffering caused by the forced-labour system did not endear the Sui emperors to their people. A serious rebellion broke out in 614, at the same time as the Sui armies were engaged in heavy fighting against the forces of the kingdom of Koguryo in Korea. In the following year the emperor himself was besieged by a force of eastern Turks, allies of the Koreans, in a town just south of the Great Wall. More uprisings occurred, and by 618 the Sui had been brought to an end. Like the Qin dynasty which preceded the Han, and established a governmental system which laid the basis for Han success, so the Sui brought about its own downfall through the harshness of its government, but laid the foundations for another of China's great dynasties, the Tang.

The Silk Road and Maritime Trade

Throughout the unsettled period from the last years of the Han dynasty until the founding of the Tang, goods from China had continued to find their way westwards to the Roman and, later, the Byzantine empires across Central Asia. The land routes were to remain in heavy use until the middle of the eighth century. This was an extremely important period in the history of contacts between East and West. The arrival in China of Buddhism has already been discussed, and some mention has been made of domestic plants which made the journey in one direction or the other. During the centuries after the end of the Han dynasty China had made great advances in science and technology, and some Chinese inventions and discoveries had set out on the journey westwards. Paper had been known in China since before AD 105. Its transmission was very slow, first into Central Asia and then gradually beyond, arriving in Europe only as late as the twelfth century, via Moorish Spain. There is still much argument about whether Chinese printing had any influence on its development in Europe, but there is no doubt that without paper European printing would have been hamstrung. The parchment used previously could not have been produced in sufficient quantity.

The foot-stirrup for horse-riding was also a Chinese invention, probably first coming into use in about AD 300. It appeared in Europe only during the early eighth century. The Chinese were also using the modern type of collar harness on horses from about 500, some 300 years in advance of Europe. Various machines for spinning and weaving, developed in connection with the silk industry, must have reached Europe at about the same time as the arrival of silkworms in the middle of the sixth century. The crossbow, standard weapon of the Han armies and largely responsible for their successes against the Huns, appeared in Europe centuries later. Other inventions and discoveries already known to the Chinese at this time were not transmitted until an even later period. These include the wheelbarrow, used by the Chinese in the third century AD but not known in Europe for another thousand years, magnetism, long known in China at this time but not yet applied to navigation in the compass, and cast iron, which the Chinese had known as early as about 600 BC. From about AD 900 the Chinese first began to develop gunpowder, which was to have an enormous effect on European society after its introduction in about 1300.

It is difficult now to trace exactly the flow of techniques and ideas along the Silk Road at this period, but it is certain that much exchange did take place. Though undoubtedly remote from Europe, China has rarely been as totally isolated as is often imagined. When the Tang dynasty re-established a long period of order and stability in China, which lasted for more or less 300 years (618–907), foreign contacts flourished. At first these were mainly overland, but later the sea routes became more important.

LAND ROUTES

The land route of the Silk Road began at Chang'an. Running north-west through the Gansu Corridor, it reached Dunhuang, an oasis among the deserts of north-west Gansu. From here there was a choice of direction. The shortest route was due west, along the southern edge of the Tarim Basin at the foot of the great mountain ranges edging the Tibetan plateau. This road was at first much used, but became difficult later because of increasing desiccation (a process which seems still to be continuing in this region). The most northerly route, in use from about AD 5, ran up to Turpan at the foot of the Tian Shan range, and continued just south of the mountains. A third road ran via Loulan, near the shore of the lake of Lop Nor, but this city was abandoned in about 400 because of desiccation, making the road impassable. All these routes rejoined at Kashgar at the western edge of the Tarim Basin. From there there was again a choice. A southern route ran over the Pamirs to Bactria and then to Merv. A more northerly one reached Merv via Ferghana and Samarkand. From then on the road was easier, passing across Persia via Ecbatana (modern Hamadan) and arriving at the Tigris near modern Baghdad. Many routes led onwards into Syria and thence across the Mediterranean. Apart from these major routes, there were many others of lesser importance. Some diverged around the northern side of the Tian Shan mountains, thus bypassing Kashgar, and there were of course routes from Kashgar and Bactria southwards into India. It was possible to avoid Persia altogether by going south to the Indus and taking ship around the Arabian Peninsula into the Red Sea.

Sea routes were to become increasingly important because of difficulties with the overland routes. In 670 the Tibetans seized Kashgar and held it for twenty-two years. This was also the great period of Muslim Arab expansion, and in 751 a major battle took place on the Talas River, east of Tashkent, in which Chinese forces were defeated by the Arabs. This decisive battle caused the destruction of Chinese power in Central Asia, all of the oases around the Tarim Basin gradually falling under Muslim influence (though centuries later Marco Polo still found the inhabitants of Hami to be 'worshippers of idols', that is, Buddhists, as almost all Central Asians had formerly been). With the destruction of Chinese prestige in this region, trade must have been seriously impaired, with a corresponding transfer of business to other routes, the easiest of which were now by sea.

SEA ROUTES

The earliest sea-borne contacts between China and other nations probably occurred during the Han dynasty. It is likely that Indian shipping regularly sailed around the coasts of South-east Asia as far as what is now Guangdong province during the second century AD. Chinese ships began to venture along the same routes after about 300, reaching Penang by about 350 and Sri Lanka a few decades later. During the next century they probably sailed as far as the Persian Gulf and the mouth of the Red Sea. In 762 Chinese prisoners taken at the battle of the Talas River returned to China from the Persian Gulf in Chinese ships. Such long-distance Chinese navigation continued throughout most of the period of the Tang dynasty, declining after about 900.

But for most of the Tang period much of the shipping in this region was Arab or Persian. By 758 the Muslims were strong enough to burn and loot Guangzhou, and subsequently established a considerable presence along the east China coast as far north as Hangzhou, with colonies of merchants in the major trading ports. There is still today a minaret at a mosque in Guangzhou which dates from the Tang dynasty. The major Chinese exports at this period were silk and pottery, while in return imports were largely of luxuries such as pearls and precious stones, glass, spices and curious rarities, some of them thought to have magical or medicinal properties, such as rhinoceros horn. There was generally a balance of trade in China's favour, with gold and silver flowing in from the other nations involved in the trade. It has even been suggested that the heavily adverse balance of the oriental trade of the Roman Empire was a major factor leading to its economic decline. Not all of the Roman gold went to China, of course, much being absorbed by the middlemen of Central and West Asia.

The Tang Dynasty

INTERNATIONAL RELATIONS

Even the Tang imperial family was partly of 'barbarian' descent, coming from a border region in the north-west. Turks played a large part in the overthrow of the Sui dynasty, and there were Turks in the army which helped to place the first Tang emperor on the throne. Many non-Chinese served as high officials of the new dynasty, especially in military posts. Throughout the Tang period, China's foreign relations were of crucial importance. The first task of the newly-founded dynasty was to consolidate its position against its northern neighbours. These had, after all, regularly encroached upon and conquered various parts of northern China ever since the end of the Han dynasty, some 400 years previously; it had become their habit to make raids into China whenever they felt a need for the commodities which could be seized there. Even the repair of the Great Wall by the Sui had not succeeded in keeping them away, for such a great defensive work is only effective when properly manned. The eastern Turks repeatedly invaded throughout the 620s, so that in 624 it was even proposed that Chang'an should be abandoned in favour of a capital more distant from the threat from the north. In 626 the Turkish forces reached a point only ten miles from the city, and were only persuaded to turn back by an improvised show of force and a negotiated treaty. Famine and disunity among the Turks then turned the tide, however, and by 630 the Tang armies had conquered all of the northern region up to the Gobi Desert. A further Turkish invasion in 641 was repulsed with heavy losses to the invaders, and there was little further trouble from that direction for a long period thereafter.

Buddhist images dating from AD 672–6 at the Longmen Caves near Luoyang

In the north-west Chinese armies were also victorious. A people called the Tuyuhun, who lived on the north-eastern edge of the Tibetan plateau, in what is now northern Qinghai, were causing trouble in the Gansu Corridor. A large Chinese army was sent against them, and after a series of defeats the Tuyuhun were forced to accept Chinese suzerainty. This did not intimidate the Tibetans, however, who invaded Chinese territory in what is now Sichuan. They also were repulsed, but remained a power to be reckoned with. Along the route of the Silk Road, the Tang armies pushed westwards, conquering Hami in 630 and Turpan some ten years later. Several states further west were conquered or voluntarily submitted during the next decade, until Chinese power extended even beyond the Pamirs.

Chinese prestige in Asia was now as great as at any time before or since. Campaigns in Korea at first met with only partial success, but by 668 succeeded in pacifying the whole of the peninsula and bringing it under Chinese suzerainty. During the Korean campaigns, Chinese forces clashed for the first time with the Japanese, who had come to the aid of one of the Korean states. The Chinese routed them, burning 400 Japanese ships.

It was at this time of strong Chinese influence along the Central Asian trade routes that the famous Buddhist pilgrim, the monk Xuan Zhuang, set out from Chang'an to go to India and bring back Buddhist sutras. His journey took some sixteen years, for he travelled extensively around India, eventually returning with a large quantity of holy texts. These were translated into Chinese and stored in a pagoda specially built for the purpose. This still stands in modern Xi'an, and is known as the Great Wild Goose Pagoda. The numerous adventures of the monk on his long wanderings became the subject of many popular stories, which eventually were rewritten into the great Chinese novel *Journey to the West*. They also formed the basis of a series of Chinese operas.

The Tang armies were not universally victorious, however, particularly in the later part of the seventh century. In 663 a clash with the Tibetans resulted in a defeat. The Tibetans went on to cause trouble all along their borders with the Chinese, seizing a large part of the Tarim Basin and pushing back Chinese influence in what is now western Sichuan and north-west Yunnan. During the last decade of the century Chinese armies suffered defeats at the hands both of the Tibetans in the Tarim region and also of the Turks, who had again begun to harass the Chinese. Though there were several Chinese successes during the first half of the eighth century, the battle of the Talas River in 751 saw the final destruction of Tang power in Central Asia. At the same time Chinese forces were defeated by the new power of Nanzhao in what is now Yunnan. This then became an independent kingdom that was to survive until the Mongol conquests five centuries later. A large Tang army was also defeated in the north-east by the Khitan, a rising power who were to play an important part in Chinese history a few centuries later. Thus, while at the height of Tang power in about 645, Chinese rule had extended far across Central Asia, northwards to the Gobi Desert, into Korea and well into the remote south-west, by the 750s it had been pushed back within the line of the Great Wall in the north and north-west and had lost the south-west to Nanzhao. Outside of

China Proper only part of northern Vietnam remained under Chinese sway. The borders were to remain at more or less these limits for the rest of the Tang dynastic period, that is until just after 900.

DOMESTIC POLICIES

The vicissitudes of Chinese fortunes outside China Proper were closely interrelated with domestic affairs. During the early Tang period there had been several energetic rulers, who had reorganized and consolidated the system of government and thus made China strong enough to undertake successful military campaigns. The first of these was Li Shimin (ruled 627–49), son of the founding emperor, who had played a major role in the wars which established the dynasty. Though he himself showed leanings towards the Buddhist faith, particularly in his later years, he made it a matter of policy to encourage Confucianism because of its strong connections with the scholar–official class. In 630 he decreed that a Confucian temple should be established in every province and county (there were more than 1,500 counties under the Tang). The examination system for entrance to the Chinese civil service was regularized and formalized, thus gradually reducing the power of the old aristocratic families who tended to monopolize appointments. Examinations were now written. Colleges for the education of examination candidates were encouraged, the Confucian classics being a major part of the studies.

EMPRESS WU

Unfortunately Li Shimin was succeeded by a much less capable son. This emperor soon fell under the spell of a young concubine of his father's, whom he took as a concubine himself. The young lady proved extremely capable and by a long series of intrigues managed to become empress and the power behind the throne, and later was even able to succeed to the throne herself, the only woman in Chinese history ever to hold such a position officially. Though the Empress Wu was totally ruthless, probably even going so far as to murder one of her own sons, many of her policies were of great benefit to the country. She had naturally quarrelled with many of the old aristocratic families, and therefore speeded up the process of replacing their members in

Female attendants from a mural in the tomb of
Princess Yongtai: Tang dynasty, *c.* AD 705

government office with less exalted scholars recruited by examination. She also removed the capital from Chang'an to Luoyang, which was much more easily supplied. In eleven of the last twenty-six years of her husband's reign the court and the whole of the central administration, with its masses of files and records, had had to be removed to the secondary capital at Luoyang because of scarcities at Chang'an. Such costly removals were obviated by the permanent transfer.

XUAN ZONG

Eventually the Empress Wu's excesses and particularly her patronage of Buddhism, which alienated the Confucian officials, led to her downfall. In 705 she was forced to abdicate, and died shortly afterwards, after roughly fifty years as the dominant power in the Chinese court. A period of intrigue and confusion after her death was ended in 712 with the accession of the Emperor Xuan Zong, who was to reign for forty-four years. He restored the capital to Chang'an, but also improved the transport system linking it with the south. The taxation system and land tenure arrangements were overhauled, with some success, and many Buddhist monks and nuns were forced to return to lay life and engage in productive activities. But Xuan Zong's reign was later marred by the rise to power of palace eunuchs and by his growing infatuation with the famous concubine Yang Guifei.

Eunuchs had originally been used in the palace as servants in the imperial harem, where they obviously could be more fully trusted than entire males. Under Xuan Zong they took on many other roles – as purchasers of supplies for the palace and political messengers, for example. Their easy access to all parts of the palace gave them an advantage over other officials, and they quickly acquired considerable power. Later in the dynasty the palace eunuchs were to play an unpleasant part in corrupting and weakening the court. Under Xuan Zong, however, they seem at least to have remained loyal to the emperor, and it was more the palace ladies who were to cause the emperor's undoing.

During the course of Xuan Zong's reign the military, who had been reorganized in 678 from militia units into standing armies, were again reformed. Conscription was relegated to emergency use, and permanent professional armies were created, mainly based in frontier regions. In order to reduce the risk that the commanders of these armies might acquire too much power and attempt to seize the throne, a policy was adopted of appointing barbarians as generals, for they were outside the main Chinese political system with little experience of intrigue and civil administration. One of these, of Sogdian and Turkish blood, was An Lushan, who became a military governor on the north-east frontier in 744.

The Decline of the Tang

THE REBELLION OF AN LUSHAN

An Lushan became something of a favourite of the emperor and Yang Guifei, and was showered with gifts and honours. In 751 he was additionally made the governor of a second military district, so that he controlled some 200,000 troops, not much less than half the total Tang forces. In 755, after a power-struggle with a new chief minister who was a cousin of Yang Guifei, he rose in open rebellion. Almost immediately he was able to capture Luoyang, and in 756 he also took Chang'an, the emperor being forced to flee. En route his loyal troops demanded the death of Yang Guifei, to which the emperor could only agree. He then abdicated in favour of the crown prince. The court found refuge in Sichuan, and was soon able to take advantage of dissensions among the rebels. An Lushan himself was assassinated by his son in 757. Local revolts broke out all over the country, and it seemed that China would once more split apart. But the Tang court, with help from barbarian allies, was able to restore order by 763.

THE UIGHURS

Chief among the foreign allies of the Tang were the Uighurs, a Turkic people who had created their own empire in Central Asia, in parts of what are now Mongolia and northern Xinjiang. In November 757 a force of as few as 4,000 Uighur cavalry played a crucial role in battles for Chang'an and then Luoyang. Both were retaken, and as a reward for their services the Uighurs were allowed to plunder Luoyang for three days. In 759 Uighur troops were again sent to assist against the rebels, but without repeating the successes of 757. In 760 Luoyang again fell but was recaptured two years later, the Uighurs again assisting in its recapture, and again plundering the city. The Tang government needed Uighur aid so much that they were prepared to accept humiliating treatment at their hands, and they were allowed to loot the whole area around Luoyang for many weeks after its recapture. Once the rebellion had been crushed the next year, the Uighur leaders were rewarded with ranks and titles.

The Tang empire was now so weakened by the rebellion that in 763 the Tibetans were able to raid from the west and occupy Chang'an itself for a few days. In 764 they and the Uighurs joined a disaffected Tang general in another revolt. At first they were defeated, but the following year the rebel forces surrounded and threatened Chang'an. At this point their leader died, and the Tibetans and Uighurs quarrelled. The latter were persuaded to change sides and the Tibetans were then defeated.

The Uighurs received ample rewards, particularly of silk cloth, and returned to their own country.

Chinese silk was in great demand within the Uighur empire. After they had assisted in the defeat of An Lushan, they imposed a trade agreement on the Chinese by which Uighur horses were regularly brought to China and exchanged for silk. This trade was generally very disadvantageous to the Chinese, but they clearly felt unable to force the Uighurs to stop it. It in fact persisted even after the downfall of the Uighur empire in 840. The Uighurs were very active traders, and a considerable community of them established themselves more or less permanently in China, engaging in trade and money-lending.

The Uighurs also took advantage of Chinese weakness after the An Lushan rebellion to extort large amounts of money in tolls for crossing their territory. This was important because of Tibetan encroachment on Chinese territory in the Gansu Corridor, which by about 770 had resulted in the isolation of the most westerly Chinese provinces. Communication was only possible by passing through lands controlled by the Uighurs, who took immediate advantage of the situation by charging heavy transit tolls. The arrangement backfired to a certain extent because it antagonized not only the Chinese but also some groups of Turkic people living near the Chinese western provinces, who were not exempted from the tolls even though they were subjects of the Uighurs. They therefore transferred their allegiance to the Tibetans. Chinese and Uighur forces together attacked the Tibetans and their allies, but were defeated in 790. After this the Chinese western provinces were completely lost.

After the downfall of the Uighur empire in 840 as the result of a major defeat by the Kirgiz, the Chinese felt able to take measures against foreigners, at least within the borders of the Chinese empire. Many of the Uighurs resident in Chang'an were arrested and executed, and the foreign religions of Nestorian Christianity, Manichaeism and Zoroastrianism were persecuted. During the last decades of the Tang dynasty the Chinese seem to have become much less tolerant towards foreigners in their midst. This was probably a result of the excesses of the Uighurs, who had on occasion literally got away with murder in Chang'an because the Chinese were so frightened of them. Buddhism also became a target of the general hostility to things foreign. In 845 the great majority of Buddhist monks were forcibly laicized, and much monastic land was seized by the state. This measure resulted in some improvement in state income (the monks and monasteries had paid no taxes), but was not sufficient to halt the decline in Tang imperial fortunes.

THE REBELLION OF HUANG CHAO

A major rebellion broke out in 875, and in 879 rebel forces led by Huang Chao seized Guangzhou. This had very serious consequences for the sea-borne trade of the Chinese empire, which had greatly increased in importance since the virtual closure of the overland route as a result of the Tibetan conquests. Among the large number of inhabitants of Guangzhou slaughtered by the rebels were many Arab traders.

Huang Chao soon left Guangzhou to march north, and seized the two capitals in the winter of 880–1. Not until 883 were imperial forces able to expel him from Chang'an, with the aid of a force of Turks. The Tang dynasty was never able to restore its control over China after this rebellion, local military commanders commonly acting more or less autonomously. Power strugles went on for a further twenty years, but finally in 907 the last Tang emperor was deposed. China again fell into disarray and disunity.

Disintegration and Reunification

The following period is generally known to Chinese historians as the period of the Five Dynasties and the Ten Kingdoms. As it lasted for only some 50–70 years, it can be readily appreciated that it was a time of considerable disintegration. Once again China's northern and western neighbours were quick to take advantage of the situation, the Tibetans consolidating their hold on what is now Gansu, and Turks founding no less than three of the Five Dynasties. These dynasties all held sway over only a limited area of north China. They have been rather arbitrarily accorded primary status by later historians because they controlled the region around the old capital city of Luoyang, though Kaifeng, further down the Yellow River, was actually used as the capital for most of the period. In fact some of the Ten Kingdoms (there were actually more than ten) which ruled various parts of southern and western China were just as important in carrying on the Chinese cultural tradition. It was in Shu (modern Sichuan), for example, that Chinese block-printing first became a developed art. Knowledge of the process was carried to Luoyang in about 930 and the first printing of the Confucian classics was completed in 953.

The situation in about 940 was that most of north China was held by the Later Jin dynasty, while Sichuan was independent as Shu. The Yangtze valley was largely under the control of the Southern Tang, with the small state of Southern Ping holding the area from Lake Dongting westwards to the Yangtze gorges. South of this, roughly in the area of what is today Hunan, was Chu, and along the coast from the Yangtze estuary southwards lay Wuyue, Min, Southern Han and Annam. Nanzhao continued as an independent entity in Yunnan. To the north, a new force from Manchuria was establishing an important presence. The Khitan had grown in strength throughout the early years of the tenth century, and by the 930s were playing a major role in north China. They destroyed the Later Jin in 947, took the Chinese dynastic title of Liao, and held the most north-easterly area of China, including the region around Beijing, for some 150 years. It was at this time that Beijing (then called Yanjing) first became a capital city, of the southern half of the Liao empire.

One example of the important foreign influences acting upon China at about this period is that the chair became thoroughly established as an item of household furniture. The Chinese were the only Far Eastern people to use chairs before modern times. A kind of large folding camp-stool had been used out of doors since the period of the Han dynasty (probably an import from the Roman Empire), but the Chinese had continued to sit on these cross-legged, just as they did on the mats used inside their houses. A painting from the Southern Tang dynasty provides the first pictorial evidence of chairs being used as indoor furniture in China. This had many other effects, for the use of chairs instead of mats requires a redesign of much other furniture and allows changes in styles of dress.

The strength of the tradition of unity in China by this time was such that the fragmentation of the country, which in Europe at the same period would have been thought entirely natural, was not allowed to last for long. In 960 a new emperor was raised to the throne by his army while campaigning against the Khitan, and the Song dynasty which he established conquered all the other Chinese states within the next two decades. Though the far north, the north-west and the south-west were never brought under Song rule, most of China Proper was controlled by the dynasty for the next 160 years.

The Song Dynasty

PROSPERITY AND WEAKNESS

One of the first acts of the founder of the Song dynasty was to induce his generals to leave their posts in return for lavish pensions. The power of China's neighbours caused a terrible dilemma for anyone who wished to exert supreme authority over all China, for to repulse raids from outside large standing armies had to be maintained near the frontiers, but the generals appointed to head these armies could easily become powerful enough to throw off central control. Thus it was necessary either to risk invasion by reducing military strength, or to risk revolt by powerful Chinese generals. Having himself been placed on the throne by his army, the first Song emperor was only too aware of this problem. Whereas the Tang emperors had in general tried to maintain military strength, and had suffered loss of authority as a result, the Song dynasty usually chose to accept military weakness in order to reduce the risk of overthrow by their own subordinates. Barbarians could, after all, always be bought off, and under the Song they commonly were.

The first Song emperor began the consolidation of his position not by immediately attempting the conquest of all China, but by reforming the civil administration. Procedures for appointment and promotion of officials were regularized and the quality of the bureaucracy was improved. Alongside the written examinations sponsorship was utilized, particularly to fill the lowest grades in the administration. This system had some drawbacks (it tended to promote factionalism, for example), but as sponsors stood to suffer punishment if those they sponsored performed badly, it helped to raise standards.

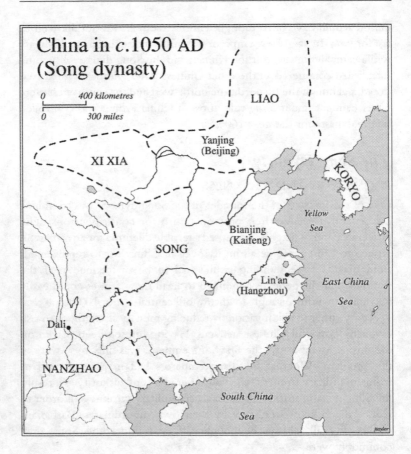

China in *c.*1050 AD (Song dynasty)

0   400 kilometres
0   300 miles

LIAO

XI XIA

Yanjing
(Beijing)

KORYO

Yellow
Sea

Bianjing
(Kaifeng)

SONG

Lin'an
(Hangzhou)

East China
Sea

Dali

NANZHAO

South China
Sea

When the civil administration was in reasonable order, the Song armies moved against the other Chinese states. The little state of Southern Ping was easily forced to capitulate in 963. The first major campaign took place in 965, with the conquest of Shu. Song naval forces played a vital role in this operation, attacking up the Yangtze River. Having taken control of the rich Sichuan basin in addition to the north Chinese economic zone, the Song dynasty was well placed to take on the remaining states. Southern Tang, holding the important lower

Yangtze valley, was left until 975, after most of the rest of the country had already been subjugated. By the end of the reign of the first emperor, only two rather small states remained independent. These fell early in the following reign. The Song did not feel strong enough, however, to move against the Khitan, and contented themselves with establishing close contacts with Korea as a possible ally against their northern neighbours. Skirmishes along the border became frequent, but no decisive campaign was mounted by either side.

TRADE AND ADMINISTRATION

The reunification at once led to much improved prospects for inter-regional trade. The south of China, formerly sparsely populated and poorly developed, had by this time advanced to a much higher economic level, largely as a result of considerable settlement by Chinese from the north. The Yangtze valley had become the major population centre of China. Kaifeng, chosen as capital by the Song dynasty, had become prominent not because it had any tradition of being a capital city, but because it was a major centre of communications and therefore of trade. The merchant class, formerly despised by the scholar-officials and discriminated against in the Chinese social and legal systems, attained much greater prestige. Opportunities for profits from trade and industry were such that many of the great land-owning families were attracted into these activities. As the populations of the great cities, and especially of the capital Kaifeng, expanded, shortages were felt which had to be supplied. Charcoal for cooking and heating, for example, became very scarce in Kaifeng shortly after the founding of the dynasty. The problem was not solved until coal replaced it.

The administrative system established by the Song had at its head the emperor and a Council of State. Immediately below were three main bodies, the Secretariat Chancellery, the Finance Commission and the Bureau of Military Affairs. The role of the latter is explained by its title, the other two dividing between them the activities of civil administration. The principal unit of local government was the prefecture (*zhou*), of which there were more than 300 in about AD 1000. Under each of these were several (usually about four) subprefectures or counties. Higher officials oversaw the activities of the prefectural administrators on behalf of the central government. A Censorate was set up to keep watch on all aspects of bureaucratic activity and report problems and abuses to the emperor.

In 1004 the long series of inconclusive hostilities against the Khitan Liao dynasty were terminated by a treaty, which provided that the Song should pay annual tribute of 100,000 Chinese ounces of silver and 200,000 bolts of silk. This could be easily found from the rich resources of the Chinese empire. The treaty ensured peace for some time to come, a further encouragement to economic development.

A great revival of educational and intellectual activity occurred during the Song dynasty. It particularly affected Confucianism. There was a great reinterpretation of the Confucian classics, at least partly because of the impact of Buddhist and other foreign ideas on Chinese thought, which led to a considerable enrichment of Confucian philosophy. The civil service examination system, based solely on knowledge of the Confucian classics, was now firmly established, so that the Confucian scholar-officials were securely in control of the government. This security allowed room for questioning and reappraisal. There were even some who said that examining candidates for office purely on their knowledge of the ancient classics was a perversion of scholarship, and attempts were made to introduce more practical subjects into the examination syllabus. Only in conditions of peace and economic security could such learning flourish in this way, and the Confucian literati undoubtedly had a strong interest in persuading emperors not to become engaged in large military adventures.

Some military activities were nevertheless forced upon the Chinese. Though the Khitan had been bought off, another force arose in the north-west where the Tanguts (northern Tibetans) had become increasingly powerful. They established their own state, known in China as Xi Xia, and in 1040 began invading China's north-western border areas. At first Chinese armies sent against them suffered defeats, but eventually the numbers of men recruited into the Song armies and the Chinese knowledge of gunpowder (a kind of hand-grenade was used during this campaign) enabled the Tanguts to be repulsed. Nevertheless, the Song had to agree to pay tribute to the Xi Xia as the

Winnowing and ploughing, from a mural at
Dunhuang, Gansu province: Song dynasty

price of peace, and were also forced to increase the amounts paid to the
Khitan.

WANG ANSHI'S REFORMS

There also began to be internal unrest at this time, mainly because of
the extreme inequality in the distribution of wealth and the imposition
of extra taxes to cover military expenditure. Early in 1069 a thorough
programme of reforms was instituted under the guidance of a former
governor of Nanjing called Wang Anshi. The payment of taxation in
kind to the capital, which involved the transportation of huge amounts
of grain and other goods over very long distances, was replaced by a
system whereby produce was sold by local officials. A state marketing
system could therefore be established, allowing commodity prices to be
partially stabilized by government intervention. Tax assessments were

revised, and peasants were allowed to take loans from the state at lower rates of interest than were available from private usurers. To improve military recruitment and strengthen public security, Wang introduced the *baojia* system, whereby families were grouped together in tens and made responsible for providing a certain number of men to the local militia and for ensuring the good behaviour of all the individuals within the group. If one member broke the law, the others were responsible for delivering the person up for punishment, failing which they could all be punished.

Wang Anshi also took several measures to improve the quality of the bureaucracy. At the same time there was a strengthening of the navy, which had been neglected for a long time; in 1077 it saw action against Annam in an inconclusive war. Merchant shipping was also encouraged, and the volume of overseas trade increased greatly, the duties imposed adding to government revenue. Wang Anshi would not contemplate military action against either the Khitan or the Xi Xia, however.

The reforms soon provoked great opposition because of their attack on so many entrenched interests. Famine in north China added to the dissatisfaction, and in 1074 Wang resigned. Though he was soon reinstated, his position had been seriously weakened and he finally retired in 1076. Nevertheless, some of his reforms remained in force and many of his policies were carried through by later statesmen. His name has come down to later generations as one of the greatest political and economic reformers in the long history of China.

The period of the Song dynasty saw the highest development of the Chinese economy, industry and technology, as well as seeing a great flourishing in literature and art. The quantity of copper coinage circulating in the empire was higher than was ever to be achieved afterwards, and paper money came into general usage. Overseas commerce was highly developed, and contributed greatly to government revenues. The coal and iron industries expanded enormously, with a great rise in the level of technology not only in these industries but also in engineering (shipbuilding, bridge-building, hydraulic engineering), architecture and armaments (especially the use of gunpowder). The magnetic compass came into use and printing reached a high stage of development (including the use of movable type), so that now all the major inventions of the pre-modern world – paper, printing, gunpowder and the compass – were known and used by the Chinese. The population of Kaifeng grew to more than a million (as much as the total population of England at the same period), and several other cities, especially in the rich south, reached a similar size. China was undoubtedly the most advanced nation in the world at this time, attaining a level which Europeans would have found hard to believe. Indeed, a little later the account by Marco Polo of what he had seen in China was not believed by contemporary Europeans, and he saw only a remnant of the great glories of the Song.

Invasion and Defeat

In the twelfth and thirteenth centuries events beyond China's northern borders were once again to exert a crucial influence on the course of Chinese history. A series of invasions were eventually to lead, for the first time, to the conquest of all China by a foreign power. This occurred in several stages, the first of which affected the Song only indirectly. Their northern neighbour, the Liao dynasty of the Khitan, was overthrown by a people who had formerly been their vassals.

The Khitan had been declining in power from the beginning of the twelfth century. In 1112 the Jurched, a tributary people from beyond their eastern borders in Manchuria, refused to submit any longer. Two years later a Liao army was disastrously defeated by the Jurched and their allies. The Jurched then established their own dynasty, the Jin, and began a campaign against the Liao which resulted in the conquest of most of their territory by 1125. The Khitan fled westward, setting up a new empire, the Qara-Khitai (Western Khitan) in Turkestan, which lasted until 1211.

The Jurched were not content merely to overthrow the Liao, however, and soon embarked on a series of attacks on the Song. North China quickly fell to them, Kaifeng being captured in 1126. Most of the Song imperial family were seized with the city, and were carried away into captivity. An imperial prince who escaped fled southwards and carried on the dynasty in southern China.

The loss of the north was a great blow to the Song, but was not the terrible disaster it would have been earlier in China's history. The south had developed to the point where it was contributing 70 per cent of government income. The move southwards during the second half of the Song dynasty marked the culmination of a long process of development of the southern half of China as a major component of the nation. From this time onwards southern China was at least equal in importance to the old economic, cultural and political centre in the north.

After the fall of Kaifeng, the new Song emperor had a hard fight for several years to survive in the face of the Jurched onslaught (at one time he only escaped by taking to his ships off the south China coast). But eventually the tide turned somewhat, and with the reorganization of the Song navy into river and sea-going squadrons in 1132 the situation was stabilized. In 1140 Song armies advanced almost to the Yellow River. At this point the emperor decided that it would be politic to come to terms with the Jurched. The old worry about the power of the generals again came to the fore; after one victory against the Jin puppet state of Qi, the emperor is said to have commented: 'What makes me happy is not that Qi has been defeated, but that the generals have obeyed orders.' So the borders between the Song and Jin states were fixed roughly along the line of the Huai River, Song agreed to pay annual tribute of silver and silk to Jin, and an uneasy peace was made. The Song emperor took the opportunity of peace to consolidate his position, executing some of his most successful generals and organizing the government finances. Foreign commerce was greatly encouraged, and by 1131 taxation on the trade was contributing something in the order of one-fifth of government income.

In 1161, however, the Jin again invaded. A cavalry force moved into Sichuan, an attempt was made to cross the Yangtze near Nanjing and a naval force of 600 ships sailed against Hangzhou, which had been fixed upon as the 'temporary' capital of the Southern Song. Fortunately, intelligence was received of the despatch of this fleet, and a Song fleet already at sea intercepted it off the southern coast of Shandong and destroyed it. The Song ships were equipped with formidable weaponry, including iron rams, rockets and catapults for hurling incendiary missiles. The Song naval squadron on the Yangtze was equally successful, twice preventing Jin attempts to cross the river, using bombs, rockets and fire-rafts. So terrible were these weapons that rather than make a third attempt, the Jin armies mutinied and killed their emperor. The Song navy was also using boats driven by paddle-wheels (turned by treadmills), which enabled them to operate effectively whatever the direction of the wind. Such boats had been made in China since at least as early as the fifth century.

These defeats ended the Jin attempt at invasion. In 1165 a peace treaty was signed which ended hostilities. The navy was maintained as a strong and efficient force until the end of the century, and the Song state remained at peace until after 1200. The Chinese court settled down to enjoy the new way of life in the warmer and more prolific south, and Chinese prosperity continued to grow. The greatest of the Neo-Confucian philosophers, Zhu Xi, undertook his great work of reappraising the Confucian classics. Hangzhou, formerly a provincial town of no great importance, became, as the capital of the Southern Song, the greatest city in the world, with a population which grew to exceed a million by 1275. As building land was scarce in the city, sandwiched between an estuary and a large lake, houses several storeys high were constructed – a new phenomenon in China. With its bustling streets and busy canals, its gardens, restaurants, taverns and tea-houses, it must certainly have been, as Marco Polo (1254–1324) found it shortly after the end of the Song dynasty, 'the most noble city and the best that is in the world'.

CHENGHIZ KHAN

But Marco Polo never saw it at the height of its glory. In 1206 a new power had arisen on the steppes, when Temujin (*c.* 1162–1227) was declared Chenghiz Khan, or universal ruler, of the Mongols. The Jin dynasty was in decline, suffering the effects of a great flood of the Yellow River in 1194, when it burst its banks and altered course, and of its failure to handle paper currency properly, which had led to severe inflation. Having forced the submission of Xi Xia, Chenghiz Khan moved against the Jin, mounting campaigns in 1211 and 1212. In the winter of 1213–14 Mongol armies advanced to the gates of Beijing, but were bought off with presents. The Jin emperor moved his capital to

Kaifeng, and in 1215 Beijing fell to the Mongols. Chenghiz Khan then became involved in other campaigns further west, so that it was not until 1233 that Kaifeng was finally taken, the Jin state being completely extinguished shortly afterwards. Chenghiz had died in 1227, but by then a large part of Central and East Asia was under Mongol dominion and Mongol armies were campaigning in Europe. Song China proved one of the toughest of the Mongols' opponents, and was not finally subjugated until 1279, after many years of warfare.

CHAPTER SEVEN

China under Foreign Domination, 1279–1842

The Mongols

When the Mongols first began their great conquests early in the thirteenth century they were not even a literate people. Though Chenghiz Khan's ambition was to rule the world, as summed up in his slogan 'one sole sun in the sky, one sole sovereign on earth', the Mongols had little conception of how a large empire could be governed. They were undoubtedly highly proficient in warfare, but as a nomadic people interested mainly in obtaining grazing land for their flocks and herds, the concept of establishing a civil form of government over settled agricultural peoples was at first entirely alien to them. Traditionally, Mongols engaged in hostilities against their neighbours on the steppes usually either massacred or enslaved those they conquered, taking over their lands for their own use. It is quite extraordinary that this people, with a total population of only about one million, was able to overrun such huge areas of Asia and Europe in so short a time, but even more remarkable that they were able to hold and administer the conquered territories.

The early conquests of the Mongols were indeed accompanied by great slaughter, and parts of northern China that had grown crops for many centuries were put to use as pasture for Mongol horses, cattle and sheep. The old Jin capital of Zhongdu (Beijing) was razed to the ground. According to the Chinese histories, most of Chenghiz Khan's advisers counselled him that the Han Chinese were of no use and should be killed. Fortunately for China, however, remnants of the Khitan who had formerly ruled parts of northern China had some influence among the Mongols. One of them, Yelü Chucai, a descendant of the Liao royal house, pointed out to the khan that through taxation of the conquered Chinese he could obtain large amounts of silver, silk and grain every year. Chenghiz Khan evidently saw the sense of this, and the behaviour of the conquering Mongol armies was gradually modified. The policy of massacre was abandoned, and administration on traditional Chinese lines began to be organized.

The conquest of southern China several decades after that of the north was a very different affair, and much less destructive. The Mongols actively tried to persuade elements of the Chinese population to come over to their side. By this time several khans had succeeded each other at the head of the huge Mongol Empire, and it was under Khubilai Khan (1215–94) that the final overthrow of the Southern Song was completed. This was only possible because the Mongols adapted to

A Mongol cavalryman: after an old Japanese painting of a battle fought in 1281

different methods of warfare. The extraordinary prowess of their cavalry had gained them enormous successes on the steppes and plains of Asia and eastern Europe, but was of much more limited usefulness in the wet and mountainous south of China. Cavalry charges could not be mounted across rivers, marshes and paddy-fields. Only after the Mongols had absorbed Chinese naval techniques, employing many Chinese sailors to handle the vessels they had captured or which had voluntarily submitted, were their armies successful in the south. They had also taken over the use of gunpowder from the Chinese, which was of great assistance not only within China but also in the Mongol campaigns in western Asia. It was to a large extent due to Chinese influences on the Mongols that they were able to conquer and hold their huge empire.

THE MONGOL ADMINISTRATIVE SYSTEM

The Mongols did not at first follow Chinese administrative practices, but divided their early conquests in northern China into appanages held by various members of the Mongol nobility. These were not necessarily territorial, as certain social groups, such as various kinds of artisans, were assigned to some of the Mongol overlords, but as the Chinese peasantry were tied to the land and could hardly be made to follow their lords on nomadic migration (as steppe peoples could have been), many of the assignments consisted of the inhabitants of defined areas. Thus north China came to be broken up into a series of local administrations governed by Mongol overlords. As the central government lacked any means of collecting taxes, it used tax-farming as an expedient; tax-collecting concessions were sold, frequently to Muslim merchants from Central Asia. This system operated throughout the Mongol empire. Trade flourished under these conditions for, whereas in China the central government had controlled commerce through taxation and other devices imposed by a powerful bureaucracy, under the Mongols the merchants suffered no such restrictions. The drawback was that there was a constant tendency for the labouring masses to be squeezed for every possible ounce of profit, which in the long run was counterproductive and caused unrest.

Under Chinese influence, Mongol administrative techniques gradually became more sophisticated. Commercial taxes of a form previously employed under Chinese rule were introduced as early as 1230. When the south of China was conquered, the Chinese system of government was taken over more or less intact, the main innovation being the division of the country into large provinces, adding another tier of administration to the bureaucratic hierarchy. Under Khubilai Khan a major revision of Mongol government practices was undertaken, resulting in the establishment of a strongly centralized and autocratic state. In most respects the new system was entirely Chinese in form, the attempt to impose Mongol forms of administration on the very different society of China being recognized as a failure. The major difference from previous Chinese practice was that the bureaucracy was made hereditary, the civil service examinations therefore being abolished. The highest posts in the bureaucracy were generally assigned to Mongols or to other non-Chinese (hence the apparent ease with which Marco Polo gained high office under Khubilai Khan). The Mongols remained very suspicious of the Chinese, deliberately attempting to preserve their own national character against the natural tendency to assimilate Chinese customs and habits.

KHUBILAI KHAN'S EMPIRE

During the course of operations against the Song domains in southern China the Mongols had, in 1253, taken Dali, the Nanzhao capital, and Yunnan was then brought within their empire. Annam was attacked in 1258 and accepted Mongol suzerainty. Korea was completely subjugated by about 1260. Xi Xia had fallen long before, being finally overrun in 1227. The Tibetans also acknowledged Mongol suzerainty; even part of Burma was for a time forced to submit. Together with the Mongol homeland, the empire directly under the rule of Khubilai Khan included not only virtually all of present-day China, excepting only Taiwan and most of Chinese Turkestan, but also vast areas to the north extending as far as Lake Baikal. Moreover, all the rest of the vast empire of Chenghiz Khan, divided since his death in 1227 into four khanates, owed allegiance (even if sometimes only nominally) to the Grand Khan in the east. Thus for the first and only time the whole of the overland route between the Near and Far East was under one authority. Though this lasted for only a short period, it was of great importance in allowing comparatively easy contact between the countries of the Old World.

The court of the Grand Khans at Karakorum, and later at Dadu (Beijing), attracted artisans, merchants, ambassadors and men of religion from far and wide. William of Rubruck, a Papal legate who reached Karakorum in the 1250s, found there Russians, Syrians, French, Germans and Hungarians, besides many other nationalities. He himself was not the first envoy of western Christianity to reach the court of the Grand Khan, for in 1246 John of Plano Carpini had come to try to persuade the Mongols to support the Crusaders against the Saracens. The khan, however, considered that the Mongols had a divine mission to rule the whole world, and demanded the Pope's submission as a precondition of any co-operation. Western Christians had been encouraged to seek such contact by reports that the Mongols were themselves Christian. This was partly true, for some tribes adhered to Nestorian Christianity, and several wives and ministers of khans were of this faith. Most of the Grand Khans, however, favoured Buddhism most strongly. Within the Mongol realms, and even within China at this time, all the major religions of Eurasia were represented, including Nestorian, Roman and Byzantine Christianity, Islam, Judaism, Manichaeism, Daoism, Confucianism and Buddhism. These were all generally tolerated, though the Daoists suffered persecution after about 1258, but gradually the Tibetan form of Buddhism gained greatest influence. Western Christians did not give up hope of converting the Mongols, however, and in 1294 John of Montecorvino arrived at Beijing and established a permanent mission. Several thousands of converts were baptized, and in 1307 he was appointed Archbishop of Cambaluc, the European name for Beijing (derived from the Mongol *Khan balik*, meaning 'city of the Khan'). The mission did not persist after the fall of the Mongols, however.

BEIJING

It was under Khubilai Khan that Beijing was rebuilt and made the winter capital of the Grand Khans. From 1267 a whole new city was erected more or less on the site of the destroyed Zhongdu of the Jin dynasty. The general plan of the existing Imperial Palace (Forbidden City) dates from this period, though the buildings now seen are largely of the early

The Meridian Gate, main entrance to the Forbidden City, the former
Imperial Palace in Beijing: the walls were built early in the Ming dynasty
(*c.* 1400), the buildings on them were built or rebuilt during the Qing
dynasty, mainly in the eighteenth century

fifteenth century with later additions and alterations. This was the first
time that Beijing had been the capital of the whole of China, a position
it has maintained throughout the greater part of the seven centuries to
the present day. Marco Polo described it as having walls forming a square
of six miles on each side, with extensive suburbs outside each of the
twelve city gates, stretching for as much as four miles, so that there were
more people living in the suburbs than in the city itself.

Though it was within the farmed area of China, Beijing quickly
outgrew its local food supply, and grain had to be moved north to make
good the deficiency. By this time the old Grand Canal had fallen into
total disrepair, for it had of course not been used after the Song had lost
northern China; it had in any case never extended as far as Beijing. It
was therefore decided to rely upon seaborne transport. This worked
well some of the time, but there were quite often losses because of
typhoons. In 1286, when there was a poor harvest in north China, a

quarter of the grain shipped north was lost at sea. This disaster led to a reappraisal of policy, and the Grand Canal was repaired and extended, linking Hangzhou directly with Beijing, a distance of 1,100 miles. The northern section of the canal crossed country which was much less level than the plains around the Yangtze and Huai Rivers, and could only be completed as a result of advances in engineering, particularly in the construction of locks.

Sinicization and Decline

Khubilai Khan's shift of capital southward into China Proper (even if close to its northern limits) marked an important shift in Mongol policies. From about 1270 onwards the outlook of the Grand Khan was increasingly a Chinese one, despite all the Mongol attempts to resist sinicization. In 1271 Khubilai even adopted a Chinese dynastic title, Yuan. China was the richest part of the domains of the Grand Khan, supplying his court with all or most of the major commodities it required, especially grain, silk and porcelain. Because of China's rich resources, the Mongols were able to live in a luxurious style which their old steppe homelands could never have afforded them. Having accepted the necessity of using Chinese forms of administration to govern China, the influence of Chinese officials gradually permeated even into the upper layers of the Mongol hierarchy. Although many Confucian scholar-officials remained hostile to the Mongol conquerors and refused to take office under them, others were not so reticent. Mongol princes began to be educated in the Chinese manner, and after the death of Khubilai Khan's grandson, Timur, who succeeded him to the throne in 1295 and reigned until 1307, Chinese influence grew rapidly. The civil service examinations were reintroduced in 1313. Although the inheritance of office continued in parallel with the examinations and preferential treatment was accorded to Mongols and other foreigners who took them, this marked the end of Mongol resistance to the sinicization process. Mongol emperors now became proficient in traditional Chinese accomplishments such as calligraphy, painting and the composition of poetry. Unfortunately for them, this did not make them any more acceptable to their Chinese subjects, and as the dynasty began to decline in power revolts became increasingly common.

The first serious rebellion broke out as early as 1315. Revolts in the south, where anti-Mongol feeling ran highest, could easily cause severe difficulties if they disrupted the shipment of grain to the north. This became increasingly common after 1330, the situation being worsened by floods of the Yellow River. The Mongol position was further weakened by dissension within their own nobility and they soon began to lose control of large parts of southern China. Within a century of their final conquest of all China they were to be pushed back beyond the Great Wall.

The Mongol conquest was a turning-point in Chinese history. There had been a more or less continuous development of Chinese civilization up to the Song dynasty, and there is no doubt that many of the achievements of the Chinese, particularly in science and technology, reached a high point under the Song. The Mongols caused a distinct shift of direction, destroying a great deal and bringing little to compensate. Chinese culture was by no means annihilated, but it became more introverted. The earlier Mongol emperors had withdrawn all imperial patronage from Chinese cultural activities, leaving the Chinese literati to paint and write mainly for private enjoyment only. Non-traditional forms such as the novel and drama increased greatly in importance. The Mongols also left a legacy of a more strongly centralized and autocratic system of government, restrictive of individuality and innovation. As a result, Chinese culture lost much of its vitality and vigour. The shock to Chinese pride of being subjected to foreign rule also greatly increased Chinese suspicion of outside influences.

Chinese Rule Restored

THE MING DYNASTY

In the 1350s a serious uprising against Mongol rule occurred in the Yangtze valley. A rebel state was founded with its capital at Nanjing, declaring itself legitimate successor to the Song dynasty. Large areas around the Yangtze fell under its control. In 1366 a man of humble origin called Zhu Yuanzhang (1328–98) took control of the rebellion, declaring himself Prince of Wu. Further territory was added, and in

1368 he declared a new dynasty with the name Ming, the capital remaining at Nanjing. Most of China was conquered the same year, leaving only Shaanxi, Sichuan and Yunnan, which fell in 1369, 1371 and 1382 respectively. The rule of a native Chinese dynasty had, for the last time, been imposed on the country.

Mongol power in East Asia collapsed. Chinese armies were able to drive north well beyond the Great Wall, burning the old Mongol capital at Karakorum and pursuing the Mongols as far as the Yablonoi Mountains, the furthest north any Chinese army has ever penetrated. Manchuria was seized, and for the first time large numbers of Chinese began to settle there. The Chinese were not, however, able to reassert their old dominance in Central Asia, where the Mongol khanates remained strong. The line of the Great Wall, which since the Khitan conquest of north China had ceased to have much significance,

A tower on the Great Wall at Mutianyu, north of Beijing, built during the early Ming dynasty (*c.* 1400) to help keep the Mongols out of China

gradually re-emerged as the boundary between the settled agricultural districts of north China and the pasture lands of the nomads of Mongolia. Though many Mongol tribes submitted to the Ming emperors, their allegiance was often uncertain, so the Wall was completely restored and rebuilt early in the Ming period. The Great Wall as seen today dates mainly from this time. In fact, as the Mongols regrouped in the steppe region after being driven out of China, they were able to regain some of their power and become once more a threat on the northern borders.

TIMUR

Further west, at just the time that the Ming dynasty was being established, another great conqueror in the mould of Chenghiz Khan was beginning his career. Timur (1336–1405), known as Timur Leng ('the Lame') because of a limp (hence 'Tamerlane' in European languages), was chief of one of the Turkic tribes which had been allied with the Mongols. In the 1360s he gained control of Kashgar and Khorazm, and subsequently began to enlarge his domains rapidly. By 1385 he had conquered all of eastern Persia, and went on to overrun virtually the whole of western Asia, including Asia Minor. Only his death early in 1405 prevented a planned attack on China. Ming relations both with Timur and with his son Shahrukh Bahadur were strained, the Chinese emperors attempting to treat them as vassals but being forced to accept the fact of their independence.

MING EXPANSION

With no possibility of extending Chinese dominion along the traditional routes to the north-west, the early Ming emperors looked to the south and the sea routes as outlets for their desire to dominate the world. Beginning in 1403, a series of remarkable long–distance voyages were made with large fleets of ocean-going junks, reaching to the East Indies, southern India, the Persian Gulf and the Red Sea, and as far down the East African coast as Kenya. These were not merely trading exploits, for the ships were despatched by imperial command and carried diplomatic missions. States contacted during these voyages were expected to accept Chinese suzerainty, and the king of Sri Lanka and two Sumatran chieftains who defied Ming power were forcibly taken to China to make their submission. Any trade was usually much to the advantage of the Chinese, who were able to exchange goods of little real value beyond that of prestige for rare commodities. Many luxuries were brought back for the Ming court, as well as strange animals such as giraffes and zebras.

In connection with these voyages Annam was conquered in 1407 and made a province of the Chinese empire. It did not remain so for long, for by 1428 Chinese armies had been driven out. This reverse greatly diminished Ming prestige in south-east Asia and further afield, and many of the countries which had acknowledged Chinese superiority no longer did so. The long ocean voyages became much less profitable, and the last took place in 1431–3. They then ceased as suddenly as they had begun, though no doubt less ambitious private trading ventures were still undertaken. After this time the Ming made no further attempts at foreign expansion.

DOMESTIC PROBLEMS

There were, in fact, many domestic problems almost from the beginning of the Ming dynastic period. The first emperor had made the classic mistake of giving too much power to his own family, creating principalities for each of his twenty-six sons. Though their administration was placed under central government control, the princes had authority over considerable military forces, giving them a great deal of power and the ability to usurp more. This weakened central authority, and also imposed a strain on the nation's finances which increased with time, for every direct descendant of a Ming emperor was given some kind of title and salary. Towards the end of the dynasty the total number of imperial clansmen ran into tens and even hundreds of thousands, the financial burden incurred being correspondingly huge.

The power of the imperial princes soon made itself felt. The first Ming emperor's eldest son was made crown prince, but died before his father. Rather than appointing another son as heir, the emperor bequeathed the throne to his dead son's son. To prevent a power-struggle when he died in 1398, the imperial princes were forbidden to come to their father's funeral at Nanjing, where his tomb in the hills east of the city may still be visited today. The Prince of Yan (Beijing), however, ignored the order until a further command from his nephew, the new emperor, given force by the presence of an army, persuaded him to turn back. This and other measures proposed shortly afterwards to reduce the power of the princes goaded the Prince of Yan into revolt, and in 1402 he succeeded in seizing the throne. A large number of supporters of the defeated emperor were executed, often along with the whole of their families, and measures to weaken the other princes were enforced. The usurping prince, who became the Yongle Emperor, thus effectively if ruthlessly secured his position.

REIGN-TITLES

During the Ming dynasty the period of each reign was given a title of auspicious meaning, such as 'Prosperous Tranquillity' (*Jiajing*). It has become usual to refer to the emperors of this and the following dynasty by their reign-titles, though this was not in any sense a personal name. Under previous dynasties reign-titles were often changed during the course of a single reign. From the Ming dynasty onwards this ceased to be the case, one title being used throughout each emperor's rule. Chinese emperors in fact had several names, including personal names of the usual Chinese form and honorific names given them after death. During their own period on the throne they would be referred to by title only, never by name. The names of their reign-periods are therefore a convenient label, which will be used in the form 'the (reign-title) Emperor'. The first Ming emperor was the Hongwu Emperor, *Hongwu* meaning 'Boundless Martial Spirit', in keeping with the many military campaigns he had to mount to win the empire. *Yongle* means 'Eternal Happiness'.

THE YONGLE EMPEROR AND HIS SUCCESSORS

The Yongle Emperor began his reign by making Beijing, his own power base, subsidiary capital. In 1421 he moved his court there, making it the main capital with Nanjing relegated to subsidiary status. The imperial palaces at Beijing were extensively rebuilt, the present Forbidden City dating largely from this time. He reformed the government system set up by his father, simplifying control of provincial affairs and consolidating his own authority at the centre. Eunuchs were given increasingly important roles; it was a eunuch, Zheng He, who commanded the fleets of the great voyages. The eunuchs were very much creatures of the emperor, and could usually be relied upon to do his bidding unquestioningly much more than the strongly-principled Confucian officials, who often argued bravely against what they felt to be wrong imperial decisions. The eunuchs had to be carefully controlled, however, as they were always liable to abuse their positions of power for their own personal advantage. The Yongle Emperor created a kind of eunuch secret service, which later came to be used as an organ of terror and was often difficult even for emperors to control. Giving too much power to eunuchs was always dangerous, and caused problems for the Ming emperors as it had for those of the Tang.

Though the Yongle Emperor was a vigorous ruler, during the latter part of his reign there were already signs of dynastic decline. The army and navy became much less efficient, with widespread desertion weakening the forces. Oppression of the common people by the gentry began to lead to unrest. After the Yongle Emperor's death a series of short reigns by young emperors led to a serious worsening of the situation. Already towards the end of his reign corruption had set in at court, and economic decline had begun because of heavy expenditure on military campaigns and such extravagances as the emperor's tomb (the Chang Ling, earliest and largest of the thirteen Ming Tombs outside the city of Beijing). In 1448 severe revolts broke out in Zhejiang and Fujian provinces, at a time when there was a serious threat of invasion from the north. The Mongols had begun to fall under the dominance of a single tribe, the Oirats, and had again become a power to be reckoned with. In 1449 they invaded north China and captured the ruling emperor. Moving freely about the north with their captive, they plundered extensively. They had hoped for a large ransom for their imperial prisoner, but in the event the Chinese decided to place his brother on the throne. After a time the Mongols returned the former emperor free of charge, thinking to embarrass his successor, whom he in fact overthrew several years later. Fortunately for the Chinese, the Mongols were unable to follow up their success in 1449 in later years because of famine and internal squabbles. The power and prestige of the Ming dynasty had been very seriously weakened, however. Less than a century after its foundation it had already fallen into decline.

The civil service examinations became increasingly stereotyped. The emphasis was on learning orthodox interpretations of the Confucian Classics by heart, and creative thinking was discouraged. In the latter half of the fifteenth century the situation was worsened by the introduction of the 'eight-legged' essay as the prescribed way of answering questions. This was rigidly divided into eight sections, and the style and even the number of characters in the essay had to conform to ordained standards. The sterility of this system was a strong disincentive to all but strictly orthodox thought. This naturally caused a reaction. Innovative scholars of independent mind organized private academies where unorthodox philosophies were expounded and people of similar political persuasions met. The situation became so vexatious to the government that private academies were proscribed in 1537. The proscription was not thoroughly enforced, however, and many academies survived. After 1600 they caused factional disputes among officials of the central government, weakening the administration at a crucial period.

European Ships reach China

Early in the sixteenth century an event of great moment occurred. Europeans had begun their maritime exploration of the world shortly after the time when the Ming had ceased theirs. Sailing down the western coast of Africa and around the Cape of Good Hope, the Portuguese had established positions in India, and then traded directly with the 'spice islands' of the East Indies. They seized Malacca in 1511, and immediately began to explore the routes to the south China coast. As early as 1514 the first Portuguese ships reached China. An official embassy was despatched from Malacca to Guangzhou in 1517, but was not allowed to proceed to Beijing until 1520. The ruling emperor died in 1521, however, without according the Portuguese ambassador an audience. At the same time envoys arrived from Malacca seeking Chinese help against Portuguese rapacity. Shortly afterwards trade with the Europeans was banned, and the members of the Portuguese embassy were thrown into prison on their return to Guangzhou; they were never released. Clandestine trade continued, however, as local Chinese merchants were always ready to take advantage of opportunities when they presented themselves. The imperial navy was too delapidated to prevent such activities, and local officials were often easily bribed. Besides, Japanese pirates, who had been active on the China coast during much of the dynasty, were causing far worse problems. There was also renewed strife with the Mongols on the northern borders at this time.

The Portuguese were soon able to establish footholds on the Chinese mainland, and in 1535, by the use of bribery, obtained official permission to dry their cargoes at Macao. Their settlement there became steadily more permanent and it effectively became a colony during the 1550s. It was never officially ceded by China, however. European power in the region continued to increase; the Philippines were occupied by the Spanish in 1565. The Portuguese tried to maintain their monopoly of trade with China but by the 1570s the Spaniards had gained official Chinese sanction to trade on the Fujian and Zhejiang coasts. In 1626 they established a land base on Taiwan, but were expelled in 1642 by the Dutch. A year earlier the latter had seized Malacca from the Portuguese and were to go on to control most of the East Indies. Soon all the seafaring nations of Europe were contending for their share of the China trade, the English arriving in 1637. To the north, the Russian expansion across Siberia brought them into contact with the Chinese by 1618.

Accompanying European trading activities came attempts to convert the Chinese to Christianity. At this early period it was the Jesuits who were the most active. They decided to begin the process by learning the language and customs of China, and attained a remarkable degree of success. Having arrived in Macao in 1577, they moved on into Guangdong province, and by 1601 Matteo Ricci had established himself at Beijing, where he won acclaim and high position through his scientific knowledge. In particular, his skill in astronomy enabled him to regulate the calendar better than native astronomers could. Ricci not only received imperial favour, but also began to convert high-ranking officials. His was a great personal success, and his death in Beijing in 1610 was a major setback to the Jesuit mission. It nevertheless continued to be active, and the Jesuits were of great service to the Ming dynasty in its last years, assisting them to cast cannon for use against their enemies.

THE END OF THE MING DYNASTY

This was not enough to save the Ming, however. The eunuchs were in virtual control at court, the civil service was rent by factional jealousies and expenditure was exceeding income. The court wasted huge sums on extravagant ceremonial and on renovation of the palace buildings, particularly after fires in 1596 and 1597. There were no less than 70,000 palace eunuchs and 9,000 palace women at this period. After 1590 there was also a great increase in military expenditure, with further war in Mongolia, campaigns against aboriginal peoples in the south-west and a war against Japan in Korea. The Korean campaigns, which continued for several years before the Japanese withdrew, were especially costly. Heavy increases in taxes were imposed to pay for them, with a corresponding stifling of economic activity and growth of unrest.

In the early seventeenth century the empire was torn by internal revolts. The most serious of these broke out in 1629, and soon began to ravage most of the area between the Yangtze and the Huai Rivers, from Sichuan and Shaanxi in the west to the Nanjing area in the east. The problems caused in the major economic zone along the Yangtze valley increased government difficulties. After 1640 the rebels showed signs of becoming powerful enough to replace the ruling dynasty, and in 1643 one of their leaders, Li Zicheng, actually did declare a new dynasty with its capital at Xi'an. Shortly afterwards his armies marched on Beijing. The Ming emperor was unable to raise sufficient forces to resist, and in the spring of 1644, as the rebels entered the city, he hanged himself from a tree on Coal Hill (Jing Shan), which stands on the northern side of the Forbidden City. The Ming dynasty had ended.

The Manchu Invasion

Li Zicheng's success was not to last long. Within a few weeks he was forced out of Beijing, and a year later his forces were defeated and he himself killed (though some sources claim that he escaped the field of battle and became a monk). It was not loyal Ming forces which caused his destruction, however, but a new power from the north-east which was to overrun all China and impose a further two and a half centuries of foreign rule. The Manchus, descendants of the Jurched who had earlier established the Jin dynasty in north China, had begun a gradual rise to power from about 1590 onwards. By 1644 they were poised on China's frontier all ready to move south.

NURHACI

The Jurched had of course fallen under Mongol rule during the first half of the thirteenth century, and remained Mongol subjects until the fall of the Yuan dynasty. Under the Ming they had regained a considerable degree of independence, although they regularly presented tribute to the Chinese court. In 1583, after internal disputes among the several Jurched tribes, a new leader, Nurhaci, came to the fore. He soon proved himself a skilful and forceful manipulator of affairs, and through marriage alliances and military action rose rapidly in power and status. By 1600 he had embarked on the conquest of all the Jurched tribes and was already becoming influential among the neighbouring Mongols. In 1607 they awarded him the title of Kundulen Khan ('Respected Emperor'). The following year he entered into an agreement with the Ming general in Liaodong (southernmost Manchuria) which defined the borders of his territory; Chinese were forbidden to cross the line. By 1613 all but one of the Jurched tribes had fallen under his control.

In 1601 Nurhaci organized his followers into military and administrative units called 'Banners', of which there were at first four and later eight. As increasing numbers of Chinese and Mongols came under his rule, a further eight Chinese and eight Mongol Banners were created. The banner organization managed registration, taxation and conscription of the banner members, providing the framework of administration in peace as well as in war. With this basic governmental system established, Nurhaci felt able to declare his own dynasty in 1616, reviving the old dynastic title of Jin. In 1618, with the aid of the Khalkha Mongols, he attacked China and successfully overran the more northerly part of Chinese-administered Manchuria, taking the important city of Fushun almost at once. Mukden (Shenyang) and Liaoyang fell in 1621. In the course of these campaigns, the last independent Jurched tribe was also conquered. In 1625 Nurhaci moved his capital to Mukden. The next year a further attack on the Ming forces was repulsed, with the assistance of cannons cast under the direction of the Jesuits. Shortly afterwards Nurhaci died.

ABAHAI

His son Abahai carried on the campaigns. First Korea was attacked and forced to send annual tribute of silver. Then another raid was made on Chinese territory, Beijing itself being looted in 1629. By about 1635 more or less all of Manchuria as far south as Shanhaiguan, where the Great Wall reaches the sea, was under his control, and many of the Mongols of Inner Mongolia had recognized his supremacy. In 1631 Abahai set up a civil administration patterned very much on that of China, but with the higher posts carefully divided between Manchus, Mongols and Chinese. Unlike the Mongol conquerors four centuries previously, the Manchus had been partly sinicized for a long period, and adopted Chinese government practices even before their conquest of China Proper.

In 1635 Abahai changed the name of his people from Jurched to Manchu, and shortly afterwards dropped the old dynastic name of Jin in favour of a new one, Qing. Probably the reason for these changes was a desire to throw off the associations of the old names, which were reminders of past defeats and subjugation both by the Mongols and later by the Ming. The dynastic name of Jin was particularly unfortunate as it means 'gold', while Ming means 'bright' and the character shows the sun and moon together in combination. As fire can melt metal, and Ming could be associated with fire, the name Jin was inauspicious. Qing, on the other hand, is written with an element which means 'water'; clearly water can overcome fire, and thus it was no doubt hoped that the Qing would conquer the Ming.

In 1636 and 1638 Manchu armies again made raids into northern China, penetrating as far as Ji'nan in Shandong. In 1640 all remaining areas to the north-east of the Great Wall were conquered, large Chinese forces being routed. Then the most northerly areas of Manchuria, everywhere south of the Amur River, were firmly subjugated. In 1643 Abahai's health faided and he died at the age of fifty-one. A six-year-old son succeeded him, with Jirgalang and Dorgon as regents. Meanwhile Beijing had fallen to the rebel forces under Li Zicheng, giving the Manchus a great opportunity. The commander of Ming forces at Shanhaiguan, Wu Sangui, faced by the advancing rebel armies, turned to the Manchus for assistance, inviting them through the gate in the Wall. Li Zicheng fled before the combined forces and the Manchus entered Beijing. Though they declared that they had come to avenge the Ming and destroy the Chinese rebels, they had no intention of giving up their position. Late in 1644 they moved their capital again, from Mukden to Beijing. Though remnants of the Ming held on in various parts of south China for several years, by 1660 only Taiwan and parts of the Fujian coast remained under their control. Taiwan fell to the Qing in 1683. Once more the whole of China was ruled by a foreign dynasty.

The Qing Dynasty

The effective ruler of the Qing empire immediately after the conquest was the regent Dorgon. Though he acted in a high-handed manner, dismissing his co-regent Jirgalang in 1647, he was energetic and talented and undoubtedly made a great contribution to the consolidation of the Qing position. In civil administration he retained most Ming practices and encouraged Chinese officials to serve the new dynasty. The Jesuit Adam Schall von Bell was kept on as director of the Imperial Board of Astronomy. It was at Dorgon's order, however, that Chinese men were forced to adopt the wearing of the pigtail, an unpopular measure. Though Westerners were later to consider the pigtail an essential part of Chinese fashion, it was in fact alien to the Han Chinese. One of the first acts of rebels against the Manchu regime was usually to cut off their pigtails. There was also resentment among the Chinese because of the appropriation of land to reward Manchu and Mongol princes and nobility.

Dorgon died late in 1650, the young Shunzhi Emperor then beginning his personal reign. He learned Chinese so that his Chinese officials could communicate with him directly, and generally continued Dorgon's policies even though Dorgon himself was posthumously disgraced. But his rule was not to last long – in 1661 he contracted smallpox and died when still in his early twenties. His third son was chosen to succeed for the practical reason that he had already been infected with smallpox and had survived. He took the throne at the age of six with the reign-title Kangxi. His was to be one of the longest and most prosperous reign-periods not only of the Qing dynasty but of the whole of Chinese history.

CHINESE SOCIETY UNDER QING ADMINISTRATION

Among the reasons for the great prosperity of China during the early part of the Qing dynasty were changes in Chinese agriculture. These had begun during the last century or so of the Ming dynasty, but had not taken full effect at that time. There had been great improvements in rice cultivation, with faster-ripening varieties coming into use, allowing more crops to be harvested each year. But perhaps the most significant of these changes were brought about by the introduction of new food crops, principally from the New World, which came sometimes by sea to the coast of south-east China, and sometimes less directly from south and south-east Asia into Yunnan and Guangxi. The most important were maize, sweet potatoes, peanuts and potatoes. The great significance of these new crops was not simply that they increased the variety of food plants available to Chinese farmers, but that they enabled land which was not suitable for growing traditional crops to be put to productive use. Maize and sweet potatoes were especially important in this respect; sweet potatoes in particular will produce a reasonable crop on very poor soil even in years of drought. An agricultural treatise written towards the end of the Ming period advocated their use to avoid famine in years when other crops failed. In Shandong province today they are still considered to be the food of poor peasants, principally grown to avoid hunger in areas where the soil is poor and water scarce. The new crops could also be planted on hill slopes unsuitable for traditional crops. This led to a gradual rise in the area of land under cultivation, with an increase of about 35 per cent between 1660 and 1760. Over the same period the population more or less doubled. Such growth was only possible because of improvements in the quantity and certainty of food supply.

There were, however, problems associated with this agricultural expansion. Much of the land newly brought under cultivation was poor, giving lower yields than old-established fields. More critically, the clearance of hillsides for crops commonly led to more rapid run-off of rain-water, causing soil erosion and increasing the danger of flooding of the valleys where the best land lay. Before the end of the eighteenth century such effects were already noticeable, and they have generally increased in severity ever since. Between 1812 and 1833 there was actually a decrease in the area of land under cultivation because of 'natural' disasters, of which many were really man-made.

But during the seventeenth and eighteenth centuries such problems were not severe. The increase in population and cultivated land area correspondingly increased government revenue, most of which derived from the land and poll taxes. These taxes had been more or less combined since 1581, under what was known as the 'single-whip system', the poll tax being levied as a proportion of the land tax. In 1712 the Kangxi Emperor decreed that the poll-tax quota should be permanently based on the contemporary population figures, no increases being made as a result of increase in population because it was rising much faster than the area of cultivated land. Government income for much of the eighteenth century comfortably exceeded expenditure.

CENTRAL ADMINISTRATION

The Qing administration was divided into several major groups of offices. Some of these had overlapping functions, for it was policy to ensure that no single office could usurp too much power. The highest offices were the Grand Secretariat and the Grand Council, which gave advice to the emperor, helped to draft decrees, suggested appointments and dismissals, and so on. The two bodies overlapped considerably in function and at first only the Secretariat existed. The Council was created in 1729, originally to handle a military crisis, and then took over many of the functions of the Secretariat. The Grand Secretaries usually held other high posts concurrently, and eventually appointment to the Secretariat became more or less a purely honorific matter. The Secretaries and Councillors had no direct executive functions, only the emperor having the power to issue orders to the next tier of government.

Below the Secretariat and Council were the six boards, which fulfilled the functions of ministries, being responsible for Civil Office, Revenue, Rites, War, Punishments and Public Works. The Board of Civil Office was the administrative body of the civil service. That of Revenue was responsible for taxation and tribute payments and all connected matters, including the census of population and the land registers, currency and coinage, and the auditing of central and provincial accounts; it had fourteen subsidiary bureaux, each responsible for one or two provinces. The Board of Rites not only handled all ritual matters but also education and the administration of the civil service examinations. The Board of War dealt with all military matters, except that the Imperial Bodyguard was under the direct control of the emperor. It also oversaw the official communication system, which used relays of horses to transmit urgent communications; the degree of urgency was matched to the required speed of transmission – the fastest speeds would take a message the 766 miles from Nanjing to Beijing in three or four days for example, the slowest taking twice as long. Routine communications were carried on foot and took 23 days for this journey; from Guangzhou it was 56 days.

The Board of Punishments handled all matters of law, and in conjunction with other government offices reviewed all cases involving death sentences. It had eighteen subsidiary bureaux, mostly handling affairs for one province. Two had authority over two provinces, and one handled the three Manchurian provinces; one other dealt with certain affairs involving Banner members. It should be noted that legal affairs in China were not handled in the European manner: civil matters were normally settled outside the courtroom, resort to the legal process being had only in exceptional circumstances. Arrested criminals were considered guilty unless they could prove their innocence. The courts were intended to be terrifying places, which good citizens would avoid at almost any cost, and to this end punishments were harsh. However, it is probably true that until the nineteenth century they were no more severe than in most European countries at the same period.

The last of the Boards, Public Works, oversaw the construction and repair of public buildings, including the imperial palaces and tombs. The control of rivers, canals and irrigation systems was an important part of its function, and it also had responsibility for the regulation of weights and measures.

Apart from these major offices of central government, there were a number of others directly under the emperor. These handled such matters as relations with the Mongols, Tibetans and other border peoples, official literary activities (including the collection of material for official histories), the receipt of communications from the provinces, and the regulation of the calendar. The Censorate had an important function in criticizing (and praising) government officials and remonstrating with the emperor about dubious policies. Provincial governors and governors-general usually held junior office in the Censorate, and in addition there were about a hundred other censors. They helped to ensure that mismanagement and corruption in the civil service were kept within limits.

Imperial household affairs, including those of the imperial clan, were handled by a number of separate offices, such as the Imperial Clan Court, the Imperial Study, the Court of State Ceremonial and the Imperial Medical Department. These did not form part of the main administrative structure of the empire.

PROVINCIAL ADMINISTRATION

Under the central administration were the provincial governments. For most of the period of the Qing dynasty there were eighteen provinces, excluding Mongolia, Tibet (including Qinghai), Xinjiang and Manchuria, which were administered in a different way from the Chinese provinces. Provincial administrations were headed either by a governor or a governor-general, some governors-general heading two or even three provinces. All provincial civil and military officials were subservient to the governors. Each province was divided into circuits and prefectures, and at the lowest level into counties (*xian*). The average population of a county was about 200,000. The local government was scarcely adequate for the control of such a large unit and relied heavily on unofficial aid through powerful local families, village headmen and so on. A *baojia* system was established in 1644 to assist police control, and another system, *lijia*, to facilitate tax collection. These were both systems of mutual responsibility which required local populations to govern themselves to a large degree. The extent of government control in China, even during periods of dynastic strength, was in fact usually much less complete than in contemporary Western states, and certainly much less than in any modern state with modern means of communication. As long as taxes were paid and there was no disorder or direct challenge to imperial authority, most areas away from the seats of local government were left largely to their own devices.

Yongzheng and Qianlong Emperors

The Kangxi Emperor died in 1722 after a reign of sixty-one years. The succession was controversial as the late emperor had not named his heir. The son who took the throne as the Yongzheng Emperor probably gained the position by intrigue, and several of his brothers were imprisoned shortly after his accession. He proved to be an energetic and hard-working, if ruthless, ruler who directed the empire strictly and efficiently. His father, he felt, had been too relaxed and tolerant in his later years. The Yongzheng Emperor certainly was not tolerant: a scholar who wrote a book considered to be anti-Manchu was condemned to the 'lingering death', his son and all his students being beheaded. Had he reigned longer, his autocratic behaviour might have begun to cause unrest, but he died suddenly after thirteen years on the throne before he had reached the age of sixty. His successor, his fourth son, had been a favourite grandson of the Kangxi Emperor and was destined to follow very much in his grandfather's footsteps. Though already in his mid-twenties when he took the throne late in 1735, the Qianlong Emperor was to rule for sixty years, and could have ruled longer had not respect for his illustrious kinsman moved him to abdicate rather than exceed his grandfather's length of reign. He died in 1799, not far short of ninety years of age.

FOREIGN CONFLICT AND THE ORIGINS OF DECLINE

The century or so after 1680 was a period of Qing strength. In the west they were able to overcome much opposition from Mongol leaders and bring Xinjiang back within the empire. More importantly, in the north-east they were sufficiently strong to push back the advancing Russians, who had begun to penetrate the Amur region during the 1640s. There were many minor clashes throughout the 1650s and 1660s which were inconclusive overall. In 1663 a Russian settlement was established at Albazin, on the north bank of the Amur River at about 124° E. Further Russian encroachments continued throughout the next twenty years. Early in the 1680s the Manchus began making thorough preparations for a campaign on the Amur, linking the Liao and Sungari Rivers with a canal and obtaining intelligence about Russian positions. In 1683 a Qing army moved north and soon cleared all Russian settlements from the lower Amur and its tributaries. Two years later Albazin was taken and burnt, but no Chinese garrison was left there and the Russians returned. The next year a Qing force again besieged the fort. The Russian defenders were on the point of being overrun, their numbers greatly reduced by Chinese attacks and by starvation and disease, when Russian overtures led to a truce. Further negotiations followed, and in 1689 a treaty was signed at Nerchinsk which bound the Russians to give up Albazin and placed the border along the Argun River to the Amur and then along a tributary to the Stanovoi Mountains. The most easterly stretch was left to be decided later. The Qing had achieved a considerable success, and had for the first time negotiated a treaty with a western power.

After the signing of this treaty several Russian missions entered China for trade and diplomatic purposes. In 1693 permission was granted for a Russian trade caravan to go to Beijing every three years; in fact they arrived more frequently. In 1727 another treaty delimited the frontier between Mongolia and Siberia, regulated trade arrangements, and allowed the Russians to establish a religious mission in Beijing. Both this treaty and the earlier one were negotiated with the aid of Jesuits from the Beijing mission, and to a great extent embodied western conceptions of international law.

TRADE WITH THE WEST

Western contacts on China's southern coast were handled very differently, however. The Portuguese had not made a favourable impression upon the Chinese because of their seizure of Malacca and forcible occupation of Tamao on the coast of the Pearl River estuary. Reports of the Spanish conquest of the Philippines must also have caused alarm. Nevertheless, trade developed gradually throughout the sixteenth and early seventeenth centuries, the major problems being caused by animosity between the various European nations involved rather than Chinese attempts at obstruction. The Portuguese were very jealous of their established position, and constantly tried to exclude other nations from the trade at Guangzhou. The ill reports which they gave of the other Europeans did not improve the Chinese opinion of these foreigners from the Western ocean. The imperial court was suspicious of their motives and continuously tried to limit the extent of contacts with them. Nevertheless Chinese merchants in the traditional ports of foreign trade were happy to do business whenever profitable opportunities presented themselves, and in the years after 1644 there was much trade with the Ming loyalists on the south China coast, particularly at Xiamen and on Taiwan. In 1685, after the Qing forces had occupied Taiwan and thus finally suppressed opposition to the new dynasty in south-east China, the Kangxi Emperor allowed maritime trade to proceed. Customs houses were opened at Guangzhou, Zhangzhou in Fujian, Ningbo and Yuntaishan in Jiangsu. The English East India Company established a regular trade with Guangzhou, the largest of these ports, during the last two decades of the seventeenth century. This continued, with numerous interruptions, until the 1750s, when attempts were made to re-establish trade further north at Ningbo. The customs duties and irregular exactions of the Chinese officials at Guanzhou caused continual irritation to the Western traders. It was thought that trading through a port closer to the main regions of tea and silk production would be more advantageous as these major commodities should be cheaper there. Indeed, the number of ships calling at Guangzhou decreased considerably from 1754 to 1757 as the trade shifted northward.

The argument often advanced by the Chinese at the time, that foreign trade was of no benefit to the Chinese empire but was allowed to the foreigners as a favour, was demonstrated to be false by the reaction of the officials at Guangzhou to the reduction in trade. They petitioned the emperor for a sharp increase in duties at Ningbo so that trade would return to their port. The finances of the province of Guangdong in fact gained great benefit from the various levies on the trade, besides the large amounts which the local officials were able to divert into their own pockets. During most of the eighteenth century, the balance of trade ran very much in China's favour, with considerable amounts of silver flowing into the empire in payment for the commodities exported.

The major export by the late eighteenth century was tea, which accounted for well over half the total value of commodities bought at Guangzhou. Raw silk was also important, other items including porcelain, lacquerware, various spices and sugar. It is extraordinary how quickly tea became fashionable in Europe (particularly in England). No tea had ever been seen in Europe until about 1640, and until about 1700 only very small quantities (five or six chests a year) were bought by the British East India Company. During the first quarter of the eighteenth century this amount increased to some 400,000 pounds of tea per annum, and by 1800 the yearly amount stood at no less than 23 million pounds. Tea-drinking had become a British national habit. It is curious that the cup of tea which seems so natural a part of everyday life today was a luxury 200 years ago and almost unknown a century before that. The import duty on Chinese tea in around 1800 provided the British government with one-tenth of its total revenue.

In response to the petition of the Guangzhou authorities, the Qing emperor restricted trade with Westerners to Guangzhou. The Manchu rulers of China seem to have been worried not only by the possible aggressive intentions of the Western nations (Britain was in the process of conquering India at this time), but also by the danger of their Chinese subjects taking advantage of assistance from the foreigners to rise up against the Qing dynasty (in fact, the Taiping rebels during the next century did gain some foreign support and came close to being given a great deal more). They were aware that Ningbo was very close to the estuary of the Yangtze River, and that foreign ships might easily penetrate the Chinese interior by sailing up this vast waterway. It was much safer to keep the Westerners as far from the centre of the Chinese empire as possible.

The Westerners chafed at the restrictions imposed upon them, and tried constantly to improve their position. In 1793 a British embassy led by Lord Macartney arrived at Beijing, and was accorded a gracious reception by the Qianlong Emperor at the Summer Palace at Jehol (Chengde), despite the fact that Macartney refused to perform the *ketou* (kowtow). This question of ceremonial assumed enormous importance, and was much discussed throughout this early period of Western intercourse with China. The *ketou* involved kneeling and performing a prostration so that the forehead touched the ground. Before an emperor, three kneelings and nine knockings of the head were normally demanded. This was considered humiliating by Westerners, however, and was correctly seen as offering effective submission to the emperor of China. An official envoy performing the *ketou* placed his country in a tributary relationship with China, as far as the Chinese were concerned; great efforts were always made to obtain this submission from foreign envoys. The refusal of Lord Amherst, second British ambassador to China, to perform the *ketou* resulted in him not being received by the emperor in 1816. On both occasions, the attempts made by the ambassadors to negotiate with the Chinese regarding trade relations produced no concrete results, but it was noticed at Guangzhou that the local officials became more accommodating.

In view of the way the world was developing after 1800, there was little prospect of the Qing policy of allowing only very restricted contacts between China and the West being successful for very long. When European ships had first arrived on the coasts of China in the sixteenth century there had been little difference between the relative stage of advancement of the Western nations and the great empire of the Far East. Certainly the Europeans at that time could not have contemplated a major war with China. The Industrial Revolution tilted the balance very much in favour of Europe. Nineteenth-century Britain was a great power, with enormous military resources and a vast empire. The British of the period were scarcely in the mood to continue to tolerate Chinese attempts to humiliate them. The absolute refusal by the Qing court to treat the maritime European nations as equals was bound to cause friction, especially as the latter knew that Russia was accorded better treatment. The Russians had a permanent ecclesiastic mission in Beijing, and were allowed to send students to learn the

Chinese language. No other Western nation was permitted to send a resident to the Chinese capital and Chinese were forbidden to give them language tuition. Whatever the rights and wrongs of the situation, the attitude of the Qing court was totally unrealistic, and bound to cause serious problems.

The Decline of the Empire

The Qing dynasty after the death of the Qianlong Emperor was in fact a spent force. Even during the later years of this great ruler the empire was already showing signs of decline. Lord Macartney had noticed this, describing China as 'an old, crazy, first-rate man-of-war' doomed to destruction 'whenever an insufficient man happens to have the command upon deck'. After the Qianlong Emperor, the Qing produced no more 'sufficient' rulers. Even during his long reign the seeds of decline had been sown. Since the 1770s an official called He Shen had been the old emperor's favourite and had been able to practise corruption and extortion on a massive scale. His personal fortune, confiscated after the Qianlong Emperor died in 1799, was estimated at some 800 million taels (Chinese ounces of silver), when the annual revenue of the whole empire was only about 40 million. Almost all of this wealth must have been ill-gotten. He Shen's influence spread throughout China, encouraging corruption and moral degeneration. There was also vast military expenditure during the Qianlong period, on campaigns in Xinjiang, Burma, Annam and Nepal, and against rebels in Taiwan and western Sichuan. This began to cause financial difficulties. The final blow was a serious uprising under the leadership of the White Lotus Sect, a secret society pledged to overthrow the Manchus and restore Chinese rule. This first broke out in 1793, and was not finally suppressed until 1804 at a cost of 200 million taels. One of the major reasons for serious unrest among the peasants was the large increase in population, which was not matched by a corresponding increase in land under cultivation. From the 1790s the Qing empire fell into a decline from which it never recovered.

Just at this time of degeneration in China, the Western nations began to reach the peak of their power. By 1800 Britain was firmly established in India, giving her a strong base not too far from the China coast. Moreover, possession of India at last provided the answer to the problem of the trade balance with China, for in India the opium poppy was cultivated. In about the middle of the eighteenth century it was discovered that there was a demand for opium in China, and trade in the drug developed rapidly.

OPIUM

The smoking of opium seems to have become widespread in China during the seventeenth century, though the poppy from which it is derived had been known and grown for very much longer. At first the opium consumed by the Chinese was home-produced. As early as 1729 an imperial prohibition of the sale and smoking of opium was promulgated, but this apparently had little effect. The Portuguese soon found that there was profit to be made selling opium to the Chinese and began the trade between India and China. The British soon followed them and by 1773 were the main dealers. In 1796 its importation and cultivation were banned by the Qianlong Emperor, but again the prohibition had little effect because many officials smoked the drug and therefore connived at its illegal distribution and use. The East India Company nevertheless found it politic to disassociate itself officially from the the trade in opium, all exports to China from India being shipped on 'country' ships (private trading vessels operating under the Company's licence). Once these arrived off Guangzhou, the opium was sold to Chinese dealers and run ashore in special fast boats. Local officials were commonly bribed to close their eyes to the illegal trade.

The opium trade developed so rapidly that by the 1820s the overall balance of trade began to run against China. Silver actually began to flow out of the empire, most rapidly during the middle and late 1830s. This economic effect increased the Qing government's concern about the drug and further efforts were made to ban it. But with so many government officials themselves smokers (probably about 20 per cent), such efforts were doomed to failure. Qing naval forces were anyway quite inadequate to suppress opium smuggling. The problem became more and more acute, especially after the East India Company's monopoly of the China trade was abolished in 1834. The Company had certainly connived at the trade and made large profits from it, but had at least exercised some restraint in the way it dealt with the Chinese officials. The private traders were often much less orderly and more ruthless. A crisis was not long in coming.

In 1836 a movement arose among some high-ranking Chinese officials to legalize opium. When the foreign traders heard of this, they ordered large supplies from India in anticipation of increased demand after the prohibition was lifted. But late in the same year the emperor decided to take the opposite course, and strict measures to stamp out the illegal trade were ordered. A new governor-general arrived at Guangzhou and took vigorous action. By the end of 1837 the native smuggling networks had largely been crushed. The foreign opium dealers found themselves with large quantities of virtually unsaleable opium, and prices fell through the floor. By the beginning of 1839 the trade was dead; in March of that year, a special commissioner sent by the emperor demanded the surrender of all the opium stocks held by the Western traders at Guangzhou.

At first the traders prevaricated, and the commissioner, Lin Zexu, took various measures to try to coerce them. Finally, the British government representative in Guangzhou took responsibility for the opium held by British traders and handed it to the Chinese authorities. Thus the matter ceased to be one involving private traders and the Chinese authorities, the British government taking over the interests of its subjects. The opium was destroyed under Commissioner Lin's supervision. The British considered themselves insulted and entitled to compensation, and an expeditionary force was despatched to blockade Guangzhou. Fighting broke out in November 1839, several Chinese war junks being sunk or damaged. Thus began the infamous Opium War.

THE OPIUM WAR

Once the main British fleet arrived it quickly proceeded northwards, blockading all the major ports of the China coast. When it reached Bei He near Tianjin, the emperor was sufficiently disturbed to send a reprimand to Commissioner Lin and authorize the governor-general at Tianjin to negotiate. With the promise of negotiations at Guangzhou, the British withdrew southwards. Early in 1841, by threat of force, they compelled the Chinese negotiators to accept a draft convention, by which Hong Kong would be ceded to Britain, an indemnity would be paid, the trade at Guangzhou would be resumed, and direct and equal intercourse would be established between British and Chinese officials. But when the draft was submitted to the emperor he was furious; the chief negotiator was recalled in chains. The British government was almost equally dissatisfied with the bargain, considering that the Chinese had been let off far too lightly! Hostilities were recommenced, the British soon destroying the outer defences of Guangzhou. Reinforcements arrived from India, and by the summer of 1842 several major Chinese ports along the coast and on the Yangtze had been occupied. With British warships threatening Nanjing, the Qing government decided it had better negotiate before its loss of face encouraged its Chinese subjects to revolt. The Treaty of Nanjing (1842) gave the British Hong Kong Island, improvements in trading facilities, including the opening of the ports of Xiamen, Fuzhou, Ningbo and Shanghai in addition to Guangzhou, and equality in official correspondence. The indemnity to be paid by China was set at $21 million. Further treaties were signed shortly afterwards with the Americans and French. Curiously, in the Sino-British treaty, opium was not even mentioned.

The opium question was not, in fact, the ultimate cause of the war, which really resulted from the strong conflict of attitudes of the Chinese and Westerners. The Western nations could not accept the claim of the Chinese emperor to rule the world, and demanded relations based on equality. They also demanded the right to trade under what they considered to be reasonable conditions. The Manchu court and its officials were appallingly ignorant of conditions in the West, and had ludicrous ideas about foreigners. Commissioner Lin believed that the British could not survive without tea and rhubarb! The superior weaponry of the Westerners took the Chinese entirely by surprise: they could only think that the accuracy of the fire from British warships was due to sorcery. Despite more than 300 years of direct contacts with the Westerners, the Chinese had almost entirely failed to learn anything about them.

The Opium War began a new era for China, an era of humiliation and painful adaptation to a world in which Chinese civilization could no longer see itself as the centre of world culture. Riven by internal dissensions and almost constantly facing aggression from outside, China was to remain weak for more than a century, only re-emerging as a great power during the last fifty years. The process of adaptation to a modern world dominated by Western ideas and values is still continuing today.

CHAPTER EIGHT

The Collapse of Empire,
1842–1911

After the Opium War, every major development in China was influenced to a greater or lesser degree by the Western impact. Though the Manchus can at first hardly have believed that the foreigners could be capable of conquering China, they certainly feared the loss of face that Western military strength could cause them. If their Chinese subjects perceived Qing authority to be weak, they might be encouraged to rise up and overthrow their Manchu overlords. The Qing emperors therefore felt it essential to take a hard line with the Westerners, even though their comparative military weakness warranted a more cautious approach. The greatest fear of the Manchus was the possibility of collusion between the Chinese and the Westerners, which was an important reason for their attempts to limit Western penetration of their empire. That such fears were by no means unjustified was soon made very clear by a serious outbreak of rebellion early in 1851.

The Taiping Rebellion

The Taiping rebellion was a curious affair. Led by a failed candidate for the Confucian examinations who claimed to be the younger brother of Jesus Christ, it affected most of the provinces of China Proper, and in particular those of the rich lower Yangtze valley, for more than a decade. The rebels held Nanjing as the capital of the 'Heavenly Kingdom of Great Peace' from 1853 until 1864. For some years it seemed as though they might be capable of overthrowing the Qing regime, but the revolt finally crumbled, due largely to internal weaknesses. It caused appalling bloodshed and destruction, the effects of which remained obvious for many decades and are still discernible today. It was also a severe shock to the Qing dynasty and altered the balance of power between Chinese and Manchus; future revolutionaries were to draw inspiration from it. It is in fact possible to argue that it was potentially just as great a revolution as those which were to shake China during the twentieth century.

The Chinese word for revolution is *geming*. The character *ge* means 'change', and *ming* is the character for the 'mandate of Heaven', the divine authority by virtue of which dynasties ruled the empire. Thus the literal meaning of *geming* is 'change of the mandate of Heaven'. The implications of this are far less sweeping than the corresponding English term. 'Revolution' means a complete turn, a change in everything, whereas to change the mandate of Heaven it is sufficient for one dynasty to replace another. Every change of dynasty in Chinese history theoretically involved a change in the mandate of Heaven. In fact, although the revolutions in China during this century have wrought many changes, they have also left a great deal unaltered. At one time during the early 1980s official Chinese newspapers declared that, though China had experienced more than one revolution during the twentieth century, the Chinese were unfamiliar with reform, and urged greater efforts to change old ways.

Had the Taiping rebellion succeeded in 'changing the mandate of Heaven' it would almost certainly have brought about changes in China as great as any seen in more recent years. Unlike many peasant uprisings, it had a complete ideology of its own, largely based on partly-assimilated Christian ideas which were completely hostile to old Chinese philosophies. Wherever the Taiping rebels went, they destroyed temples and religious images and forbade the traditional sacrifices to the ancestors. They promulgated Ten Commandments based on those of Moses, and preached egalitarianism and abstention of a kind which Protestant missionaries would have (and, indeed, did) admire. Had they been better led and organized, they might well have brought about the downfall not only of the Manchu dynasty but also of a large part of Chinese tradition. Their theories were certainly revolutionary, and had it been possible to put them fully into practice would have changed the whole basis of land and property ownership and swept away Confucianism and Chinese religion.

ORIGINS OF THE REBELLION

Hong Xiuquan came from a peasant family of moderate means living about thirty miles outside Guangzhou. As a boy he studied for the civil service examinations and later became a village teacher, but failed the first level of examination four times. When in Guangzhou for his second attempt, he came into contact with Protestant Western missionaries, and later began to have visions of God. In 1843, after his fourth attempt at the examinations, he began to preach his own form of Christianity, in which he himself figured as younger brother of Jesus Christ. One of his associates organized a Society of Worshippers of God in Guangxi province, which made rapid progress. Hong sought further instruction in Christian doctrines from a Western missionary in Guangzhou in 1847, but soon left to continue his preaching activities. As a result of famine in 1849–50, there were many uprisings in Guangxi and neighbouring provinces, mainly organized by the secret societies. The Worshippers of God were not directly involved but gained many new adherents and benefited from the difficulties of the local government authorities. By early 1850 Hong's followers numbered more than 10,000. In January 1851 they rose in open revolt. Hong was proclaimed 'Heavenly King' of the 'Heavenly Kingdom of Great Peace'. The rebels cut off their pigtails and wore their hair long as an open act of defiance against the Manchus.

The Taiping army moved northward through Guangxi, defeating all government forces and living by plunder. After some setbacks during 1852, they reached the Yangtze River and took Wuhan and then Nanjing in 1853. There they settled, establishing a court on imperial lines and beginning to organize an administration. The British plenipotentiary in China soon made contact, with a view to ascertaining the attitude of the rebels to foreigners, particularly in view of their professed Christianity. It would have been very much to the advantage of the rebels to have gained foreign support, but they behaved less than astutely in their reception of the British. Their peculiar beliefs, especially regarding the divinity of Hong Xiuquan, led to a guarded Western reaction. The foreign powers in general decided to maintain neutrality, though the Catholic French and Orthodox Russians inclined strongly to the Qing side.

The Manchu imperial armies were by this time in severe decline. The Taiping fighting forces were better organized and fought with all the zeal of religious fanatics. A Taiping expedition to the north in 1853–5 reached almost to Tianjin before its extended lines of communication forced a retreat. Had it been better led and adequately supported and reinforced, it could almost certainly have taken Beijing. Faced with such an onslaught and with its existing forces in no state to check the main Taiping forces under their best leaders, the Manchu court called on some of its high Chinese officials to organize local militia forces. The Hunan Army of Zeng Guofan, organized in 1852–3, was the first of these, followed by Li Hongzhang's Huai Army, raised in 1862. Meanwhile the attitude of the foreign powers towards the Taipings was hardening, largely because of rebel attacks on Shanghai. Official neutrality was maintained, but an army of volunteers (mainly ruffians from the Shanghai waterfront) was raised and paid for by merchants and businessmen. It was at first led by an American adventurer, Frederick Ward, and after his death in action came to be commanded by the famous British soldier, Charles Gordon, known now as Gordon of Khartoum but to his contemporaries as Chinese Gordon. This foreign-led 'Ever-victorious Army' defeated the Taiping armies several times, acting in concert with the Huai Army.

The Downfall of the 'Heavenly Kingdom'

In 1856, after major victories over Qing forces near the Yangtze, the Taiping Heavenly Kingdom was shaken by an internal conflict which resulted in the deaths of most of its leaders. Hong Xiuquan was not himself threatened by the events but lost faith in his subordinates. He appointed two of his brothers to run the government, but they did not have the talent to do so properly. Together with the rise of the power of the Hunan Army, this brought a turning-point in Taiping fortunes, although it was not until 1864 that Nanjing was finally recaptured, Hong Xiuquan committing suicide just before the end. The rebellion, which had cost an estimated 20 to 40 million lives, was soon completely suppressed.

The fundamental reason for the ultimate failure of the Heavenly Kingdom of Great Peace was its leadership. There can be little doubt that Hong Xiuquan was mentally ill, and failed to exercise sound and rational control over his subordinates. He committed many tactical blunders, and because of his religious fanaticism and delusions about his personal importance failed to make good use of opportunities for co-operation with the secret societies and with the Western powers. Had he set aside his claim to be the younger brother of Jesus Christ and accepted further instruction from the Western missionaries who came to Nanjing after it fell to his armies, he might well have obtained some active support from Britain and the United States at least. An accommodation with the Western interests in Shanghai could have left the city open to Taiping occupation. The extreme fanaticism of the rebels also alienated many Chinese, particularly of the gentry class, who were deeply shocked by the Taiping destruction of temples and antipathy to Confucianism. It must also be said that the Taiping leaders themselves failed to comply with the strict code of moral behaviour they enjoined. Hong Xiuquan had a personal harem of eighty-eight concubines.

OTHER REBELLIONS

Had Hong Xiuquan wished, he could have made good use of alliances with other rebels. The Nian rebellion, for example, raged in the area just south of the Yellow River, in Shandong, Henan and Anhui, from 1853 until 1868. The Taiping northern expedition actually received much support from the Nian rebels when it passed through the areas where they were active. There were Muslim rebellions in Yunnan from 1855 to 1873 and in the north-west from 1862 to 1878. This period was one of tremendous turmoil, which left the Qing court in a much-weakened position. The various rebellions were only suppressed with the aid of loyal Chinese such as Zeng Guofan and Li Hongzhang, who with their personal armies began to acquire the sort of power which earlier dynasties had always feared to allow their generals. Although after the mid-1870s the Qing government appeared to be firmly in control again, the position of the Manchus had suffered an irreversible setback.

The Arrow War

There had also been further conflict with the Western powers. The position at Guangzhou had continued to be unsatisfactory, the officials appointed there after the Opium War being particularly anti-foreign and obstructive. Some of the articles of the treaties made after the war were not complied with, causing great dissatisfaction to the nations trading at Guangzhou, but no firm action was taken for some time. The Western nations claimed the right to negotiate a revision of the treaties after twelve years, as had been stipulated in most of them, but the Chinese authorities obstructed all attempts to discuss such revision. The prevailing atmosphere became very strained, and further war seemed inevitable.

In 1856, an incident involving a small vessel registered with the British at Hong Kong, the *Arrow*, was the spark that ignited the flame. The Chinese authorities at Guangzhou refused to apologize for boarding the ship, which was flying the British flag, and seizing twelve of its crew. The British eventually moved gunboats up the river to bombard the city and the war had begun. In Britain, there was much consternation in Parliament, but a general election confirmed the government's majority. An expedition was sent to reinforce the existing British forces on the China coast.

The French joined the British in action, demanding reparation for the murder of a French missionary in the interior of China. The other nations for the moment stood aside, though the USA and Russia offered peaceful co-operation. Guangzhou was seized in December 1857. The next year the foreign forces took Tianjin and the Dagu forts which commanded the mouth of the river on which the city stood. Treaties were concluded with the four powers in June 1858. They provided for the opening of ten more ports to foreign trade, increased freedom for foreigners to move about within China, limits on the level of duties levied on foreign goods in transit inland, and indemnities for Britain and France. Later in the same year, a British envoy was sent to exchange ratification of the treaty at Beijing but the Chinese tried to prevent him proceeding beyond Shanghai. An attempt to force a way to Tianjin failed when the Dagu forts opened fire with surprising accuracy. Though the British envoy was criticized by the home government for his precipitate use of force, the British and French sent a further expedition which marched into Beijing in late summer 1860. The Xianfeng Emperor and his court fled to Jehol (Chengde). Finding no one to negotiate with, the foreigners decided to punish the emperor by burning the imperial Summer Palace on the north-western outskirts of Beijing. The Yuan Ming Yuan ('Round Bright Garden') had been largely constructed during the early part of the Qing dynasty, and included buildings in Western style designed by the Jesuit missionaries. The Western troops looted it and put its buildings to the torch, one of the most appalling acts of vandalism of the late nineteenth century. The exact reasons for the decision to destroy this palace complex have never been fully explained. Today the Chinese authorities have restored some of the buildings.

New peace treaties were eventually forced upon the Qing court, giving the foreign powers the right to have ministers permanently resident at Beijing. The stipulations of the treaties of 1858 were confirmed. In addition, Kowloon Peninsula opposite Hong Kong Island was ceded to Britain, and increased indemnities were payable to Britain and France. Tianjin was added to the list of open ports. The Russians, who had cleverly offered themselves as mediators between the two sides, in return gained large territorial concessions from the Qing government, all the land north of the Amur and Ussuri Rivers being transferred to their sovereignty. They also gained the right to trade and residency at Urga (now Ulaan Baatar) in Outer Mongolia and Kashgar in Xinjiang.

This settlement of 1860 was one reason for the changed attitude of the Western powers towards the Taiping rebels. While there had been some expectation that the policies towards foreigners of the Heavenly Kingdom of Great Peace might be more accommodating than those of the Qing court, the Westerners had been inclined to favour the rebels against the government. When Western hopes of the rebels proved largely illusory, neutrality had been maintained. But with the advantages gained by the treaties of 1860, together with a new realism shown by some of the Manchu nobility, the Westerners decided that it was to their benefit to support the Qing dynasty. The Ever-Victorious Army, especially after it came under the command of Gordon, made a great contribution to the suppression of the rebellion, as Li Hongzhang himself recognized. For a decade or so after 1860 it seemed as though the Westerners and the Qing government might be able to achieve a more harmonious relationship.

The emperor having fled to Jehol, it was left to one of the imperial princes, the emperor's half-brother Prince Gong, to negotiate in Beijing with the Western representatives. Like most of the Manchus and Chinese, the prince was extremely suspicious of the foreigners, and wrote to the emperor, 'If we think the barbarians are sincere we shall be greatly deceived . . . In my opinion all the barbarians have the nature of brute beasts.' But as a result of his contact with the negotiators his opinions altered greatly. He was astonished that the foreigners openly offered to assist China to modernize her defences, and were prepared to share the secrets of their superior weaponry. Their readiness to evacuate their troops from Beijing once a settlement had been reached revealed that the foreign powers had no major territorial designs on China and were not utterly lacking in reason and good faith. Prince Gong was completely won over, and advocated dealing diplomatically with the Westerners to try to maintain peace while China was strengthened by learning and applying Western military techniques. For their part, the Western diplomats, who were now at last allowed to reside in Beijing, began to acquire a greater understanding of the Chinese position. As recently as 1840, during the Opium War, the British Secretary of War had addressed Parliament thus: 'What does anybody here know of China? Even those Europeans who have been in that empire are almost as ignorant of it as the rest of us.' With increased communication between Westerners and Chinese, and the easier access to the Qing government afforded by residence at Beijing, the mutual lack of understanding began at last to break down a little.

FOREIGN AFFAIRS

One of the major innovations in Qing relations with the West after 1860 was the establishment of a foreign office, the Zongli Yamen. Previously foreign affairs had been largely handled by the governors-general at Guangzhou and, after 1842, at Nanjing. The Zongli Yamen provided a specialist body at the highest level to deal with foreign relations, and also took on a major role in promoting Western science and technology. Another important development was the employment of large numbers of Westerners in Chinese government service, especially in the Imperial Maritime Customs. Foreign collection of the customs levies on foreign trade had begun during the 1850s, when a secret society had taken advantage of the disorder caused by the Taiping rebellion to occupy the Chinese city of Shanghai. The Chinese customs inspectorate had been unable to operate. Western traders were happy to take advantage of the situation, but the Western consuls in Shanghai decided that it would be fair to collect the customs dues on behalf of the Chinese until normality could be restored. It was soon found that the Westerners collected the dues more fairly and remitted more to the central government, being less open to corruption than the Chinese officials had been. In 1860 this *ad hoc* arrangement was formalized and extended, the Western customs inspectors being taken into Chinese government employ. Under Robert Hart, who became inspector-general in 1863, the customs service became a valued part of the Chinese civil service, though many of its officials were Westerners. Hart himself, through his courtesy and consideration towards the Chinese, became a trusted adviser on foreign affairs to the Qing court and was awarded many high honours by it. He remained at his post through all vicissitudes until his death in 1911.

The Self-Strengthening Movement

The *rapprochement* between China and the West after 1860 took practical effect within China in a movement of self-strengthening. As early as 1840 Commissioner Lin Zexu had begun cautiously to advocate learning about the superior technology of the West, and had purchased foreign guns to strengthen Guangzhou's defences. After 1860, with wider awareness of Western power, particularly in court circles, a large number of projects were begun to bring Western technology into China. In 1862 Li Hongzhang established three gun factories at Shanghai and engaged Westerners to teach the men of his army the use of modern cannon and rifles. During the course of the next decade several more such gun factories and arsenals, as well as modern shipyards and machine factories, were set up at various places along the China coast and the Yangtze. Students were sent to study in the USA, and colleges for the study of Western languages and Western science were opened. From the mid 1870s, the emphasis on acquiring modern armaments shifted towards a more general modernization of industry to strengthen the economy of the empire. Despite considerable opposition from conservative elements, telegraph lines, textile mills, mines, ironworks and many other projects were completed. Unfortunately, in the vast area of China the number of modern enterprises was very limited, and traditional institutions maintained their dominance. Li Hongzhang wrote despairingly to a friend:

> I had the honour of meeting Prince Gong and explained to him thoroughly the advantages of railways . . . Prince Gong agreed with my suggestion, but said that nobody dared to promote such action . . . The gentry class forbids the local people to use Western methods and machines . . . Scholars and men of letters always criticize me for honouring strange knowledge and for being queer and unusual. It is really difficult to understand the minds of some Chinese.

China was also short of capital and lacked sound direction from the top: many of the modernizing projects were undertaken at provincial level with no central co-ordination. Pressure from the Western imperialist powers also continued unrelentingly. From 1871–81 the Russians occupied the Ili region of Xinjiang. The French seized Annam and fought a short war with the Chinese in 1884–5. For the first time the newly-modernized Japanese nation, which had been much quicker than China in adapting to the impact of the West, made its power felt, invading Taiwan in 1874 and annexing the Liuqiu (Ryukyu) Islands in 1879. At the same time Japan also began to behave aggressively in Korea.

The Sino-Japanese War

Korea had been tributary to China throughout the Ming and Qing dynasties as well as at earlier periods, and was viewed by the Qing court as a valuable outer buffer state under strong Chinese influence. The Japanese, however, also had a long-standing interest. After their modernization in the mid-nineteenth century they were eager to take their place among the Western powers in obtaining concessions from China. Taiwan and Korea were the obvious areas to begin. Throughout the 1870s the Japanese pushed for a strengthening of their influence in both areas, but it was Korea, closer to the Japanese mainland and economically richer, which most attracted their attentions. In 1894, taking advantage of a rebellion in Korea which had been partly fomented by a Japanese secret society, Japan sent troops to the peninsula. China crushed the rebellion and tried to negotiate a Japanese withdrawal, but in July 1894 the Japanese navy sank a troopship carrying Chinese forces to Korea, and war was declared. For the Chinese it was a disastrous humiliation, its forces being routed both on land and at sea. In a few months the fighting was over, the Chinese Beiyang ('Northern Ocean') fleet having been annihilated. In April 1895 the Treaty of Shimonoseki was signed, by which Korea became independent, a large indemnity was to be paid by China, Taiwan was ceded to Japan, several new treaty ports were to be opened and China was to be opened to Japanese industrial activity. Only pressure from the Western nations prevented Japan also taking possession of the Liaodong peninsula.

REPERCUSSIONS OF THE WAR

This war had tremendous repercussions within China. It aroused strong nationalistic feelings in a way earlier wars with the Western powers had not. The Japanese had long been despised by the Chinese, who considered them a tributary nation of 'dwarf pirates'. To be defeated by the British or French was one thing, for they were unruly barbarians from outside the pale of traditional Chinese influence, but to be thus humiliated by former tributaries was another. Moreover the Japanese attempt to seize the Liaodong peninsula, which only Western intervention had prevented, was the most alarming move yet attempted by any foreign power, for its possession would have allowed the Japanese to dominate the Gulf of Bohai and thus threaten the security of Tianjin and Beijing. The rapid defeat had also shown that 'self-strengthening' had not achieved its aims. After 1895 the fortunes of the Qing empire reached their nadir, with the foreign powers scrambling to win more and more concessions and with ever-increasing internal problems. The Chinese empire was once again beginning to fall apart.

Russia had played a leading role in preventing the Japanese seizure of Liaodong, and had facilitated a loan to pay the indemnity to Japan. The Russians were of course furthering their own interests, for they had no desire at all to see Japan secure a strong position in southern Manchuria, a region on which they themselves were casting covetous eyes. Nevertheless, the Chinese were happy enough to play off one lot of foreigners against another, and entered into an agreement allowing Russia to complete their Trans-Siberian Railway by constructing a line across northern Manchuria to Vladivostok, a shorter and easier route than one skirting around the edge of Chinese territory (as the present Trans-Siberian line does). In return Russia promised to defend China against Japanese aggression. Li Hongzhang, who was pro-Russian and negotiated this deal, was extremely pleased with it, announcing that it would give China peace for twenty years. But China was to be allowed no such respite.

In 1897 the Germans fulfilled a long-held ambition by seizing the Jiaozhou bay and Qingdao on the south coast of Shandong, in retaliation for the murder of two German missionaries in the province. The Chinese were forced to grant them a lease for ninety-nine years. The Russians promptly occupied Port Arthur and Dalian on the pretext of protecting them from the Germans; they were given a 25-year lease on the two ports. The British thereupon negotiated leases for Weihaiwei in Shandong for twenty-five years and the New Territories of Hong Kong for ninety-nine years. The French took a 99-year lease on Guangzhou Bay. Even the Italians, newly arrived in the Far East, tried to gain a foothold on the coast of Zhejiang, but were successfully resisted. Only the USA did not take part in this scramble. In addition to the leased areas, 'spheres of influence' for each power were also recognized, so that China lost much freedom of action and appeared to be on the verge of being carved up by the competing foreign powers. It was probably only increasing tensions between the powers which in the event stopped this happening during the decade or so after 1900.

The failure of the self-strengthening movement to prevent humiliation at the hands of Japan led to more radical approaches being advocated within China. Knowledge of the West had become more widely disseminated in China through the activities of mission schools, the study of Western languages and technology and the sending of Chinese abroad. Gradually it had become appreciated by at least some members of the educated classes in China that the strength of the Western nations was not solely dependent on military technology; their social and governmental systems also conferred advantages. Western political ideas began to diffuse slowly into Chinese minds; a translation into Chinese of Huxley's *Evolution and Ethics* which was serialized in a Tianjin journal and then appeared in book form in 1898 made a

The façade of the Catholic Cathedral in Qingdao,
Shandong province, formerly a German concession port

particularly strong impression. The Darwinian theory of evolution expounded by Huxley, with its doctrine of the 'survival of the fittest', had obvious implications for China at the period. If the Chinese nation were to survive in the face of foreign aggression, it had to take positive steps very quickly.

The 'Hundred Days of Reform'

One man emerged as the leader of the radical reform movement in China, a Cantonese scholar named Kang Youwei. He was thoroughly familiar with Confucian learning and passed all three stages of the traditional government examinations, but also became impressed with Western learning. He reinterpreted the Confucian Classics in an entirely original way which lent support to the reform movement by saying that Confucius himself had advocated reform. In 1895, while in Beijing to take the metropolitan examination, he prepared a long memorial to the emperor protesting about the capitulation to Japan and advocating institutional reform. He was able to persuade several hundred of the other examination candidates to sign it with him. Though it was blocked by the Censorate before reaching the emperor's eyes, it had some impact on the highest levels of government.

Eventually Kang did succeed in bringing his views to the emperor's attention. His reputation increased steadily, both among the scholarly class in general and at the court. Though his views were anathema to many conservative high officials, he enjoyed the emperor's personal support. Between June and September 1898 a series of reforming decrees were issued, designed to change the whole face of education, political administration and economic activity in China. Conservative opposition stiffened, and it soon became clear that a major power-struggle was in progress. The fate of the reform programme was in the end to be decided by the notorious Empress Dowager Ci Xi. At this time she was officially in retirement, but in fact little important business could be transacted without reference to her. She had been the power behind the throne for many years, and she intended to ensure that she continued to enjoy that power.

DOWAGER EMPRESS CI XI

The young Manchu girl Yehe Nara (Yehonala) entered the imperial palace as a junior concubine in 1851 when she was just fifteen. She soon became a favourite of the Xianfeng Emperor, particularly after 1856 when she gave birth to the emperor's only son. When the Anglo-French armies occupied Beijing in 1860, she fled along with the rest of the court to Jehol, taking her young son with her. The emperor died there the following year, and Yehe Nara's child succeeded to the throne as the Tongzhi Emperor. Eight regents were appointed to rule until he reached a sufficient age to take power himself. Yehe Nara and the dead emperor's chief wife, Ci An, were both raised to the rank of dowager empresses, but this did not satisfy Ci Xi, as she was now titled. She was not content to allow control of the government to pass into the hands of others, and was able to arrange the downfall of the eight regents. The two dowager empresses thereupon took over as joint regents, but Ci Xi was always dominant, Ci An being neither very able nor ambitious.

The young emperor married in 1872, the regency ending the following year. It seems, however, that the emperor was fond of slipping out of the palace in disguise to amuse himself with the low-class prostitutes of Beijing, and very soon he began to show symptoms of a distressing disease. By January 1875 he was dead, officially of smallpox. He left no heir. With the death of her son, Ci Xi should have found herself outside the main circle of government. But she managed to contrive a succession which contravened all the normal rules and had another young boy placed on the throne as the Guangxu Emperor. The dead emperor's wife, who should herself have become Empress Dowager if the succession had been arranged in orthodox fashion, realized the difficulties of her position and committed suicide. Thus the two dowager empresses once more became regents. Ci Xi's dominance of the court continued, and in 1881 the death of Ci An left her in sole control.

To be fair, Ci Xi was a clever woman who was quite prepared to countenance certain reforms. The self-strengthening movement took place during her regency, and Li Hongzhang was one of her trusted advisers. Her personal position always took priority over other matters, however. Funds which should have gone towards the modernization of China's navy were diverted to the rebuilding of the Yiheyuan Summer Palace in 1886–91. She was also preparing to spend huge sums on the celebration of her sixtieth birthday in 1894, but reluctantly had to abandon her plans when defeats in the war against Japan rendered celebrations out of the question.

In 1889 the Guangxu Emperor came of age, and Ci Xi retired to the Yiheyuan. The emperor had recently married a niece of the dowager, whom Ci Xi no doubt expected to help her to control the young man. Certainly she still managed to exert considerable influence. During the reform movement of 1898 the conservatives at court managed to win her support against the emperor, in part resorting to subterfuge to persuade her to their cause. She was retailed a fabricated story that the emperor was attempting to gain support from the foreign legations in eliminating her. She therefore plotted to stage a coup. The emperor was warned, however, and tried to take precautions. A young officer in the imperial army, Yuan Shikai, who was training an army of 7,000 men near Tianjin and was thought to be sympathetic to the reformers, was approached to assist. But Yuan betrayed the emperor's trust, and shortly afterwards the Guangxu Emperor was placed under detention at Ci Xi's command, it being officially announced that he was incapacitated by illness. Only intimations from the foreign legations that it would be taken amiss if he were deposed saved him from a worse fate. Many of the leading reformists were executed, Kang Youwei only surviving by fleeing the country (with British assistance). The 'hundred days of reform' were over. The poor emperor spent the remainder of his life more or less under house arrest in the palace, and in 1908 died, according to official announcement, one day before Ci Xi. There is a strong suspicion that his was not a natural death.

ANTI-FOREIGN FEELINGS

After the failure of the reform movement, conservative Manchus dominated the court. A major reason for antagonism to reform was, as one reactionary Grand Secretary said, that it benefited the Chinese but hurt the Manchus. After 1898 hopes of reforming the Manchu government and modernizing China began to fade. Even loyal Chinese officials became unwilling to obey all the edicts passed down to them from above. Provincial administrations increasingly began to follow their own independent policies, as events were very shortly to make clear.

The intervention of the foreigners to save the emperor from being deposed (and probably murdered), and their aid to the reformers like Kang Youwei, who fled the country, caused great irritation to the Empress Dowager. Strong anti-foreign feelings permeated the court, with a great desire for revenge. Anti-foreign feeling was also becoming widespread among the people of China, especially after the war with Japan and the scramble for concessions which had followed. The activities of Christian missionaries, who had moved into China in large numbers after the treaties of 1860, also often caused resentment. They erected churches which broke all the Chinese rules of *fengshui* (geomancy), thus, in Chinese eyes, impairing the flow of beneficial influences through the earth. They preached against long-established customs, and condemned the worship of 'idols' and sacrifices to ancestors. Some of them used their status as foreigners to bully local Chinese officials in law cases involving Chinese converts. The Roman Catholics were particularly obnoxious in this respect, and even went so far as to obtain official sanction from the Qing government for their claim to status. In March 1899 Catholic missionaries in China were allowed official ranks corresponding to those of the Chinese bureaucracy. A bishop, for example, was accorded a grade equivalent to that of a provincial governor. The Chinese gentry, who regarded Confucianism as the very foundation of society, commonly resented missionary activity. Rumours were spread that children taken in to missionary orphanages were murdered, their hearts and eyes being extracted for use in foreign witchcraft. The high mortality rate among the diseased and starving infants whom the missionaries tried to assist did not help to disprove such stories. In 1870 there was a dreadful incident in Tianjin, sparked off by the stupid behaviour of the French consul, as a result of which he and his assistant were murdered by a mob which went on to burn down a French-run mission church and orphanage. In all, about a score of foreign priests, nuns and others were killed. Foreign demands for reparation were of course immediate and insistent.

The Boxer Uprising

During the 1890s a more serious and co-ordinated anti-foreign movement appeared. This had its origins among the secret societies, but was greatly strengthened by a certain amount of encouragement from government officials. The exact history of the early stages of the movement are obscure, but its activities during 1898–1900 are very well known for they then surfaced in the form of a terrible outbreak of violence against foreigners and Chinese Christian converts, known as the Boxer uprising.

The Boxers were so called because they practised a form of Chinese martial art. The Chinese name of their organisation was *Yihe quan*, or 'Righteous and Harmonious Pugilists'. A society with this name had existed at least as early as the beginning of the nineteenth century, when it was fundamentally anti-Manchu. The connection with the later society of the same name is uncertain, but it seems that at least some groups of Boxers retained the anti-Manchu stance. Most, however, used the slogan 'Support the Qing and exterminate the foreigners'. From 1897 they were particularly active in Shandong province, where they received official support from reactionary governors. Feelings were especially acute there because of the German seizure of Qingdao. The province had also been severely affected by droughts and floods ever since the change of course of the Yellow River in 1855, so that many of its people were driven to desperation by poverty. Soon attacks on missionaries and their converts became common and many churches were destroyed. In 1899 the provincial governor Yuxian reported to the court that the Christians were arrogant and had 'bullied the good people. There is absolutely no such thing', he continued, 'as maltreatment of the Christians.' This interpretation found favour at court, where Ci Xi was impressed with the Boxer claims that their charms and magical practices made them invulnerable to foreign weapons. It was decided not to take action to suppress the movement.

Foreign pressure, however, resulted in the removal of Yuxian from Shandong in December 1899. Yuan Shikai was appointed governor in his place and proceeded to put down the Boxer rising with considerable energy. Soon Shandong had been pacified, but many of the Boxers crossed into neighbouring Zhili (now Hebei) province and continued their activities there. The governor-general of Zhili, the metropolitan province, dared not act against the wishes of the court, so that the Boxers were allowed freedom of action within the area under his jurisdiction. They began to destroy railways and telegraph lines as symbols of foreign encroachment. Meanwhile Yuxian, having praised the Boxers to the court in Beijing, was appointed to the governorship of Shanxi, where attacks on missionaries soon became frequent. On 9 July 1900 he personally supervised the execution of 46 missionaries (including 20 women and 11 children) in the provincial capital, Taiyuan.

Potentially even more serious was the situation in Beijing. The foreign legations there had become increasingly alarmed as the ravages of the Boxers came closer to the capital, and had brought up guards from Tianjin towards the end of May 1900. From early in June Boxer adherents were seen in Beijing in increasing numbers. The court not only refused to suppress them but also brought in troops from outlying provinces to support them, principally an army of Muslims from Gansu, who hated Christians. On 11 June these Muslim soldiers murdered the Japanese legation chancellor; on 20 June a similar fate befell the German minister, Baron von Ketteler. A few hours later the legation quarter in Beijing was attacked by Boxers and imperial troops, and the next day war was offically declared by the Chinese court on all the foreign powers. The Boxers were placed under the command of princes and other high-ranking members of the Qing court.

The foreign response had already been put in hand. An attempt to send further reinforcements to the aid of the legations in mid-June had failed because the Beijing–Tianjin railway had been cut. Heavy fighting broke out in Tianjin by 14 June, and to prevent the situation of the foreigners there and in Beijing becoming virtually hopeless, the Dagu forts were seized by forces from foreign ships offshore on 17 June. Reinforcements were brought up during the course of the next few weeks, and on 4 August a multi-national force of about 18,000 men left Tianjin to march to the relief of the Beijing legations (without waiting for the German contingent, which arrived too late to take part in the main action). Despite much confusion, as no overall joint command of the whole mixed force could be agreed, the foreign troops arrived outside the walls of Beijing by 12 August. On the evening of the next day assaults were made on several of the city gates. On 14 August the siege of the legations was ended. Beijing was again occupied by foreign troops, and the court fled into Shanxi and eventually to Xi'an.

It is certain that the attacks on the legation quarter were not pursued with the fullest possible ferocity. There were still those in authority in Beijing who realized the stupidity of the court's decision to support the Boxers and attempt to wipe out the foreigners. Though they could not openly oppose the decisions of government they undoubtedly did their best to frustrate their implementation. In the south, the governors and governors-general formulated their own policies entirely, suppressing all Boxer violence and refusing to comply with imperial decrees. After the occupation of Beijing, they strongly advised the court to make a settlement as soon as possible. This was not easily arranged, however, as the foreigners had difficulties agreeing among themselves what the terms should be. Eventually their demands were formulated and put to the Qing court, which reluctantly accepted them. A large number of officials who had supported the anti-foreign movement were punished – several, including Yuxian, being executed; a large indemnity was to be paid. Missions of apology were sent to Japan and Germany, the Dagu forts were destroyed and foreign troops were stationed at key points between Tianjin and Beijing. In addition, the official examinations were suspended for five years in areas where the Boxers had been active. Following the signing of the agreement, the foreign troops withdrew from Beijing in September 1901, though the court did not return until the following January.

THE QING GOVERNMENT

The weakness of the Manchu administration in the face both of the foreigners and of its own Chinese subjects had been amply demonstrated by the events of 1900–1. It became increasingly clear that there was little hope of the Qing government ever putting its house in order. After 1900, even the respectable Chinese gentry became convinced of the need for a radical change, and movements to overthrow the Manchus won wider sympathy and support. If the lot of the Chinese people were ever to be improved, then they were going to have to seize control of their own destiny.

The Qing government was not yet a totally spent force, however. Ci Xi was as determined as ever to maintain her own personal position, and after 1901 spent considerable effort in reconciling the foreigners, even going so far as to entertain the wives of Western diplomats personally in the Imperial Palace. Seeing the inevitability of making changes, she initiated a number of reforms, generally along the lines of those which had been attempted during the ill-fated movement of 1898. Many of these were, however, cunningly contrived so as to concentrate power in Manchu hands, and there is little doubt that Ci Xi's real intentions were not those openly professed.

The Chinese people remained dissatisfied. After the Russo-Japanese war of 1904–5 (largely fought on Chinese soil in Manchuria), there was a growing popular demand for constitutional monarchy along Japanese lines. The victory of the Japanese over the Russians impressed the Chinese greatly. A small, newly-modernized East Asian power had inflicted humiliation on the vast Eurasian Russian empire. The victory of Japan was seen very much to be a result of its political reforms – a constitutional monarchy had defeated an autocracy. Surely China could follow Japanese example, and being a much larger state could become even more powerful?

Ci Xi could not contemplate genuine constitutionalism, but in face of growing pressure from many quarters resorted to delaying tactics. Commissions were appointed to investigate constitutional monarchy and make recommendations, a time-consuming process. Eventually it was decided that constitutional monarchy would be introduced gradually over a period of nine years from 1908. Ci Xi apparently felt herself strong enough to go on for several more years at least, but she was already seventy-three. Towards the end of the year she fell ill, and died on 15 November. The poor emperor, who had shown signs of anticipating the liberation her death would bring him, died just one day before her, possibly poisoned at the vengeful dowager's command. Her two-year-old grand-nephew Puyi (1906–67) succeeded to the throne as the Xuantong Emperor, his father acting as regent. The death of Ci Xi did not result in a liberalization of attitudes at court, however.

Though provincial assemblies were at last inaugurated in 1909, their demands for the convocation of a national parliament were dismissed out of hand. With attempts at constitutional reform thus continuously blocked, the only way forward for China was revolution.

The Republican Movement

Anti-Manchu sentiment had never entirely died out in China. Though the Manchus had to a great degree become sinicized, absorbing Chinese culture and ideas and often even forgetting their own language, they remained distinct in a number of ways. Manchu women, for example, did not keep their feet small by binding them like Chinese women. Intermarriage between Chinese and Manchus was forbidden until 1902. Manchus were given precedence in official appointments. All revolts from the beginning of the dynasty until late in the nineteenth century aimed to throw off the Manchu yoke; the Boxer movement was exceptional, the secret societies generally remaining anti-Manchu. But this underlying current of nationalistic protest had no further aim than the restoration of Chinese rule over the Chinese people; many secret societies continued to use slogans supporting a restoration of the Ming dynasty. But the impact of foreign ideas soon began to have an effect; even as early as the 1850s the Taiping rebels had been influenced by Western thinking. As more and more Chinese came into contact with the West, either through foreign penetration of China or through themselves travelling abroad, Western political philosophy became increasingly widely understood in China. Nationalism, it was realized, was not enough. If China were to revive its fortunes fully, political reform was also necessary.

SUN YAT-SEN

Republican organizations began to appear in China in the 1890s. One of the first was the 'Revive China Society' organized in 1894 by Sun Yat-sen (Sun Zhongshan, 1866–1925). In 1895 it took advantage of the problems caused by the war with Japan to stage an uprising in Guangzhou. This was unsuccessful but marked the beginning of serious republican agitation in China. Sun Yat-sen survived and fled abroad, first to Japan and then to Europe. The Qing authorities were anxious to arrest and execute him, however, and in London he was kidnapped and held at the Chinese legation. Fortunately he was able to get a message to a British doctor who had been his teacher in Hong Kong. The Foreign Office was alerted, and the Qing legation was shortly obliged to release Sun. The publicity he gained from this incident made him world-famous virtually overnight.

Remaining in Europe for two years, Sun studied Western political and social trends and developed a complete revolutionary philosophy. The revolution would not only be nationalistic and democratic but also socialistic, with controls on the accumulation of private capital and redistribution of land. Throughout the early 1900s Sun travelled extensively, gaining support among the Chinese communities in the USA, Japan and elsewhere, and organizing further revolutionary societies. There was another attempt at revolt, which again failed. The turning point came when Sun entered into close co-operation with the secret societies and with disaffected elements within the modern units of the Qing army. More attempts at revolution occurred throughout the period from 1906–11. The winning over of more and more elements of the Qing New Army continually strengthened the revolutionary position.

THE REPUBLIC OF CHINA

In 1911 disorder broke out in Sichuan as a result of controversy over the construction and financing of a new railway. The Sichuan Provincial Assembly found itself at loggerheads with the central government. The situation became so serious that government troops moved to quell disorder, provoking a violent reaction. Qing army units from neighbouring Hubei were ordered into Sichuan, and in their absence an uprising occurred in Wuhan. Local units of the New Army mutinied, and the provincial assembly threw in its lot with the revolutionaries. Hubei declared itself independent of the Qing regime. Within a month and a half it had been joined by fourteen other provinces.

Sun Yat-sen was abroad at the time this successful uprising broke out, and immediately began to canvass support among foreign governments. The British and French received him favourably. Sun returned to

Shanghai and at the end of December was elected provisional president of the Republic of China. A government was organized in Nanjing. Sun's dreams had at last been partly fulfilled, but the Qing dynasty still existed and much remained to be done in reunifying the country and pushing through republican reforms.

CHAPTER NINE

Chinese Revolutions,
1911–98

The Young Republic and the Warlords

The first problem was to unify the country. The Manchu government still existed in Beijing, even if it had lost control of most of its empire. If it could rally support from the military it might yet find the strength to crush the infant republic. In this period of uncertainty the attitude of one man was crucial and that man was Yuan Shikai. In return for his support, Yuan demanded that the Qing government place him in full control of all army and navy units (with a guarantee of sufficient military funds). In late October 1911 this was agreed, and Yuan responded by sending units under his command to retake Hankou, which fell to the Qing forces early in November. At almost the same moment Yuan was appointed premier, with a promise from the court to inaugurate constitutional monarchy within a year. Yuan had become the most powerful man in China. It was now a question of either civil war between the republican revolutionaries and the Qing court dominated by Yuan, or negotiation for an accommodation.

Complicated negotiations began. It was proposed that, if Yuan would support the republican cause and force the abdication of the emperor, he would be made president of the Republic of China. This was so attractive to Yuan that when Sun Yat-sen was elected provisional president at the end of December 1911, he broke off negotiations. Eventually Yuan was won over, however, and on 12 February 1912 he published the imperial announcement of abdication. Sun resigned in his favour, and a new republican government was inaugurated in Beijing with Yuan Shikai as president.

Unfortunately many compromises had been made to assure the success of the revolution. Many of the supporters of the republican cause were interested only in removing the Manchus from power and re-establishing a Chinese government. Sun Yat-sen's democratic and socialist ideals meant little or nothing to them. The readiness to compromise evidenced by the speedy accommodation with Yuan boded ill for the future. It was indeed only a matter of months before Yuan, in his new capacity as president, set about consolidating his personal power. It was evident that he intended to make himself a virtual dictator. When the newly-organized Nationalist Party (Guomindang) won a landslide victory in parliamentary elections at the end of 1912, Yuan resorted to bribery and assassination to ensure personal support in the parliament. A rift developed between Yuan and the revolutionaries, and in the summer of 1913 seven southern provinces declared independence. Yuan's armies had little trouble in crushing this 'Second Revolution', however. Sun Yat-sen fled to Japan.

Yuan's ambitions were such that, having achieved virtual dictatorship over China, he began to consider taking the final step of elevating himself to imperial status. In this he was, indeed, following the normal practice of Chinese militarists who were able to achieve supreme power after the downfall of a dynasty. But there had been changes in the Chinese outlook as a result of contacts with the West, and monarchism was no longer acceptable to many influential Chinese. Moreover, Yuan himself was not very popular. His acceptance of the humiliating 'Twenty-one Demands' made of China by Japan in 1915, which greatly extended Japanese power and influence in China, caused a nationwide outcry. Chinese students in Japan returned home in protest, and a boycott of Japanese goods was organized. But Yuan pressed ahead with his plans, announcing that he would begin his reign as emperor at the beginning of 1916. Yunnan thereupon declared its independence, and was followed by several other southern provinces. Yuan tried to backtrack, postponing his enthronement, but more and more provinces deserted him. In the midst of these troubles, in June 1916, he suddenly died.

Lacking a strong and powerful leader, China fell apart. In July 1917 there was a short-lived attempt by some of the northern military leaders to restore the Manchu dynasty. Once again the young Puyi, the last emperor, sat upon the throne, but within a few days the restoration was ended by other northern forces. Civil war between the various warlords and the republican government, which Sun Yat-sen was able to re-establish in Guangzhou in 1917, continued sporadically for the next decade. Throughout this period a warlord government in Beijing existed simultaneously with the Nationalist government in Guangzhou, with many provinces under the control of more or less independent warlords. Sun Yat-sen died in 1925, a disappointed man. His will urged his comrades to carry on the unfinished struggle to establish a progressive republican government over all China.

CHIANG KAI-SHEK

Sun was succeeded as leader of the Nationalists by the young general Chiang Kai-shek (Jiang Jieshi, 1887–1975). The republic had been gaining in strength, and between 1926 and 1928 the Nationalist armies were able to regain control over a large part of China. A new government was established at Nanjing (Beijing, meaning 'northern capital', being renamed Beiping, 'northern peace'). Sun Yat-sen's remains were placed in a splendid mausoleum in the hills outside the new capital city. It seemed that most of the problems which had beset China ever since the downfall of the Manchus had been resolved. Unfortunately, not all had disappeared, and new ones had arisen.

Japanese Encroachment and the Rise of the Chinese Communist Party

The Japanese had become a power to be reckoned with in the Far East during the last couple of decades of the nineteenth century. Their successful wars against China in 1894–5 and Russia in 1904–5 had clearly demonstrated their capabilities. At a time when the European powers were beginning to turn away from the aggressive empire-building which had characterized their foreign policies during the nineteenth century, and were in any case becoming preoccupied with problems closer to home, Japan was strengthening herself in readiness to acquire an empire of her own. First the Ryukyu Islands, then Korea and Taiwan, had fallen under her sway. The defeat of Russia had allowed Japan to replace her in Manchuria, taking over the concession ports of the Liaodong peninsula and some of the railway interests. Then with the outbreak of the First World War in 1914, Japan threw in her lot with Britain and France and quickly seized the German concession of Qingdao in Shandong. Yuan Shikai's acceptance of most of the Twenty-one Demands allowed Japan to take over all the German rights in that province and greatly to extend her influence within China. China's belated entry into the First World War in 1917 allowed her a place at the Peace Conference at Versailles, but Chinese interests were taken little account of there. Some of the Chinese delegation seem to have betrayed their own country in return for Japanese bribes.

In Beijing a great demonstration was held on 4 May 1919 outside the Gate of Heavenly Peace, demanding the return of Qingdao and other measures to restore Chinese sovereignty where foreign encroachment had eroded it. This was the beginning of a great nationalist movement, which for the first time involved large sections of the population in the attempt to push China forward along a progressive path towards modernization and reassertion of national pride. The movement was reflected by an intellectual ferment which saw the discussion of every kind of ideology, the publication of many highly popular political and literary magazines, and reforms such as the abandonment of the classical written language, which, rather like Latin in Europe, had continued to be used for centuries after it had ceased to be spoken. The use of a written language based on the vernacular completely changed the face of Chinese education and made the acquisition of literacy much more easily available to the masses.

EARLY CHINESE COMMUNISM

While the Versailles negotiations left the Chinese disillusioned with the Western democracies, events in Russia were observed with great interest. The October Revolution seemed to offer another way forward. The renunciation by the Bolsheviks of many of the privileges extorted from China in the past by the Tsarist regime made a great impression on the Chinese, and Marxism quickly began to make progress in China. The Comintern soon offered encouragement, and in 1921 the Chinese Communist Party was able to hold its first general meeting. Labour unions were organized, and with Russian encouragement Chinese Communists joined the Guomindang in an attempt to influence its policies towards the left. Moscow saw the 1911 revolution in China as the bourgeois revolution which, according to Marxist ideas, must precede the revolution of the proletariat. The Russian Bolsheviks therefore considered that Sun Yat-sen should be encouraged, as China was not yet ready for Communism. Russian advisers gave considerable assistance to the Guomindang during the 1920s.

But the Nationalist party contained many shades of opinion. While Sun Yat-sen represented the left wing of the party, and was prepared to co-operate with the Chinese Communists, there were many Nationalists further to the right who were not. After Sun's death there was a split within the Guomindang between the right wing of the party and the left with its Communist allies. Chiang Kai-shek led the right, and in 1927 struck a severe blow at the Communists, many of whom were rounded up and shot. The left-wingers at first opposed Chiang, but soon became frightened by suspicions of Russian motives into rallying to his leadership. All Communists were expelled from the Guomindang. Pushed out of the mainstream of political action, they turned to underground activities, and soon also began to establish bases in remote and mountainous areas in the south.

The years immediately following 1928 saw no reduction in the confused political situation in China. Though the warlord government in Beijing had been defeated, this had been achieved only with considerable assistance from other warlords who had been attracted to the Nationalist cause. Their loyalty was largely a matter of expediency and could not be relied upon. Many provinces of China remained only tenuously under the control of the Nanjing government; some were completely independent. Tibet and Outer Mongolia had taken advantage of the confusion in China after 1911 to declare their independence, Xinjiang was left very largely to its own devices, and Manchuria and Inner Mongolia were strongly influenced by the Japanese. Only the lower Yangtze valley was directly under the sway of Nanjing; beyond that it was up to the local warlords whether its sway was acknowledged or not.

THE 'LONG MARCH'

Under such circumstances Chiang Kai-shek was unable to mobilize his forces against the Communists until 1930. Assistance was sought from Germany, which sent military advisers who helped Chiang increase the effectiveness of his armies. The largest Communist bases were on the borders of Jiangxi province, established by Mao Zedong (1893–1976) with the assistance of Zhu De (1886–1976), the founder of the Chinese Red Army. These two leaders demonstrated their abilities by defeating not only Chiang's first 'encirclement campaign', but also three more between 1931 and early 1933. Not until the summer of 1934 were the Communists forced to abandon their southern bases, breaking through the Nationalist lines to begin the famous 'Long March', which ended late in 1935 when a remnant of some 30,000 of an original 100,000 troops marched into Yan'an in northern Shaanxi, where a northern base had been established some time before.

JAPANESE AGGRESSION

Chiang Kai-shek was eager to pursue the war against the Communists but other affairs demanded attention. First and foremost was the aggressive behaviour of Japan, which in September 1931 had seized the major cities of southern Manchuria. By early 1932 most of the rest of Manchuria had fallen, and once again the last emperor, Puyi, was brought into the political limelight. At first he was no more than Chief Executive of the puppet republic set up by the Japanese in Manchuria, but in 1934 it became an empire with Puyi an emperor once again. In 1933 Japanese troops seized the area around Chengde and attacked the passes on the Great Wall north of Beijing. Not content with this aggressive activity in the north, Japanese troops also became embroiled in fighting against the Chinese in Shanghai in 1932, though this incident had less far-reaching consequences. Japan's behaviour was (eventually) condemned by the League of Nations, prompting Japan to walk out of the League in March 1933.

The United Front and the Second World War

Chiang Kai-shek continued to insist that the Communists must be defeated first and the Japanese dealt with later. But many of his subordinates had different ideas. The troops that had been forced out of Manchuria by the Japanese were particularly keen to get to grips with their old enemy again, and had deliberately been transferred away from the north-east to reduce the chances of their provoking incidents. But in their new base of Xi'an they were in the front line against the Communists at Yan'an, and it soon became clear that they were disinclined to fight their fellow-countrymen. Late in 1936 Chiang went to Xi'an to urge greater efforts to subdue the Communists, but the troops mutinied and Chiang was placed under arrest.

This 'Xi'an incident' was a turning-point in Communist fortunes. It was at first assumed that Chiang would probably be put to death but the Communists rapidly interceded. Zhou Enlai (1898–1976) hurried to Xi'an to negotiate. Chiang's life was spared, but in return he had to agree to form a United Front with the Communists against the Japanese. He was released amidst great popular enthusiasm at Christmas 1936, and it seemed that a united China would be able to prepare herself for what was becoming the increasingly inevitable conflict with Japan. But there was not enough time; on 7 July 1937 the first shots of the Second World War were fired at the Marco Polo Bridge (Lugou Qiao) a short distance outside Beijing.

SINO-JAPANESE WAR

Neither the Chinese Communists nor the Nationalists had the military forces necessary to repel the Japanese invasion, and large parts of eastern China rapidly fell into Japanese hands. But the Chinese did have occasional successes, and the small Japanese nation simply did not have the manpower to place effective garrisons in all the regions it conquered. The Nationalist government moved inland to Chongqing in Sichuan, a province surrounded by mountains and easily defended, where it remained out of reach of the Japanese (except for bombing by their air force) for the rest of the war. The Communists maintained their major base at Yan'an, and organized guerrilla warfare behind the Japanese lines.

In many areas the Japanese could only control the major population centres and lines of communication, leaving vast areas of countryside where few or no Japanese were ever seen. Both Communist and Nationalist units were able to take advantage of this situation to harass the invader from bases within the regions under Japanese occupation.

After 1938 the Japanese made little further military progress in China. They were preparing for further offensives elsewhere, and hoped to achieve the remainder of their aims in China by political means. Chiang Kai-shek adamantly refused to negotiate with them, but another leading member of the Guomindang was more amenable to Japanese approaches. Chiang had pushed the left wing of the Nationalist Party out of the main circle of political power, and one of its foremost members, Wang Jingwei (1883–1944), decided that co-operation with the Japanese against Chiang was in the best interests of China. A puppet Nationalist regime came into being in the area under Japanese occupation, with its capital at Shanghai. Soon it was recognized by the Germans and Italians, and by regimes sympathetic to the Axis powers such as Spain.

It soon became evident, too, that the United Front was failing to live up to its name. Chiang continued to be worried by the prospect of the Communists consolidating their position through the establishment of guerrilla bases behind Japanese lines, which they organized much better than the Nationalists. Soon he was taking steps to weaken the Communists, and clashes between Nationalist and Communist forces in north China began to be reported before the end of 1939. The Nationalists refused to allow military supplies to be sent to the Communists, and in January 1941 a Communist army in southern Anhui was attacked and scattered by a Nationalist general. Communist–Nationalist co-operation ceased.

Chiang Kai-shek felt justified in temporizing in face of the Japanese because of his conviction that sooner or later the USA would enter the war and that American might would destroy the Japanese. China had much sympathy in the United States at this time, and the Americans did what they could to support Chiang's forces. In the summer of 1941 volunteer airmen arrived from the USA to form the famous 'Flying Tigers' air force at Kunming. It was clear which way the wind was blowing, and the Japanese attack on Pearl Harbor in December forced the issue. China found herself an ally of the USA and Great Britain in their struggle against the Axis powers. The result was as Chiang had foreseen, though the final outcome perhaps took longer to achieve than he had expected. Japan could not hold out against the massive military resources which the USA was able to muster against her, and China found herself on the winning side.

The Civil War and Communist Triumph

The end of the war with Japan left internal Chinese political issues unresolved, however. The situation on the ground was very complicated. Something of the order of two-thirds of the territory nominally under Japanese occupation had, by the end of the war, become

'The People's Apple', a propaganda poster of the 1940s, shows a child in its mother's arms offering an apple to a soldier of the People's Liberation Army

'Liberated Areas' under Communist control. The Red Armies, though often poorly equipped, were huge in numeric terms. Chiang Kai-shek had not expected the sudden end of the war brought about by the use of the atom bomb, and was not in a position to extend his control over the Japanese-occupied areas immediately. Moreover, after the defeat of the Germans in Europe the USSR had declared war on Japan. While occupied with fighting on other fronts, both the Russians and the Japanese had found it expedient not to open hostilities with each other; with Japan on the point of collapse, the Russians easily overran Manchuria. Naturally the Russians were more inclined to favour the Communist against the Nationalist Chinese, and Manchuria quickly became a Chinese Communist stronghold. In most of China, however, the Nationalists, with US backing, insisted that the Japanese should surrender only to their forces. The USA provided transport to make this possible. Nevertheless efforts continued to try to arrange a peaceful settlement of the situation, but by the middle of 1946 all negotiations had broken down. Civil war followed.

At first Chiang Kai-shek's armies made spectacular progress, over-running most of the 'Liberated Areas' of north China. But the Nationalist regime had become corrupt and unpopular, and it was easy for the Communists to foment trouble within the Nationalist-held areas. Chiang could only respond by increasing repression. Public executions on street corners became commonplace. Even Chiang's American allies found his activities distasteful and reduced their support. The Nationalist armies overstretched their lines of communication in Manchuria and suffered a severe defeat there late in 1948. Beijing and Tianjin fell in January 1949, and within a matter of weeks the Communist armies had reached the north bank of the Yangtze. In April they crossed the river, and the Nationalist remnants soon found themselves forced out of the mainland to the island of Taiwan, where they remain to this day.

The People's Republic

The People's Republic of China was formally established on 1 October 1949, Mao Zedong declaring its foundation from the Gate of Heavenly Peace (Tianan Men) in Beijing. Once again Beijing became the capital of China. Within the next two years the Communist armies regained almost all the territories ruled by the Qing. Outer Mongolia, with Russian protection, remained independent as the People's Republic of Mongolia, but Tibet was reoccupied by the Chinese in 1951.

The 'Liberation' of 1949 was welcomed by the great majority of the Chinese people, not because they were Communists (or, indeed, understood what Communism meant), but because for the first time in decades China was ruled by a strong *Chinese* authority, which reunited the country, settled internal dissensions and promised land reform. This latter point was always a major issue during uprisings in China, where the vast majority of the population worked on the land. Policies in 1949 were at first moderate, the Chinese Communist Party trying to win the confidence of as many of the people as possible. Land and possessions were confiscated only from the richest sections of the population, with comparatively little persecution of the landlord class and former officials of the Guomindang. The promulgation of the Agrarian Law of 1950, however, led to more severe action. Landlords were held up for public abuse and humiliation, many being either executed or lynched by peasant mobs. Estimates of the total number killed vary widely, but it was certainly not less than a million and very possibly about two million. In a land with a population which already exceeded 500 million this was perhaps not a high figure. The Taiping rebellion had caused much greater loss of life. Importantly, however, the confiscation of land and persecution of former landlords destroyed the gentry, the class which for centuries had dominated the Chinese system of government. Henceforward, it was the Chinese Communist Party which was to hold the monopoly of power.

The redistribution of land did not take it out of private hands but merely spread ownership more evenly. The next step was to encourage the peasants to form themselves into 'mutual aid' associations, to work their land collectively. In some areas this was not a great departure from traditional practices, which had involved sharing work at busy seasons. By about 1957 this process had been taken a step further, to the organization of formal peasant co-operatives in which land and equipment were pooled and produce divided according to input. Finally, in 1958, people's communes were set up throughout the country. These were quite large economic and administrative units, under which were several 'production brigades' further divided into 'production teams'. In the early days, communes tried to collectivize virtually all aspects of the life of their members, with large communal eating halls and dormitories. This policy was quickly relaxed in the face of peasant opposition, and in any case not all of the leadership of the Communist Party was committed to such rapid collectivization.

FOREIGN POLICY

In foreign policy, the 1950s were dominated by relations with the USSR and USA. The Russians seemed to be the natural allies of the new Communist regime, and considerable quantities of aid came from the USSR, together with large numbers of advisers. Mao Zedong made a personal visit to Moscow in December 1949, his first trip to a foreign country, and a Treaty of Friendship, Alliance and Mutual Assistance was signed. Nevertheless the Russians were slow to withdraw all their forces from Manchuria and held Port Arthur (Lüshun) until 1954. After the death of Stalin old Sino-Russian hostilities began to re-emerge: the fundamental problem was that China was not prepared to accept the dominance which the Soviet Union wished to assert over the Communist bloc. China had not finally stood up against foreign imperialism only to submit to Soviet dominance; she intended to go her own way. In 1960 the differences reached a peak, all Soviet advisers being withdrawn. This rift has only recently been healed.

THE KOREAN WAR

During the period of close ties with Russia, the USA was perceived as China's main external enemy. The Americans had after all aided Chiang Kai-shek, even if most such assistance had been withdrawn, and of course 'US imperialism' was the standard Communist target of the time. This hostility came to a head during the Korean War. Korea, as part of the Japanese empire since 1910, had been under Allied occupation after the surrender of Japan in 1945; the Russians had occupied the northern part of the peninsula, the Americans the south. Each had established a regime acceptable to their own ideologies, though the leader in the south, Syngman Rhee, had quickly proved himself so corrupt and unenlightened that his American support wavered. It was hinted that the USA would not assist South Korea in the event of war with the North. It seems that the North Koreans and their Russian backers took this seriously, and in June 1950 South Korea was invaded.

The US response was immediate and American troops soon poured into Korea. United Nations support was obtained in the absence of the USSR, which was at the time boycotting UN meetings. Landings on the Korean coast north of the North Korean lines caused a collapse of their forces, and soon they had been pushed back across the North–South demarcation line. The UN forces pushed on northwards, and faced with the prospect of an American-backed regime controlling the whole of Korea, with its long border with China, the Chinese decided to send in troops. Thus US and Chinese Communist forces clashed in a major conflict. The consequences persisted long after the Korean conflict had been inconclusively settled with an armistice in 1953. The Americans had sent a fleet to the Taiwan Straits to prevent any Communist invasion of the Nationalist-held island, and also instituted an economic embargo against China. Chinese isolation from the non-Communist world was thus greatly reinforced. China did, however, benefit from a great increase in prestige, particularly in the Third World. This was reinforced by the activities of premier Zhou Enlai at the Geneva Conference in 1954, where the partition of Vietnam was settled, and at the conference of Afro-Asian states at Bandung in 1955. The successful testing of the first Chinese atom bomb in 1964 brought China the status of a great power.

The Anti-Rightist Movement

At home there were problems, however. In 1957 Chairman Mao sanctioned the 'Hundred Flowers' campaign, when criticism of government policies was actually encouraged. 'Let a hundred flowers bloom, let a hundred schools of thought contend,' said Mao. Whether there was ever any genuine intention to allow an open airing of differing views is doubtful: certainly many Chinese now believe that this was a deliberate trap. At the time many intellectuals took Mao literally, however, and there was a great outpouring of criticism of the Chinese

Communist Party and its policies. Repression quickly followed. Critics from both inside and outside the Party were arrested and sent to labour camps, where they were expected to reform their 'rightist' attitudes. Many of the victims of this 'anti-rightist' movement remained in the camps for more than twenty years. Some died there.

Most of the victims were from the intellectual class. Mao Zedong had disliked intellectuals since his youth. Some say this was born of resentment of the disdainful way in which scholars had treated him when he worked in the library of Beijing University in 1918–19. Probably more significantly, the early leaders of the Chinese Communist Party had mainly been intellectuals and Mao had opposed their policies almost from the day the Party was founded in 1921. While he had organized peasant revolts in the countryside, the leadership (and the advisers sent from Russia to assist them) had stressed orthodox Marxist reliance on the urban proletariat as the main force in Communist revolution. During the 1920s, urban uprisings organised by the Party leadership failed again and again, while Mao and his allies successfully established Communist-controlled areas in country regions. A power struggle developed in the early 1930s which Mao at first lost. His strategy of using guerrilla warfare against the Nationalist armies sent to attack Communist bases was replaced by a strategy of positional warfare. This was a disaster, resulting in defeat and the 'Long March'. During the march, in early 1935, Mao was finally able to take control of the Party at a conference at Zunyi in northern Guizhou province. After this triumph, he was determined to ensure that intellectuals were never able to threaten his leadership again.

THE 'GREAT LEAP FORWARD'

Mao was determined to advance the tide of Communism in China as rapidly as possible. With the establishment of communes in 1958 came also the call for a dramatic increase in industrial production. This 'Great Leap Forward' was intended to take place over three years and to see increases in production of steel, electricity and coal of as much as a third each year (targets were continuously revised upwards). All over China, people with no previous experience of steel production began building blast furnaces in their back yards. Often they had no supplies of iron, but if nothing else could be found, household objects (including kitchen pots and pans) were collected and melted down. The results were disastrous: many furnaces never produced anything at all, those that did often produced steel of such low quality that it was unusable. Though there were real achievements in some areas, the 'Great Leap' failed to produce the results that had confidently been called for.

This failure and problems resulting from the over-hasty establishment of the communes produced serious strains between the Maoists and the more pragmatic Chinese Communists. There began to be serious criticism of Mao within the Party leadership. In 1959 he was replaced as head of state by Liu Shaoqi (1900–69), who was prepared to be much less dogmatic and take more account of practicalities. He had considerable support, particularly from the Party secretary-general, Deng Xiaoping (1904–97). Deng's attitude was that 'it doesn't matter whether it's a black cat or a white cat, if it catches mice it's a good cat', which contrasted strongly with Mao's insistence that being 'red' mattered more than being expert.

THE SINO-SOVIET SPLIT

The fundamental problem was that Mao Zedong was not prepared to tolerate criticism. He saw himself as China's great leader and, indeed, as leader of world Communism. The low opinion of Russian Communism which he had held since the 1920s was reinforced after the death of Stalin when Khrushchev came to power. Mao considered Khrushchev a 'revisionist' and tensions between the two led to the Sino-Soviet split in 1960. All Russian advisers were withdrawn from China and Russian and Chinese leaders traded insults in official speeches. The sudden withdrawal of Russian economic assistance added to the problems of developing China's industrial base. It did not, however, prevent the Chinese from successfully building their own atomic bomb in 1964.

In August 1959 the problems facing Mao's critics were clearly demonstrated by the outcome of the Lushan Conference of the Party Central Committee. The Defence Minister, Peng Dehuai (1898–1974), who had recently returned from a visit to the Soviet Union, strongly criticised the policies of the previous few years. He referred to 'blunder after blunder' in economic management and attacked Party control of the army. Mao's response was to have him dismissed and replaced with Lin Biao (1908–71), whom he saw as his successor.

The Cultural Revolution

During the next few years the tensions within the Party gradually came to a head. Finally, in March 1966, while Liu Shaoqi was on a state visit to Pakistan and Afghanistan, Mao launched an all-out attack on his opponents. With the support of Lin Biao and the army he felt confident of being able to overthrow his critics in the Party. As Liu, Deng and their supporters were in control of the established Party structure, Mao created new organizations to further his aims. In August the Red Guards were formed to carry Mao's revolutionary line all over the country and in November a Central Cultural Revolutionary Committee was set up, composed of Mao's closest allies, including his wife, Jiang Qing (1913–91). The intention to remove power from the old Party administration was made quite explicit in Mao's call in August to 'Bombard the Headquarters'. Soon Liu Shaoqi and Deng Xiaoping (though the latter was never referred to by name) were being identified as 'capitalist roaders' and persecuted by the Red Guards. Quite unconstitutionally, Liu was forced out of office in 1968. The next year, his health broken and denied medical attention, he died.

The events of the Cultural Revolution were extremely complicated, with frequent shifts in the balance of power between factions and considerable confusion. Contradictory directives were issued by various different groups within the Party leadership: often it was hard for those at lower levels to decide which of these they ought to follow. In many areas the Red Guards split into factions which fought each other. In places there were outbreaks of what amounted to civil war, with weapons as heavy as field artillery being used. This was too much even for many of Mao's supporters: in August 1968 the Red Guards were disbanded and the army was used to restore order where necessary. During 1970 a less violent phase of the Cultural Revolution began: articles in the official press criticized those who were 'left in appearance but right in reality', implying that the Cultural Revolution had been turned in the wrong direction by some of its leaders. One of these was presumably Lin Biao, who died in mysterious circumstances in 1971. It seems that he attempted a coup and tried to flee when it failed: he is said to have died when the aircraft in which he was fleeing crashed in Mongolia. The details of this affair remain extremely hazy, however. As he was the architect of the great personality cult of Mao and the editor of the famous 'little red book' of Mao's selected thoughts, his loss was a serious blow to the Maoist faction.

ZHOU ENLAI

Throughout the Cultural Revolution one moderating figure remained untouched and apparently untouchable. Zhou Enlai (1898–1976) had studied in both Japan and Europe in his youth and had held important posts in the Chinese Communist Party since the early 1920s. He had been with Mao in the Jiangxi revolutionary base in the 1930s and was a veteran of the 'Long March'. His skills in diplomacy were considerable: he had played an important role in resolving the 'Xi'an incident' (see p. 184) and in 1945–6 was heavily involved in the attempt to negotiate a settlement with the Nationalists. After the foundation of the People's Republic in 1949 he became premier, the highest position in the government of China below head of state, and was concurrently foreign minister and held high rank in the Party hierarchy. He seems to have been a great statesman, able to steer the difficult course between opposing the Maoists outright and giving in to them altogether. He is credited with effective use of his prestige and position to moderate many of the worst excesses of the Cultural Revolution, not only in ensuring the preservation of at least some historic sites and relics from destruction by the Red Guards but in affording limited protection to some of those who came under attack. Deng Xiaoping may well owe his life to Zhou Enlai: it is unlikely to be a coincidence that after restoration to high office in 1973 he was again relieved of all posts shortly after Zhou died. Premier Zhou is remembered with affection by the Chinese people today.

It was Zhou who was the architect of the new relationship with the USA which culminated in the visits to Beijing of Dr Kissinger and President Nixon in 1971 and 1972 and the admission of the People's Republic of China to the United Nations (replacing Taiwan) in 1971.

Mao Zedong and Zhou Enlai as portrayed by a
revolutionary artist in the late 1940s

These were events of immense significance, ending China's isolation
from the international community and signalling a new era of much
more constructive foreign relations for China. Zhou wanted to see
China take her rightful place as a major state in the community of
nations. This meant that China must not only seek to strengthen
international ties, but also strive for internal development so as to stand
on an equal footing with other major states. To this end, he announced
the 'four modernizations' (of agriculture, industry, science and technology, and defence) early in 1975.

China after Mao

Zhou's death in January 1976 was a great blow to those who hoped that
the Maoist radicals would not hold power for ever. There were popular

demonstrations in Tianan Men Square when memorial meetings were held in his honour. Then in September Mao himself died and the pragmatists were able to make a comeback. In October the 'Gang of Four' (Jiang Qing, Wang Hongwen, Zhang Qunqiao and Yao Wenyuan) were arrested: their trials ended a few years later with sentences of life imprisonment or death. Mao's wife, Jiang Qing, refused to repent and confess her crimes and so received the most severe judgement. Her death sentence was later commuted to life imprisonment: she is reported to have hanged herself in May 1991, while suffering from incurable cancer.

Now the Chinese talk of the 'ten wasted years' from 1966–76 and their government has adopted very different policies from those of the first three decades of the People's Republic. Deng Xiaoping proved himself to be both a great pragmatist and a skilful politician, gradually outmanoeuvring the hardliners in the Party to push through his policies of opening China to foreign trade and investment and radically restructuring the economy. During the late 1970s and early 1980s agriculture was decollectivized, land being allocated to individual farming families to cultivate as they wished. 'Free markets' were established where produce could be sold for personal profit. Private enterprise was also permitted (within limits) in the industrial and service sectors, and a beginning was made on the restructuring of state enterprises to introduce more influence from market forces. 'Special Economic Zones' began to be established, particularly in eastern coastal areas where most import-export business is conducted. In these zones special regulations apply which allow greater freedom for what is, in effect, capitalist enterprise: there are especially favourable terms on offer to foreign companies investing there. The first of these zones was at Shenzhen, on the border with Hong Kong. When it was set up in 1981, Shenzhen was no more than a small peasant village surrounded by rice paddy. Within a few years this was replaced by skyscrapers with a new railway station and airport to link it with the rest of China and with the outside world. Many Hong Kong-based companies have established factories within this zone: the trains from Kowloon to the border now carry a daily flow of commuters from Hong Kong to Shenzhen.

The rapid development in areas like Shenzhen acted as a catalyst to the rest of China, which has experienced dramatic changes during the last two decades. The average standard of living of the Chinese people has risen to many times what it was two decades ago. In the late 1970s most Chinese could only aspire to own a radio and a bicycle: now many have colour televisions, washing machines, audio equipment (even home karaoke machines: karaoke has become extremely popular in China), refrigerators and computers. Whereas in the early 1980s most of China closed down completely by 7.00 p.m., there is now an active entertainment industry with restaurants, bars and dance halls open until late at night. People have money to spend on enjoying themselves.

But although there have been amazing changes in the economy, which have greatly affected the lives of huge numbers of Chinese, there have been very few political changes. The Communist Party holds a monopoly of power and, although its economic policies scarcely seem to be Communist any more, it does not intend to relax its political stranglehold. This does not mean that in many respects the Chinese have not begun to enjoy more freedom during the last two decades: many restrictions have been relaxed or entirely abolished. China does not enjoy democracy, however. With the example of the Soviet Union just across their borders, the Chinese leadership has considered that economic reforms must precede political reforms. The results achieved could be taken as a justification of this attitude.

Not everything has gone smoothly, however. Problems have arisen because of the inequality of development between more remote country regions and the big eastern cities. During the winter, when many peasants have little to do in the fields, huge numbers of them flood into the cities to try to find work on the many building sites. There is never enough work for them all. Together with the great increase in economic activity, there has been a rise in economic crime. From time to time there have been periods when inflation has caused problems, with wages failing to keep up with rising prices. The intellectual class has tended to become even more dissatisfied, as private enterpreneurs have begun to make fortunes while highly-qualified government employees have enjoyed only modest increases in income.

The Tianan Men Incident

In 1989 this dissatisfaction came to a head. The immediate cause was
the death in April of Hu Yaobang, former Party General Secretary who
had been dismissed in 1987. He had been among the most liberal of the
leadership and had undoubtedly stimulated opposition from hard-liners
in the Party: he may perhaps have been too liberal for Deng Xiaoping
himself. He had gained much popularity among Chinese students, who
organized mass meetings in his memory. These developed into large
demonstrations which took over Tianan Men Square for much of May.
The leadership seemed at a loss as to how to handle these demonstrations: probably there were disputes between different factions within
the highest tiers of the government and the Party. It is possible that
Deng may have been ill at this time and therefore unable to make
any final decision. The eventual outcome is well known, troops
being used to disperse the demonstrators at the beginning of June, with
considerable loss of life. It should be noted, however, that most Western
journalists' accounts of these events are highly inaccurate. It has been
difficult to obtain reliable details of exactly what happened and how

The Great Hall of the People on the western side of Tian'an Men Square in
Beijing: one of several large buildings erected for the tenth anniversary of the
founding of the People's Republic of China in 1959, this is a venue for large
political and governmental assemblies

many died, but it seems likely that troops were attacked with petrol bombs and possibly other weapons before they opened fire and that the total number of civilians killed was in the region of 400. It is certainly true that few if any died on Tianan Men Square itself: most casualties occurred on Chang'an Avenue to the west, the direction from which the troops advanced towards Tianan Men. The shooting began at road-blocks on the Avenue a mile or more from the Square. It has also emerged now that there were those among the students who deliberately intended to provoke bloodshed to further their cause. It is also quite probable that more soldiers died than civilians: the official figure of some 600 military fatalities may well be accurate.

The tragedy is that the students' demands for democracy and the yielding of power by Deng Xiaoping were not only totally unrealistic but in the long run have come to seem almost irrelevant. Though there is still an active dissident movement among Chinese intellectuals, the great mass of the population is far more interested in making the most of the new economic opportunities than in politics. At the end of October 1996 Wang Dan, one of the leaders of the democracy movement of 1989, was sentenced to eleven years' imprisonment for plotting to overthrow the government (no doubt an exaggerated charge). This provoked no significant protests within China. The general level of education in China is probably still too low for any genuinely democratic system to be successful: as many as a quarter of the population remain illiterate or semi-literate. The rapid development of the economy and rise in living-standards must necessarily lead to other changes, however, and it can be expected that in the long term political reforms will take place. Deng Xiaoping outlived the Maoist hardliners and, despite the problems currently being suffered by other Asian economies, it seems unlikely that China will now move in any direction except that of increasing economic development and liberalization.

China has, indeed, remained unusually stable throughout the period surrounding Deng Xiaoping's official retirement and death. The leadership struggle which was so widely predicted by Western journalists failed to occur. The retirement as Premier of the widely-disliked Li Peng and his replacement by the reformist Zhu Rongji early in 1998 is a clear indication that the economic reforms within China will continue: loss-making state-owned industrial concerns are being forced to reform or close down. China has struggled to repair its image abroad in the aftermath of the Tianan Men incident, but despite pressures from human rights activists and hard-line anti-Communists within the USA, President Clinton normalized trade relations with China; he received Jiang Zemin on a state visit late in 1997 and visited China himself in 1998. The handover of Hong Kong to China by Britain in the middle of 1997 went smoothly and so far there have been no very serious problems under Chinese rule in what is now the Special Administrative Region of Hong Kong. The gravest problems in the area have resulted from the economic difficulties into which South Korea, Indonesia, Malaysia and the Philippines recently plunged, with knock-on effects on Singapore and Hong Kong (as well as more widely). With the Japanese economy now also somewhat shaky, foreign investment in China and exports to nearby markets are likely to suffer, but in the medium to long term the Chinese economy is unlikely to be very severely affected, if only because it still remains less than fully integrated into the world economy. China remains on-course to become the world's largest economy very shortly and must surely play an increasingly prominent role on the world stage during the twenty-first century.

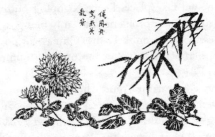

CHAPTER TEN

Life in China Today

China today is still in the process of rapid transformation, so that to some extent anything written here will be out of date even before this book has been published. Yet at the same time there is much in China that has changed very little since imperial times. It is difficult to generalize about a country so large and diverse, which in some respects has modernized rapidly during recent decades while still not altering many of its basic characteristics. It must constantly be borne in mind while reading this chapter (and, indeed, the whole of this book) that there are great differences between the various regions of China, between the urban centres and the countryside, and between the various sections of Chinese society. Foreigners in China tend to see more of the large cities and their immediate environs, and to hear the views of the Chinese of Beijing, Shanghai or other great cities, so that it becomes easy to overlook the fact that 80 per cent of the population lives in the countryside. The daily life of a resident of Beijing or Shanghai is very different from that of a peasant in, say, the Sichuan Basin or rural Shandong, and their outlooks and ideas differ correspondingly.

The great majority of Chinese have travelled little, even within their own province. The lack of contacts between regions, which was even more marked prior to the advent of modern means of communication during this century, has encouraged diversity. To take language as an example, there are commonly wide variations of dialect within very short distances. Fujian is a well-known instance, every valley having its own dialects which are usually scarcely intelligible to the inhabitants of neighbouring valleys. But even within the large area in which variants of the Mandarin group of dialects are spoken, there are often great

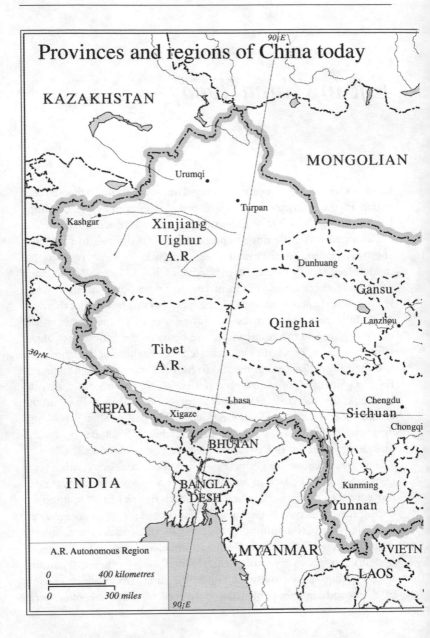

Provinces and regions of China today

differences in pronunciation over very short distances. Thus, Zou Xian in Shandong has a different dialect from Qufu, though they are only some twenty miles apart. The Chinese lose their accents only slowly. Mao Zedong, for example, used a very broad Hunan pronunciation to the end of his life. The teaching of the standard language, *putonghua*, in every Chinese school has not yet seriously eroded these differences, though perhaps the spread of radio and television, which always use the best standard pronunciation, will accelerate the decline of non-standard speech.

At the same time, China is also a thoroughly unified country. The Han Chinese all think of themselves principally as Chinese, and do not question the ideal of a united China. Though the country has often been divided into separate states, not for many centuries has there been any question of such division being acceptable in the long term. Today Taiwan is still politically divided from the People's Republic, but although there is a movement favouring independence on Taiwan now it seems that the majority of the people of the island, and certainly the majority of the people of the mainland, have no desire to see this state of affairs become permanent. This strong sense of unity coexisting with great regional diversity is only one of many paradoxes found in China, paradoxes which easily confuse observers from outside. In attempting to understand China it is essential always to keep an open mind.

Government and Society

The People's Republic of China has a system of government described by the current constitution as 'the people's democratic dictatorship led by the working class and based on the alliance of workers and peasants, which is in essence the dictatorship of the proletariat'. Theoretically this means that it is the workers and peasants who control the government system. The Communist Party is, of course, considered to be the genuine representative of the workers and peasants, and therefore in practice it is the Party which is the main controlling power. The policies of those who lead the Party become the policies to be followed throughout the country. Nevertheless, distance from the political centre in Beijing and the delicate balance of power between the top ranks and the lower echelons of government can often allow considerable latitude of action to local administrators. This is less today, however, than it was formerly, because of the great improvement in communications which has occurred in recent times.

The structure of the machinery of government in China today is fundamentally identical with what it was under the later imperial dynasties. There is no emperor at the top, but instead there is a small committee of the leading members of the Party which holds much the same position. The political centre in Beijing is indeed located in the Zhong Nan Hai section of the former imperial palaces, immediately to the west of the Forbidden City. It is almost as remote from the ordinary people as was the emperor. The Party structure is separate from the structure of government, but in effect controls the government by allowing only approved candidates to be elected to the local and national People's Congresses.

There are four major tiers of government: national, provincial, prefectural and county. At present there are twenty-three provinces (including Taiwan). Ranking at the same level are the four large municipalities at Beijing, Tianjin, Shanghai and Chongqing and the five autonomous regions of Tibet, Xinjiang, Inner Mongolia, Guangxi and Ningsia. Autonomous governments in China allow differences in administration for the non-Han ethnic groups. Below the provincial-level governments are more than 300 prefectures and municipalities and some 2,500 counties (or units of equivalent status).

This pyramidal structure of administration, with its attendant bureaucracy, is the traditional government system of China. It is, indeed, hard to imagine how China could be governed in any other way. The Chinese developed their bureaucratic system at a very early date, and it has been tried and proven as an effective means to control their large state over the course of centuries. The great problem in China is how to exercise control over the bureaucracy, which tends to develop an independent existence of its own. In the past, the bureaucracy was recruited from the Confucian scholar–official class and worked almost entirely in the interests of that class. Now there are no more Confucian scholars, but there is still a large class of officials, mostly members of the Communist Party, and there is still a strong tendency for them to arrange

Despite extremely rapid development during the last fifteen years, life for many people in China's hinterland is still very similar to what it was two or more centuries ago: transplanting rice, western Sichuan province

things to their own advantage. Corruption has not been eliminated by the revolution of 1949. Having the right connections in official circles (what is known in Chinese as *guanxi*) is still the best way to success in Communist China. Serious cases of corruption and bribery have recently hit the headlines in China. In September 2000 a vice-chairman of the Standing Committee of the National People's Congress, Cheng Kejie, was executed for taking bribes worth US$5 million. At the same time, a number of officials involved in a major corruption scandal in Xiamen were put on trial. There is still a problem in ensuring effective central control over provincial administrations. A few years ago a special commission was sent down from Beijing to investigate the administration of Guangxi, which had apparently taken its autonomous status rather too literally. During the disorder of the violent phase of the Cultural Revolution, some provinces were for a time more or less completely outside the control of the central authority in Beijing.

But such problems of control are comparatively minor when looked at in the light of China's past. The Chinese Communist Party has been remarkably successful in establishing a strong and effective administration, with a reasonable level of popular support. The real beneficiaries of the Communist revolution were the peasants, and as they form the overwhelming majority of the population it can only be considered just that their interests should be paramount. Though today many of them are still very poor in the eyes of foreigners from developed countries, they are generally incomparably better-off than they were before 1949. I remember talking to an old peasant I met walking along a country lane south of Ji'nan in Shandong in 1982, his agricultural tools carried over his shoulder. The houses in his village had floors of beaten earth, but were solid and weather-proof. Water had to be drawn from a well or, during the severe drought of the time, collected from a lorry sent by the provincial drought-relief administration. But the old man was happy: he had a roof over his head, land to till and grandchildren to delight him and look after him in old age. All this, he said, was thanks to Chairman Mao. All over China, there must be thousands and even millions of such people, who formerly eked out a precarious existence with starvation constantly at their elbows, whose lives have been immeasurably improved since 1949.

THE YOUNGER GENERATION

But for the younger generation without personal experience of the appalling conditions of the 1930s and 1940s, life in New China is often frustrating and disappointing. The post-1949 generation of Chinese, who are now easily the majority of the population, are not satisfied with such simple benefits as the old Shandong peasant. They want bicycles (or even motorbikes or cars), colour televisions, washing machines and refrigerators, and money to spare for fashionable clothes and entertainment. The old way of life in the countryside, which often involved working hard all year just to ensure that there was enough to eat, has little to recommend it to most young Chinese. Current government policies are trying to take this into account and to improve the standard of living of the whole population, but this necessarily cannot be achieved overnight. The 'responsibility system', which has in effect de-collectivized agriculture and allows the peasants (officially now to be described as 'farmers') personal responsibility for the areas of land assigned to them and lets them keep the greater part of any profits they can make, is a radical alteration to the old policies for the countryside.

It has certainly brought about a great increase in income for some of the rural population, most especially those living in fertile areas close to large cities where there are markets for their produce. Some peasant families in such locations have been able to increase their incomes by several times in the course of just a few years. Conversely, however, there have been few benefits for many people in regions distant from the major cities. There are some disadvantages too, such as the loss of use of collectively-owned machinery on large communal fields. For workers in the cities bonuses have allowed some increase in income, but there is only restricted scope for most city-dwellers to make dramatic improvements to their living standards. Indeed, the appearance of inflation in China recently, affecting particularly the price of many foodstuffs, has hit hard at the pockets of most workers. Their wages have often been allowed to rise only by less than the rate of inflation.

Despite recent relaxation of controls on economic activities, Chinese society generally remains very tightly controlled. This is not merely a result of Communism but reflects traditional Chinese practices. The old system of mutual responsibility (as, for example, under *baojia*) was a great restriction on individual freedom, and the present government has not attempted to increase individual liberty to any great extent. It is normal in any Chinese community for everyone to take a very close interest in what everyone else is doing, and there are very strong social pressures to conform. At the most basic level neighbourhood committees look after everyday affairs within their areas, taking an interest in matters which many non-Chinese would usually consider to be strictly private. It is, for example, these local committees which are in the forefront of implementing China's birth-control policies. If a young wife becomes pregnant, the street committee is sure to know almost as soon as she does, and will, if she already has the one child normally permitted, bring strong pressure to bear on her to have an abortion. When social controls are relaxed, however, the Chinese seem to be natural anarchists. Queueing, for example, is a concept totally alien to the Chinese mind, and in the absence of officials to enforce order Chinese waiting for a bus will push and struggle to be first through the doors and even climb through windows. They are also, unless traffic regulations are strictly enforced, happy to cycle on the wrong side of the road and go the wrong way round roundabouts. Recent campaigns in the major cities have dramatically improved such behaviour, and even the common traditional practice of spitting on the streets seems to have been greatly reduced, at least in some of the major cities.

Life, Death and Religion

BIRTH CONTROL

The traditional ideal in China was to have a large family, and in particular to have many sons. Family ties were very close and the family unit formed the basis of Chinese social structure. The values inculcated by Confucian morality laid particular stress on family loyalty and strong respect from younger family members for their elders. This respect continued even after death and was manifested through the making of offerings and the tending of graves. Many of these old practices and ideas have been challenged in New China, and the severe problems created by overpopulation demand drastic change.

Faced with an ever-increasing population which has already grown well beyond the thousand million mark, the government of China has taken strong measures to try at least to reduce the rate of increase. Married couples have been officially restricted to having only one child, or, in limited instances, two. This stringent policy, which has received a good deal of criticism from some quarters outside China, has become very effective in the cities but rather less so in the countryside. While it may seem very severe, it is in fact eminently sensible, for China faces disaster on a huge scale if the population continues to grow rapidly. There is very little scope for making further large improvements in agricultural production, energy resources are already scarcely adequate, and in large parts of the country there is not sufficient water even for current levels of usage. The growth in population threatens the whole of China's drive to modernize and to improve standards of living.

The policy of one child per couple is necessarily going to have a strong effect on family structure. The traditional Chinese family needs to have sons to carry on the line, for a married daughter leaves her original family to join that of her husband. This is one of the reasons for the strong desire of Chinese to have sons: not only are daughters less useful as workers in the fields, but once they marry they are more or less lost to their parents, who cannot expect support from them in old age. A son is not only a permanent asset to his family, but will also bring in a wife when he marries and provide grandchildren. In a land where old-age pensions are still enjoyed only by a minority, support by sons and grandsons is regarded as a necessity. Traditionally it was also male descendants who carried on the sacrifices to dead ancestors. The strong desire to have male heirs persists in China today, not only in rural areas, which tend to be more conservative, but even in the most modern cities. A curious example arose a decade or so ago in Shenyang, a major industrial centre in Liaoning province. A local hospital, it was reported, was determining the sex of unborn children and offering abortions if they proved to be girls. Such things undoubtedly occur more commonly in less developed parts of the country. There are still some cases of infanticide of female children, though they are not common. The policy has been relaxed slightly, couples in rural areas being allowed a second child if the first is female. This may cause problems in future, as the ratio of male to female children in China now shows about 10 per cent more males than would usually be expected.

THE POSITION OF WOMEN

One of the most remarkable changes in Chinese society since 1949 has been in the status of women. Foot-binding was already dying out, after campaigns against it throughout the Republican period, but women generally remained very much second-class citizens. Inside the family elderly matrons often exercised great power, but in their youth they frequently had to endure long years of humiliation and suffering at the hands of dominating mothers-in-law and husbands who were more or less expected to beat them occasionally. A well-known twentieth-century Chinese writer, Zhao Shuli, wrote of the 'customs. . .of seventy-five years ago' that:

> After a girl was married, she was scolded and beaten by her mother-in-law. When she grew older and became a mother-in-law herself, she scolded and

beat her daughter-in-law in turn. If she behaved in any other way, she wouldn't be considered a proper mother-in-law. The accepted attitude of a man towards his wife was summed up in the old saying: 'A wife should be treated like a horse – driven and beaten regularly.' If any husband didn't beat his wife, people thought he was afraid of her.

Among the first actions of the Communists was to set up women's associations in areas under their control. Even the idea of women meeting together to discuss serious matters was revolutionary. But soon women were discussing matters which astonished traditionalists, such as equality of the sexes and education for women. Today the position of women in China is officially the same as that of men, but inequalities remain and may actually have worsened as a result of recent policies. Women's earnings have increased more slowly than men's, leading to a growing income gap between the sexes.

HEALTH CARE

Health care is very unevenly developed in China. There is no national system. In many of the large cities there are excellent hospitals and subsidized medical care is available to the majority of the population. In rural regions, on the other hand, facilities are often inadequate and have to be paid for in full. I have had some personal experience of Chinese hospitals. In one instance I spent almost a fortnight in hospital in Kunming, provincial capital of Yunnan, with a fever (possibly typhus). Although as a student with a Chinese government scholarship (through an exchange arrangement) my medical fees were paid for by my university, I had to pay for my own food. Facilities in the hospital (the No. 1 Provincial Hospital) were reasonable, but fell a long way short of Western standards. During my twelve days in hospital, the only washing facilities available to me were a large enamel bowl and a flask of boiling water. But I was well cared for and received good treatment. Hospitals in Beijing or Shanghai are certainly of better standard. Facilities in rural areas are usually of the standard which the local administration can afford to provide. Treatment may be free or at least subsidized to local residents, but if they have a disease or injury which is too serious to be treated properly locally, they will often have to pay for treatment at a larger hospital elsewhere.

In this as in so many things in China, much depends on what kind of 'unit' you are attached to. The unit is the place of work, and normally provides many of the basics of life, such as accommodation and health-care. If the unit is rich it may be able to afford to pay all the medical expenses of all its members. If it is poor it may be able to provide only very basic medical care. Those not employed by the state may earn more money, but have to pay all their own medical fees in full. This can cause very real hardship, and occasionally people can be encountered on Chinese streets begging for money for hospital expenses. In some cases treatment may be virtually unavailable even if there is no shortage of money. Good medical facilities do not yet exist throughout the country. Nevertheless, health care in China has made great progress since 1949, when many rural regions had no medical facilities at all or relied solely on unqualified practitioners with a small knowledge of traditional Chinese medicine. Traditional Chinese medical techniques are in many respects excellent when used by well-trained personnel, however, and are still in common use in China today. There are hospitals which specialize in the use of Chinese techniques, and others where Chinese and Western methods are both practised.

FUNERAL CUSTOMS

The death of a Chinese was traditionally attended by elaborate ceremonial. It was believed that the spirits of the dead had a continuing influence on the fortunes of their living relatives, so that their burial and the regular sacrifices offered thereafter were matters of the greatest importance. Many of the beliefs and superstitions connected with death were already beginning to be questioned at the turn of last century, and since 1949 much has been done to sweep them away altogether, but among some sections of the population they remain strong. Officially cremation of the dead is strongly encouraged, and in cities it is almost impossible to avoid it. Many old graves have been levelled and the sites returned to agricultural production, but new grave mounds continue to appear in rural areas, and elaborate and expensive funerals in the old manner still occur. I have seen many freshly-raised grave mounds, often still bedecked with the circular wreaths of paper flowers commonly placed on Chinese graves, and have witnessed burials taking place.

In the past there was often a long delay between death and burial. There were many reasons for this: it was necessary to choose the right, auspicious day for the interment, and many preparations had to be made in advance; it could take some time to find the funds necessary for what was often a cripplingly expensive procedure. Sensible people ensured a proper burial for themselves by making arrangements during their own lifetimes. The large imperial tombs, for example, such as those of the Ming dynasty outside Beijing and Nanjing, were mostly prepared during the lifetime of their prospective occupants. Lesser personages would often buy their own coffins long before they were expected to be used, and would frequently also make some advance financial provision. The plot of land to be used was commonly part of a family graveyard.

Customs varied from region to region, but generally on the day of burial the coffin would be carried from the house of the departed amidst the explosion of firecrackers and the din of loud and strident music, intended to frighten away evil spirits. The coffin was slung on poles and ornamented with a light structure of bamboo and cloth which made it look like a curtained Chinese sedan chair. As the coffin was carried on its way to the burial ground, large 'coins' cut from paper were scattered along the way as offerings to the spirits. The mourners wore white, usually with white cloth wrapped around their heads also. On reaching the site of the grave, the large wooden coffin would be lowered into the pit prepared for it, and a large round or oval mound of earth raised above it. A stone tablet bearing the name of the deceased was commonly erected in front of the mound. In southern China the form of the grave was more elaborate, the mound being cut away in front to form the shape of a horseshoe or the Greek letter omega. Paper representations of offerings to accompany the dead into the afterlife were burned. Afterwards, the relatives of the deceased usually feasted together. For purposes of regular sacrifices a wooden tablet was set up, for rich families in the ancestral temple, in which the spirit of the deceased was supposed to reside.

RELIGIONS

The fact that such elaborate and costly funerals still occur, despite official discouragement, is clear evidence that the old beliefs of the Chinese have by no means entirely faded away yet. Since the persecution of religion ceased after the fall of the 'Gang of Four', most Chinese faiths have enjoyed something of a revival. There are of course far fewer shrines and temples now than previously, and the official Confucian rituals no longer take place, but the popular religion of China, which combined elements of Buddhism, Daoism and primitive beliefs, is still widely practised. There are also large active Christian communities in China today, both Protestant and Catholic, though the Catholics have been forced to break most of their links with Rome. Among the ethnic minorities other religions (especially Islam) are important.

Most Chinese in the recent past looked with more or less equal favour on Buddhism, Daoism and Confucianism. They sacrificed to their ancestors and made offerings at either Buddhist or Daoist temples as seemed most appropriate to them at the time. If favourable weather for farming was needed, then one or more of the Daoist gods would be approached, but if it was a question of praying for a male child, then the Bodhisattva Guanyin would be the right deity to go to. The Buddhists were also believed to be the most effective in offering prayers to ease the passage of the dead through the underworld, while Daoist priests would be engaged to exorcise evil spirits. Few Chinese worried too much about the subtleties of religion. Many religious or superstitious practices were continued merely because they were customary, without anyone really knowing their significance. The force of custom is very strong in China.

Today many people, particularly though not exclusively older women, still go to temples to burn incense and make offerings of various kinds. At certain times of the year some temples are packed with people. There are quite large numbers of Buddhist monks in China today, and a smaller number of Daoist priests also. During the Cultural Revolution many temples, churches and other religious buildings were seized and put to use as factories or warehouses or suchlike, but now some at least of these have been changed back to their original usage. A large church next door to the University of Shandong in Ji'nan, for example, had become a sandpaper factory, but in the early 1980s was due to be returned to the Christian community when the factory had been relocated.

Education

Before 1949 only a minority of Chinese received any education at all. Literacy was low, few people being able to read more than a small number of characters. One of the major activities of the Chinese Communists was not only to organize more educational opportunities for children, but also to provide literacy and other basic classes for adults. Throughout the early years of the People's Republic literacy campaigns were frequent. Great progress has been made. The official adult illiteracy rate is now less than 10 per cent. But the facilities to provide a good standard of education for the whole population scarcely exist yet, and in some backward areas illiteracy has actually increased recently.

There was no compulsory education in China until 1986. In the cities and large towns it was in practice hard for young children to avoid going to school even before this date, but in the countryside there are still some who receive little or no formal education. In the more backward areas there are insufficient school places and it is impossible to enforce the law fully, even though the compulsory period of education is only nine years. The Chinese educational system is divided into three levels, primary schools, secondary or middle schools, and higher educational establishments. In addition, many very young children, especially in urban areas, regularly attend kindergartens while their parents are working. In rural areas many children receive only primary education. Chinese children generally start primary school at the age of six or seven and finish at twelve or thirteen. They may then go on to junior middle school for two or three years, and perhaps also to senior middle school for as long again. There are middle school places for most children in cities, but in rural areas the situation is often very different. The introduction of compulsory education for all children has certainly imposed strains on the system in many areas where educational resources are inadequate. Recent changes in economic policies have in one way reduced incentives for parents in the countryside to send their children to school, for it can be profitable to keep them at home to share the work of the family.

Higher education is available only to a small percentage of Chinese. It is a great achievement to gain a place at a college or university, and more or less a guarantee of obtaining a desirable post after graduation. There is still not complete freedom of choice in work placements, however, and the allocation of jobs after graduation is a serious source of discontent among students. So also is the level of the salaries of the intellectual class, who may earn more than ordinary workers but find that their financial position compares badly with that of many peasants now. The intellectual class in China has had a bad time since 1949; they are still struggling for greater influence on the policies of government.

The 1911 and 1949 revolutions totally eliminated the power of the old class of scholar-officials. Their doom had been inevitable once the former Confucian examination system was abolished. A new kind of intellectual class began to emerge under the Republic, when many students went abroad to colleges and universities in Japan, the USA and Europe, and returned with ideas new to China. This process had begun early – intellectuals were in the vanguard of the pre-1911 republican movement. Many also became enthusiastic Communists, but the intellectual section of the Party rapidly demonstrated its lack of practical wisdom and was pushed aside by the more down-to-earth Mao Zedong and his supporters. Mao never really trusted intellectuals and they were targets of both the anti-rightist campaign of 1959 and the Cultural Revolution, when educational establishments were closed completely for a time and were then forced through many changes with the aim of putting 'workers, peasants and soldiers' in control. Even after the death of Mao the leadership of the Chinese Communist Party has continued to regard intellectuals as politically unsound. This distrust was one of the major causes of the appalling events in Beijing in June 1989. But China needs its intellectuals if it is to modernize successfully, so that in the long run the Party will probably be forced to give at least some ground to the demands of the intellectual class.

Holidays and Leisure

Traditionally there was a whole series of festivals throughout the year which were commonly celebrated as holidays. The most important of these was the New Year. The old Chinese calendar was very different from that used in the West, its months adhering closely to the cycles of the moon which are hard to reconcile with the annual solar cycle. The regulation of the calendar was a complex procedure, necessitating the addition of an extra (intercalary) month every few years to make up the difference between the short year of twelve lunar months and the solar year. Thus dates in the Chinese calendar vary from year to year by comparison with the Western calendar. Chinese New Year may fall at any time from about the middle of January to early March, but is usually some time in February. Though the Chinese have adopted the Western calendar for most purposes, the old Chinese calendar is still calculated and published every year as it remains in common use for agricultural purposes. Most peasants continue to regulate their sowing and tilling by the traditional calendar.

The New Year always was the most important of all the Chinese festivals. Traditionally it was the time to make a complete new start, debts usually being cleared (if possible), houses being cleaned and new images of household gods being pasted up. It was often the only time in the year when virtually everybody throughout China took several days holiday from their work. This continues to be so. Rural Chinese can usually regulate their holidays themselves, taking time off during periods when there is little to be done in the fields and working long hours during harvests and other busy times. Those employed in factories, offices and so on now normally work a five day week. Saturday and Sunday are the usual days off, unless there is a rota system (common in factories which work continuously, and in shops which normally open seven days a week) so that a certain proportion of the work-force is away on each day. Most workers now have several days' holiday at New Year, as well as days off for the socialist holidays of May Day and 1 October (the anniversary of the founding of the People's Republic). In addition, workers may be granted extra holiday once every few years, particularly if they need time to make long journeys to visit relatives. Some enterprises now give an allocation of annual leave to their employees.

Within the last few years it has become much commoner for Chinese to travel within their own country, but as a result the transport system is sometimes overstretched. At New Year it is usual for extra trains to be run, and lack of rolling stock has sometimes resulted in all kinds of wagons being pressed into service for carrying passengers. During the New Year of 1982 I travelled from Emei to Chengdu in Sichuan sitting on the floor of a box-car. It is normal at all times of year for the 'hard seat' (cheapest class) coaches of a train to be crowded, with many people standing for long distances. Nearly all Chinese trains have coaches of different classes, the cheapest being the 'hard seat' which are exactly as the name suggests. On long-distance trains there are usually also 'hard sleepers', partitioned into compartments open at the corridor end and with three bunks on each side of the compartment. Obtaining a ticket for a hard sleeper is now a great achievement. The most comfortable accommodation on trains is in the 'soft sleepers', which are divided into large, fully-enclosed compartments each for four people and with much superior bunks. Some soft-class coaches are air-conditioned. On short-distance trains which do not need sleepers there may be 'soft seat' coaches not divided into compartments and with numbered, well-cushioned seats.

LEISURE

Despite their limited leisure time the Chinese contrive to enjoy themselves whenever possible. Parks and famous sites are always well visited by the local population, and the cinema, Chinese opera and other performances are very popular, as is television and the now seemingly ubiquitous karaoke. Sporting activities are also greatly enjoyed. Table-tennis was at one time almost universal in China, though it now seems to have been replaced by pool, and volley-ball, badminton and football are very commonly played. Many Chinese spend even short breaks from work or study playing table-tennis or knocking a shuttlecock about. Great excitement is also aroused by watching sports tournaments, and China's participation in international events is always closely followed. Outbreaks of violence at a football match in Beijing a few years ago, however, led to the national team being disbanded.

May Day used to be the occasion for great political parades in the major cities, but since the downfall of the 'Gang of Four' these have ceased to be held; now it is just another holiday for most people. Much the same is true of National Day on 1 October. There are, however, many other days when traditional festivals fall, some at least of which continue to be celebrated. Thus the Lantern Festival on the fifteenth day of the first month of the Chinese year is often the occasion for celebrations. Parks are filled with displays of elaborate lanterns, and in Ji'nan (and other places) stilt-walkers in traditional costumes dance through the streets. Old temple fairs may still be celebrated with special markets, as on the 'double-ninth' (ninth day of the ninth month) at the Thousand Buddha Hill on the outskirts of Ji'nan. The festival of Qing Ming in early April, when graves were traditionally cleaned, is usually officially marked by the placing of wreaths on memorials to revolutionary martyrs, while those who still look after the graves of their ancestors go to tidy them and perhaps also make some small offerings.

The ability of the Chinese to enjoy their leisure time is strictly limited by their income. Most Chinese have to live on what in developed countries would be considered a pittance: a few thousand yuan a month (at an exchange rate which now stands at about twelve yuan to £1, eight yuan to the US$1) is a good wage in most of China (salary levels vary widely across the country). A few years ago there was still a large percentage of the peasant population whose annual cash income was below 200 yuan. The average annual per capita income is now about £900 (US$1,300) in cities and £300 (US$450) in the countryside. Nevertheless, personal savings have shown remarkable growth, indicating that many Chinese have money to spare. Food and most basic necessities are cheap in China. Many Chinese remain poor, however, and some are very poor. Peasant families who have achieved incomes of 10,000 yuan per year or more under the current economic system are comparatively rich. China's new economic policies have already brought about great changes in patterns of work and leisure in China and this process will continue. China's GDP has grown to become the world's sixth largest and its growth remains rapid: 7.3 per cent in 2001.

CHAPTER ELEVEN

The Minority Races

The greater part of China Proper is inhabited virtually exclusively by Han Chinese, who account for some 93 per cent of the total population of the country. But in isolated pockets here and there within China Proper, and in extensive areas around the borders, live peoples who are ethnically distinct from the Han. These are the minority races of China, and despite their small numbers they are by no means insignificant. The government of the People's Republic has paid considerable attention to its policies towards the ethnic minorities, and has been greatly embarrassed by problems with some of them, particularly the Tibetans (see pp. 228–32). The relations between the Han Chinese and neighbouring peoples has strongly influenced the course of Chinese history and that influence is still felt; some at least of the minorities are less than happy to be dominated by the Han Chinese, and their loyalty to the Beijing government is questionable. It is essential for the security of China's borders that unrest among the minorities be kept to a minimum.

ZHUANG

Numerically the largest is the Zhuang minority, consisting of more than 14 million people. Most of these live in Guangxi Zhuang Autonomous Region, with some also in the neighbouring provinces of Guangdong, Guizhou and Yunnan. They are probably closely related to some of the inhabitants of Vietnam, who speak very similar languages, and are likely to be remnants of the Yue peoples who inhabited large parts of south-eastern China in early historical times. Their way of life is similar to that of the Chinese, though they have their own language and some different customs.

HUI

Other minorities with their own autonomous regions are the Uighurs, the Tibetans, the Mongols and the Hui. The Hui, formerly often called Tungan, are the most numerous of these, totalling some 7.5 million. They are scattered widely throughout most of the northern provinces, mainly in rather small communities. There are larger groupings in Qinghai, Gansu and Xinjiang, and particularly in their Autonomous Region of Ningxia. They are at least partly of Chinese blood and speak Chinese, and would probably have been completely absorbed into the Han population long ago but for their Islamic faith. They appear to be the descendants of Central Asian Muslims who settled in China long ago and intermarried with Han Chinese. They still preserve their religion and distinct customs (though they seem not to worry about the Islamic prohibition of drinking alcohol), and mosques and restaurants serving Muslim dishes may be found in many towns and cities of China. The most famous mosque is in Xi'an, a large complex of buildings generally in Chinese style but with many Islamic decorative features. In the north-west the large Hui populations were in the past commonly very troublesome, frequently attacking their neighbours of Han, Tibetan or other race, and from time to time there were serious Muslim revolts, such as that of 1862–78. Sometimes such revolts spread to co-religionists among other minorities, mainly in Xinjiang.

UIGHUR

The largest ethnic group of Xinjiang is the Uighur minority of more than 6 million. They are of Turkic stock and speak a language intelligible to the western Turks of Asia Minor, but are unlikely to be directly descended from the Uighurs of the Tang dynastic period. They are a settled, agricultural people, cultivating the lands of the various oases of Xinjiang. Like the Hui they are Muslims. Xinjiang is also home to other Turkic peoples, including the Kazakhs and the Kirgiz, who are nomadic herdsmen, and the Uzbeks, who are mainly town-dwelling tradesmen. In parts of Qinghai and Gansu there are smaller ethnic groups speaking Turkic languages, the Salar and Yugur minorities, though they are not of purely Turkic blood.

In the mountains of the far south-west of Xinjiang lives the largest

Apples being sold in the bazaar at Turpan in Xinjiang: most of the
population of Turpan are Turkic Uighurs

ethnic group of Caucasoid affinities found within the borders of China
today, the Tajiks. They are speakers of an Indo-European language of
the Iranian group, and are Muslims. Altogether they number well over
20,000 living mainly in and around Taxkorgan near the border with
Pakistan. The only other ethnic group of Indo-European speech are the
small number of Russians left within the borders of China, most of
whom are remnants of the many White Russians who fled into China
after the October Revolution. At one time they numbered many
thousands, but most either moved on elsewhere or returned to their
home country so that now there are only a few thousand left. Most live
in Xinjiang, but a very few are scattered through other parts of China,
principally in the north-east.

MONGOL

Right across the northernmost part of China, from Xinjiang and
Qinghai in the west to Heilongjiang and Jilin in the east, is a band of
semi-arid country inhabited mainly by nomadic Mongols. They have
their own Autonomous Region of Inner Mongolia and number in all

more than 3 million people. Their main occupation is herding horses, sheep, camels or cattle. They are generally adherents of the Tibetan form of Buddhism, to which they were converted from the period of the Yuan dynasty onwards, the religion becoming widely accepted among ordinary Mongols after the sixteenth century. As a result of their conquest of all China during the thirteenth century and their close relations with the Manchus of the Qing dynastic period, there are still small groups of Mongols scattered throughout many parts of southern China. One group has maintained its distinct identity in Yunnan ever since the conquest by Khubilai Khan's forces in the 1250s.

MANCHU

The Manchurian region has been extensively settled by Han Chinese, large numbers of whom moved across the Gulf of Bohai from Shandong province during the late nineteenth and early twentieth centuries. The Manchus are today no more than a scattered remnant totalling some 4 million, the great majority of whom have forgotten their own language and use only Chinese. This is a result of their conquest of China and subsequent gradual assimilation of Chinese culture. The Manchu language is today in danger of falling into complete disuse, and steps have recently been taken to try to revive it. Also living within the three north-eastern provinces are small populations of Tungusic peoples such as the Oroqen, Ewenki and Hezhe, who still mainly subsist by hunting; they amount only to about 25,000 people in all. One of the largest minorities in the north-east are the Koreans, of whom rather less than 2 million are resident in China.

THE SOUTH AND SOUTH-WEST

Small numbers of non-Han peoples live scattered in remote areas in various parts of southern China, such as the mountain people of Taiwan, the She of Fujian, Zhejiang, Jiangxi and Guangdong, and the Li of Hainan Island. They are probably remnants of aboriginal peoples displaced but never quite totally absorbed by the Han Chinese. Their languages are diverse, some being Austronesian (Malayo-Polynesian), and others related to Thai or of uncertain affinities. They are an interesting reminder of the former cultural and linguistic diversity of

Houses of the Dai ethnic minority in Xishuangbanna,
extreme southern Yunnan province

southern China. In the west and south-west such diversity persists today, the greater number of the fifty-five minorities currently recognized by the Chinese government being found in Yunnan, Guizhou and Sichuan. Western Sichuan, most of Qinghai and of course Tibet are inhabited by some 4 million Tibetans.

The largest and most widespread of the south-western minorities are the Yi, totalling some 5.5 million people, and the Miao, about 5 million. Only a few of the remaining ethnic groups have populations of more than a million, but several are numbered in hundreds of thousands. Many of them speak languages of the Tibeto-Burman group, and probably migrated southwards from the Tibetan borderlands, but some are speakers of Austro-Asiatic tongues related to Vietnamese and Khmer, and the languages of the Miao and Yao minorities form a group of their own of uncertain wider relationship. These south-western minorities generally either follow their own primitive religions or are Buddhists. Some of them, like the Dai of the extreme south of Yunnan, are Buddhists of the Hinayana school.

Chinese Attitudes to the Ethnic Minorities

Since the earliest recorded times , the Chinese have tended to treat other ethnic groups with disdain. Throughout virtually the whole of their history the Han Chinese have possessed a much higher level of culture than any other people with whom they have been in contact, and they have therefore tended, naturally enough, to regard those people as savages. Their view was that the Chinese were the most civilized people in the world and that all other peoples were inferior. This attitude coloured their relations with all non-Chinese and was a major reason for their failure to understand the situation which arose when China came into direct contact with modern European states. For many of the minority peoples under Chinese rule it led to centuries of maltreatment and oppression. It is only fair to point out, however, that the Chinese rarely treated the minorities as badly as, for example, European settlers did the natives of the Americas or Australia. Racial prejudice is no worse among the Chinese than it has commonly been among other races, despite their reputation for xenophobia.

The non-Han ethnic groups within and around the borders of the Chinese state were accorded different treatment by the Chinese according to their level of socio-political organization and their distance from areas of Chinese settlement. Their military strength as compared with that of China was, of course, also an important factor. The fundamental policy of the government of China was normally to leave the 'barbarians' more or less to their own devices, as long as they recognized Chinese superiority and caused no trouble. Thus well-organized peoples with their own states, such as the Tibetans or Koreans, were usually left to rule themselves so long as they acknowledged Chinese overlordship or suzerainty and paid tribute from time to time. In times of Chinese strength there might be some interference with internal affairs, but rarely to any great extent. In times of Chinese weakness, of course, tribute was often not paid and these tributary states became completely independent. Many of China's former tributaries are today independent nations, as for example Korea, Vietnam, Burma and (outer) Mongolia, while others have been annexed by other states, such as the Liuqiu (Ryukyu) Islands which are now part of Japan. Tibet asserted its independence after the crumbling of central authority in China in 1911, but was never strong enough to take control of the whole of the territory claimed by Lhasa, which included most of what is now Qinghai province and parts of western Sichuan and north-west Yunnan. It was reoccupied by Chinese troops in 1951. Outer Mongolia retained its independence only because of strong Russian influence. The Mongolian People's Republic (now simply the Mongolian Republic) was for decades in a similar situation to that of Soviet-dominated Eastern Europe after 1945. The sympathies of many Mongols were alienated by the suppression of their religion, so that there was never any strong incentive for the Mongols of Inner Mongolia to try to join their northern relatives. Indeed, many refugees fled in the opposite direction. Since the collapse of the Soviet Union and subsequent Russian withdrawal from Mongolia there has been a big revival of Buddhism in the country.

XINJIANG

The history of Xinjiang is complex. Chinese influence has been strong in the region since the Han dynasty, but it was only intermittently under Chinese control for rather short periods until its conquest by the Manchus in the early eighteenth century. What sets it apart from regions such as Tibet is its lack of internal cohesion. When not under foreign domination Xinjiang has normally been a collection of small independent states. This has been a result of its geography, with numerous oases separated by stretches of desert. It has been rare for the ruler of one oasis to be able to extend his influence over more than a few neighbouring ones. The situation has been further complicated by the many migrations of people which have passed through the region, which is today reflected in the large number of different ethnic groups represented within its borders.

At one time the authority of the emperors of China was recognized well to the west of the present borders of Xinjiang, but as Russia expanded its influence eastwards during the eighteenth and nineteenth centuries considerable areas were removed from Chinese overlordship and incorporated into the Russian Empire. It is in fact quite astonishing that the rest of Xinjiang managed to avoid this fate during the period after 1911 when central authority in China was too weak to have much influence in the far north-west. Though large parts of the region often broke away from its control, the Chinese local government was able to maintain itself in Urumqi throughout the whole of this period, and somehow to overcome not only internal resistance to its authority but also pressure from beyond the borders. This is something of a tribute to the fact that the government imposed by the Chinese was usually preferable to anything that could be expected from local tyrants (or, indeed, from the Russians: large numbers of White Russians fought in support of the Chinese government in Urumqi during the 1930s). The Soviet Russians were also restrained by their desire to keep on good terms with the Chinese Nationalist government.

In areas such as Xinjiang, where there was no native central authority, the Chinese established their own higher administrative units while often leaving control at lower levels in the hands of native leaders. These local chiefs would be required to submit to Chinese authority, in return for which they would be given a Chinese title and symbols of office. Their freedom of action would to some extent be circumscribed, but generally they were not interfered with provided they kept good order and paid whatever taxes or tribute the Chinese demanded from them. This sort of system was used to control not only the small oasis states of Xinjiang but also the various chiefdoms of the Sino-Tibetan borderlands and the more organized non-Han communities of south and south-west China. Peoples whose social organization was at a more primitive level were quite often left completely outside Chinese administrative control. Usually such people lived in remote and difficult country which the Chinese rarely attempted to penetrate. Contacts between the Han and these peoples were normally limited to a certain amount of trade. They were sometimes treated very badly, and used, for example, as a source of slaves. It was also not uncommon for the various different ethnic minorities to exploit each other in a similar way.

Since 1949 the government of the People's Republic of China has been able to establish closer control over the minority peoples than has ever existed previously. Though they have brought what might be considered many benefits to these peoples, including better medical and educational facilities, and have helped most of them to enjoy greatly enhanced standards of living, the old Chinese attitude of superiority has not entirely faded away and there can be no doubt that Chinese rule is commonly resented. The accordance of at least a limited amount of autonomy to the minorities, which allows them to live under different regulations from those applicable to the Han Chinese, has not been enough to dispel all animosities. The situation varies greatly from one area to another, but certainly in Xinjiang and in Tibet the Chinese are unpopular. Tibetan resistance to Chinese rule is well known, particularly as a result of the 1959 uprising and the flight of the Dalai Lama, who stills lives in exile, but there have undoubtedly also been a number of smaller uprisings in Xinjiang. The greatest ill-feeling has been caused by Chinese interference in the religious practices of the minorities and by the settlement of Han Chinese immigrants in minority areas. The Tibetans at least fear that they may become a minority in their own land because of Han immigration.

Chinese Rule in Tibet

The Chinese claim to Tibet goes back a long way. Chinese accounts usually begin with the marriage of two Chinese princesses to Tibetan kings during the Tang dynasty, in AD 641 and 710, but this was no more than an inducement to good relations between two independent states. Tang China was on several occasions attacked by the Tibetans, who even occupied Chang'an for a short time in 763, during the chaos created by the rebellion of An Lushan. After the fall of the Tang dynasty, relations between China and Tibet consisted mainly of local trade in the border regions. This was the period during which Buddhism first entered Tibet, interacting with the native Bon beliefs to produce the distinctive Tibetan form of the religion. It seems to have been mainly from India, not China, that Buddhism reached Tibet.

Tibet first came firmly under the same government authority as China as a result of the Mongol conquests. Tibet in fact submitted before the Southern Song fell to the armies of Khubilai Khan. In 1264 a Tibetan monk called Phags-pa, who had impressed Khubilai Khan, was placed in political control of Tibet as well as being made head of the Buddhist church throughout the Mongol dominions. Tibet and Mongolia remained strongly connected, sharing a common religion, long after the Mongols had been driven out of China. Nevertheless Tibet continued to recognize some form of Chinese suzerainty throughout most of the period of the Ming dynasty, though actual Chinese control over Tibetan affairs was extremely limited. The prestige of the Manchus during the early period of their conquests was such that the fifth incarnation of the Dalai Lama personally made the long journey from Lhasa to Beijing in 1652 to acknowledge the suzerainty of the newly-founded Qing dynasty. But again, during the early period of Qing rule, this acknowledgement had only a very limited effect within Tibet. Actual political control of the country was exercised largely by khans of the Khoshote tribe of western Mongols, who had settled within what is now Qinghai. The whole of this region, as well as much of Xinjiang and Mongolia, was thrown into turmoil during the late seventeenth century by expansionist activities on the part of the Junggar tribe of western Mongols. The Manchus mounted several campaigns to suppress the disturbances, which resulted in the conquest of Tibet in 1720 and Qinghai in 1724. From that time onwards much closer control was exerted by the Manchus. A strong garrison was left in Tibet and from 1727 imperial residents were permanently stationed in Lhasa. The eastern Tibetan province of Kham was placed under the jurisdiction of Sichuan. Manchu control was further strengthened as a result of the suppression of a rebellion by a Tibetan chief in 1750 and of successful campaigns against the Gurkhas, who invaded Tibet in the 1790s.

The decline of the Qing dynasty during the nineteenth century naturally led to a weakening of Chinese influence in Tibet. At the same time the expansion of the Raj in India brought the British into close contact with Nepal, Bhutan and Sikkim, and led to the first attempts to enter into relations with the Tibetans. People who had become British subjects in India had for many years conducted a small volume of trade with Tibet across the high passes of the Himalaya. The British were quite naturally anxious to come to an agreement with the Tibetans about the regulation of such trade, which they hoped to expand. They were also eager to exert some influence in Tibet to counter possible moves by Russia. But the Tibetan government frustrated all attempts to negotiate, and eventually the British felt justified in sending an armed expedition into Tibet which enforced a settlement at Lhasa in 1904. The British forces then withdrew. This armed intervention curiously enough greatly strengthened goodwill between the Tibetans and British and relations were much better thereafter. The Chinese, however, took the successful British invasion as a cue to embark on a forward policy in Tibet themselves. The British had never officially questioned their suzerainty over Tibet and could be relied upon not to aid the Tibetans against them.

The first signs of this new Chinese policy were seen in the border regions of western Sichuan and north-west Yunnan, where the local Chinese administrators tried to assert much greater control over the local Tibetan population. This very shortly led to unrest, with both Europeans (mostly missionaries) and Chinese being attacked and murdered. Late in 1905 Chinese troops under the command of Zhao Erfeng were sent west to put down the disorder. This they did with considerable severity, and Zhao commanded that all the local peoples should submit to Chinese sovereignty and wear the pigtail in Manchu style. All of western Sichuan and neighbouring parts of eastern Tibet were thoroughly subjugated by Zhao and his troops. In 1908 the Qing government went on to appoint Zhao Erfeng imperial resident in Lhasa, his brother at the same time being made governor of Sichuan. Shortly afterwards an imperial decree for the first time claimed Chinese *sovereignty* over Tibet. Before attempting to move on to Lhasa, Zhao Erfeng occupied further areas of eastern Tibet during 1909 and early 1910. Chinese troops arrived in Lhasa shortly afterwards, whereupon the Dalai Lama fled to India, placing himself under British protection (clear evidence of the great improvement in Anglo-Tibetan relations).

The fall of the Qing dynasty completely changed the situation. Zhao Erfeng was murdered in Sichuan by the revolutionaries in 1911, and the Chinese troops in Tibet were repatriated via India shortly afterwards. Tibet declared its independence, but this was never recognized by any Chinese government. The Chinese were in fact able to maintain some limited presence in the Tibetan border regions. They even created a new province of Xikang, comprised of western Sichuan and neighbouring areas of eastern Tibet, though their authority there was very weak.

Tibetan women from the Sichuan-Tibet borderlands
in their colourful national costume

The present government of China, in again enforcing Chinese rule
in Tibet, has thus continued a policy first embarked upon in 1905. The
Chinese would consider it a serious affront to their prestige to give up
their claim to what they consider to have been an integral part of China
prior to 1911. The loss of Outer Mongolia was a serious enough blow
to their dignity. The Tibetans found themselves in a hopeless position
in 1951 in the face of the advancing Chinese troops and quickly came
to terms. It must be said that their situation was partly of their own
making, for had they sought to modernize and develop relations with
the outside world during the period of independence after 1911 they
might have been able to offer serious resistance to the Chinese and gain
foreign support. As it was they had little choice but to submit. Chinese
insensitivity quickly reawakened old animosities, however, resulting in

a major uprising by the Tibetans and the flight of the present (14th) incarnation of the Dalai Lama, who still lives in exile in India. Anti-Chinese feeling still runs high among the Tibetans, as has been shown by demonstrations in Lhasa during the last few years.

The Aspirations of the Minorities

There is no doubt that the great majority of Tibetans would like to be completely independent of China and ruled once again by their god-king, the Dalai Lama. Realistically this is very unlikely to be possible in the foreseeable future. The best that the Tibetans can hope for is an increased amount of local autonomy while remaining within China, though even this will be hard to achieve. The relaxation of controls after the end of the Cultural Revolution has led, as far as the Chinese can see, only to increased unrest in Tibet, so that they may well be unwilling to go any further in that direction. They have tried to coax the Dalai Lama back to Lhasa, but are clearly not prepared to make too many concessions in order to do so.

Though there has been unrest among some of the other minority peoples of China since 1949, it has never reached the serious proportions it has in Tibet. Most of the other minorities are smaller or less united, and have also been under stronger Chinese influence for a longer period. In Xinjiang and Inner Mongolia, for example, there was very considerable Chinese settlement prior to 1911. Manchuria, where a quasi-independent puppet state was established by the Japanese from 1932–45, now has a predominantly Han population. No area other than Tibet was in a position to declare and maintain its independence of China after 1911 (with the exception of the still-independent Mongolian Republic). In any case many minorities probably felt no strong urge to break away from China. Where closely-related populations are divided by international borders, as with the Mongols, the Kazakhs and the Kirgiz, there seems rarely to have been any strong desire to move across those borders to join the related peoples not under Chinese rule. Indeed, the opposite seems to have been more often the case. Many Mongols, for example, fled from the Mongolian People's Republic into Chinese Inner Mongolia and Xinjiang during the early 1930s. There was usually greater freedom of religion in China than there was in the USSR or the Mongolian People's Republic, except during the period of the Cultural Revolution.

The ethnic minorities of southern and south-western China are scarcely in any position to contemplate independence, as most of them live in small enclaves surrounded by Han Chinese. In any case, though relations with the Chinese have often been bad, and there were, for example, major uprisings by the Miao in the 1720s, 1790s and 1850s–60s, few of these minorities today seem seriously concerned to throw off Chinese domination. Provided they are reasonably well treated they are happy enough with their position. Since the post-1949 Chinese government has in general treated them well, allowing them some official autonomy and giving them certain privileges compared with the Han Chinese (such as not having to comply with such strict birth-control regulations), there has been little or no unrest.

The loyalty or otherwise of the minorities has serious implications for the security of China's borders. Most of the long land borders of the People's Republic of China run through areas principally inhabited by non-Han peoples. Should they become seriously disaffected this could make it very easy for any hostile power sharing a common border to foment trouble. The present tensions in the Muslim world caused by the fundamentalist movement must be of great concern to the Chinese government as there is a large Muslim population in China, some of whom are Shi'ites. The situation in Afghanistan must be especially worrying as that country has a short common border with China. All the might of the Soviet armed forces was unable to suppress the uprising of the much more poorly-equipped Afghan guerrillas; a similar uprising in Xinjiang might be at least as difficult for the Chinese government to handle. But so far at least the fires of Islamic fundamentalism seem to have left China largely untouched.

Problems with minority populations are a legacy to the current government of China from its imperial past. Just as the European imperial powers had to find ways to resolve such problems, so will the Chinese. Their most serious difficulties at present are with the Tibetans, but even those are probably not so bad that they could not eventually be settled by amicable negotiations. It is largely a question of trying to build up good will. Whatever the problems, it is most unlikely that any of the regions now forming part of China will break away and become independent, at least in the foreseeable future. In the long term it is likely that many of the smaller minorities will simply become absorbed into the Han population, as has already happened in large parts of southern China. The larger minorities will no doubt remain distinct for many years to come, but most will probably accept their position in the multi-racial nation of China. The Tibetans, however, are a stubborn people, and are certain to continue to aspire to independence. It is most unlikely that the Chinese would willingly concede this, and a solution to this problem does not appear to be near at hand.

CHAPTER TWELVE

Hong Kong, Taiwan and the Future

The former British colony of Hong Kong was wrested away from the Chinese Empire in three stages as a result of the Opium War, the *Arrow* War and the scramble for concessions after the Sino-Japanese War of 1894–5. Its return to China in 1997 removed the last still-effective vestige of the 'unequal treaties' of the nineteenth century, which can now be finally consigned to history. With Macao also due to be returned shortly, China's territorial integrity, as seen by the current government in Beijing will be complete – except for Taiwan.

Taiwan was returned to Chinese rule after the defeat of Japan in 1945. Just four years later, as the Nationalists were progressively driven back by Chinese Communist forces on the mainland, Chiang Kai-shek decided to withdraw the bulk of his forces to the large off-shore island, where the seas of the Taiwan Strait would at least offer hope of holding the Communist armies at bay. With the outbreak of war in Korea and a resultant shift in US policy in the region, the Nationalists found themselves protected by an American fleet. With few naval forces of any kind at their disposal, the Chinese Communists had to abandon all thoughts of an immediate invasion of Taiwan. As the years went by, continued US support allowed the Nationalists to consolidate their position on the island. For many years, the USA and its closest allies continued to recognize the Nationalist government on Taiwan as the legitimate government of all China: the Nationalists occupied China's seat at the United Nations until 1971.

But neither the Nationalists nor the Communists regarded the separation of Taiwan from the mainland as permanent or desirable. Both sides claimed to be the legitimate government of all China, including both the mainland and the island. As the years have passed and the separation has continued, an independence movement has gained some strength on Taiwan, but the great majority of its people still consider themselves to be Chinese. The Beijing government clearly still regards them as such. Having settled the questions of Hong Kong and Macao satisfactorily, Beijing would undoubtedly now like to come to some arrangement which would bring Taiwan back to 'the motherland'. The Taiwanese, however, are in no hurry to make a deal. No doubt they want to see how the situation in Hong Kong develops over a period of time before they consider any sort of negotiated settlement. A few more decades is after all a very small drop in the large ocean of Chinese history.

So far, Hong Kong seems to have taken the withdrawal of the British and the Chinese takeover pretty much in its stride. There are concerns about a number of matters, not least the complex and rather obscure system by which a new legislative assembly is to be elected (to replace the elected Legislative Council instituted by Governor Patten shortly before the handover, which Beijing – as it had promised – duly disbanded after the British had left). The domination of Beijing over Hong Kong has not yet produced any major disasters, however. If this continues to be the case for long enough, Taiwan may be encouraged to feel that a negotiated settlement with Beijing might be worth exploring. In the long term, such a settlement will probably be agreed, and Taiwan will again become an integral part of China (though no doubt with guarantees of considerable local independence for at least a few decades).

The Background

HONG KONG

Before the arrival of the British as traders at Guangzhou, Hong Kong was just another of the many small islands off the south China coast, with a negligible population and no economic importance. It attracted the attention of British merchants because of the fine harbour which lies in its lee. When the British opened hostilities against China in the Opium War of 1839–42, one of their aims was to obtain from China the cession of a small island where the British could reside under their own flag. Hostilities and negotiations alternated throughout the period of the war. In January 1841 a Convention was agreed at Chuanbi which ceded the island of Hong Kong to the British, and shortly afterwards they took possession of it. But neither government was prepared to ratify the Chuanbi Convention and hostilities were reopened. In rejecting the cession of Hong Kong, the British Foreign Secretary, Lord Palmerston, described it as 'a barren island with scarcely a house upon it', and issued a stern rebuke to the British representative in China, who was replaced. The following year, however, the Whig government fell and the Tories who replaced it were not even concerned to obtain an island at all. But as Hong Kong was already in British possession the new representative in China decided to keep it, and the cession was confirmed by the Treaty of Nanjing of 1842.

Hong Kong Island in the 1840s did not seem to offer very much. It was smaller than the present island, which has been enlarged through the reclamation of land from the harbour, and its rocky slopes fell steeply into the sea. It was subject to the onslaughts of typhoons, and had an unhealthy climate in which fever was a common affliction. It soon became clear that it was too small to be of any great use and the earliest opportunity was taken to enlarge it. Thus, by the Convention of Beijing of 1860, which concluded the *Arrow* War, the southern part of Kowloon peninsula opposite Hong Kong Island was ceded to Britain, together with Stonecutters Island. This increase in area was important for there had been a great influx of population since the colony was founded. Perhaps surprisingly, large numbers of Chinese had been attracted to life under British rule, and by 1851 there were more than 30,000 of them living on Hong Kong Island (whereas there were only some 1,500 other inhabitants).

The colony remained at this size for almost another forty years. In the aftermath of China's defeat by Japan in 1895, however, it became clear that the aggressive intentions towards China of other foreign powers might at some stage make it necessary to defend Hong Kong, almost an impossibility while the hills around the northern end of the Kowloon peninsula were not under British control. While the other foreign powers exacted their own concessions from the beleaguered Qing government, therefore, Britain sought and was granted a 99-year

The Legislative Council building in Central District, Hong Kong,
symbolically dwarfed by the new Bank of China building to its left
(the Old Bank of China building can be seen behind it to the right)

lease on the New Territories. These comprised all the land north of
Boundary Street in Kowloon up to the Shenzhen (Shum Chun) River,
together with a total of some 230 islands (the majority of them small
and uninhabited).

Hong Kong continued to attract immigrants from China, and by
1931 had a total population of almost 880,000, of which only 20,000
were non-Chinese. The colonial pattern of administration gave little
say in government to the Chinese (this remained true until very
recently), and at first an attempt was made to govern them through
Chinese officials seconded from the mainland. This soon broke down,
however, and from 1865 the official policy was changed to that of equal
treatment of all races. Hong Kong's economy thrived under the
laissez-faire policies of its government, and the number of ships using
the port steadily increased.

After the 1911 Revolution the unrest in China caused an influx of refugees from the interior into the colony. Following the First World War and the failure of the Chinese to gain their demands at the Versailles peace conference there was much anti-foreign sentiment in China, which soon affected Hong Kong. The prominent position of Britain among the imperialist powers in China made her the main target of agitation during the 1920s, when there were serious strikes in the colony. After 1931, however, the actions of Japan diverted Chinese attentions. The invasion of China by the Japanese in 1937, and particularly the fall of Guangzhou in 1938, caused another wave of refugees to pour into Hong Kong. The population of the tiny colony more or less doubled in three years. In December 1941 the Japanese invaded Hong Kong, which they then occupied until the end of the war. A large part of the population was deported, so that at the time of Japan's surrender probably only some 600,000 remained. A vast increase resulted from the Civil War and the victory of the Communists, however, and by 1950 the population had reached more than 2 million. The problems caused by such huge and sudden influxes of people were naturally enormous; food and water supplies and housing were often severely overstretched. Chinese continued to enter Hong Kong from the mainland, often illegally. The British authorities eventually began handing illegal immigrants back to the Communists, if they could catch them, but it is estimated that only about a third were actually caught. At the time of the handover in 1997 there were about 6 million people living in Hong Kong. Restrictions on passage between the rest of China and the Special Administrative Region of Hong Kong continue to be enforced.

The people of Hong Kong were undoubtedly shaken by the Tianan Men incident of 1989 and many worried what the return to Chinese control might mean. The disagreements between Governor Patten and the mainland government during the last few years before British withdrawal contributed to the uneasiness. Although the British government refused to allow the right of residence in the UK to more than a few of the more than 3 million Hong Kong residents entitled to British passports, a considerable number of those with the resources to do so managed either to leave the colony or to make arrangements to do so

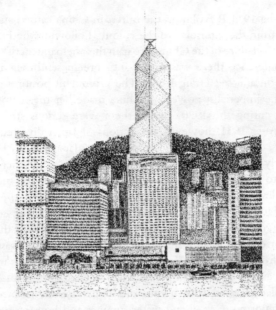

The curiously prism-shaped new Bank of China building in Central District, Hong Kong: when first erected it was the tallest building in the colony

if the need was felt. There are still worries about some issues, such as journalistic freedom, the peculiar elective arrangements for the new Legislative Council, crime and corruption, but in general life in Hong Kong has not been greatly altered since the handover. The greater worry recently has been the effect on Hong Kong of the economic problems that have afflicted so many countries in the region: the backing of the government of mainland China actually helped the Hong Kong dollar to ride the worst of the economic storms without severe losses of value.

TAIWAN

The large island of Taiwan, also known by its Portuguese name of Formosa (Ilha Formosa – the Beautiful Island), lies off the coast of Fujian province, almost 100 miles from the mainland. Though it has been in contact with the mainland since prehistoric times, it was not incorporated into the Chinese empire until a comparatively recent period. The Penghu (Pescadores) Islands off its western coast were administered from Fujian during the Southern Song dynasty, and from 1292–4 the Mongols established an administration for both the Penghu Islands and Taiwan. Subsequently, however, Taiwan was left largely to its own devices for a long period, though increasing numbers of Chinese from across the straits went to settle there. Not until the last decades of the Ming dynasty does it again figure in Chinese history.

In 1624 Dutch traders, having been driven by the Portuguese and Chinese from the mainland China coast, established themselves on Taiwan, where they were to remain for several decades. Two years later the Spanish also arrived, but were driven out by the Dutch in 1642. The Dutch settlements were destroyed in 1661 when the pirate and Ming loyalist Zheng Chenggong descended upon the island. The Zheng family maintained themselves in control of Taiwan until the Qing government was able to send an expeditionary force which drove them out in 1683. Taiwan was then incorporated into the Qing empire as a part of Fujian province. In 1885 it was raised to the status of a separate province, but as a result of the Sino-Japanese War of 1894–5 was transferred to Japanese sovereignty. It remained a part of the Japanese empire until the defeat of Japan at the end of the Second World War.

Though Japanese rule on Taiwan was often not popular, it conferred great benefits at least on the economic structure of the island. Electrical power was supplied even to remote areas at a time when little of the mainland had any electricity, and modern industries were developed. Education was also greatly improved, so that by 1945 the majority of the population was literate, a great contrast to the mainland situation. Thus, after its return to China in 1945 there was every prospect of Taiwan quickly taking a prominent position in the post-war development of the country. Unfortunately the reimposition of Chinese rule on the island was not well handled by the Nationalist regime.

The first Nationalist governor of Taiwan province, appointed in 1945, was Chen Yi. His corruption and the favour shown to mainland Chinese in preference to established Taiwan residents soon made his administration extremely unpopular. Though the Nationalists had at first been welcomed as liberators from Japanese colonial rule, resentment rapidly grew to such proportions that in February 1947 there was a violent uprising, which was put down with great ferocity. The dismissal of Chen Yi improved the situation, but much bitterness persisted among the Taiwanese against the mainlanders and even gave rise to an independence movement.

As the military situation of the Nationalists on the mainland worsened during 1948, Chiang Kai-shek looked towards Taiwan as a possible refuge. After the fall of Nanjing in April 1949 troops and resources began to be transferred to the island, the Nationalist government following in December. In 1950 Nationalist troops were evacuated from Hainan and Zhoushan (Chusan) Islands. Eventually the Nationalists held only Taiwan itself, the Penghu Islands and a couple of islands off the Fujian coast, which is how the situation remains today. Nationalist military forces on Taiwan were strengthened not only by the withdrawals from other offshore positions, but also by the return of units pushed over the Chinese borders into South-east Asia, and by more than 14,000 Chinese prisoners-of-war from the Korean conflict who preferred to go to Taiwan rather than the mainland.

It was the Korean War which saved Taiwan from the threat of invasion by Communist forces in the early 1950s, for it brought about a reversal of United States policy regarding the Nationalist Chinese. In the latter half of 1949, as the Nationalists collapsed on the mainland, the USA seemed to accept the inevitability of the fall of Taiwan during 1950. In January of that year President Truman announced that: 'The United States Government will not pursue a course which will lead to involvement in the civil conflict in China . . . [and] will not provide military aid or advice to Chinese forces on Formosa.' This continued to be US policy until the middle of the year, but after the North Korean attack on the South US perceptions changed. In the face of the Communist use of armed force in Korea the US government decided that 'the occupation of Formosa by Communist forces would be a direct threat to the security of the Pacific area and to the United States forces . . . in that area'. The US Seventh Fleet was thereupon sent to the Taiwan Straits to prevent any Chinese Communist attempt at invasion, and US military advisers arrived on Taiwan to formulate joint defence plans with Chiang Kai-shek. Thus any attempt at the invasion of Taiwan would have brought the mainland Chinese into direct conflict with the USA, and Communist plans to do so were therefore abandoned. Attempts later in the 1950s to take the islands of Jinmen (Quemoy) and Mazu (Matsu) just off the Fujian coast were repulsed by the Nationalists with US encouragement. They are still in Nationalist hands.

The change of US policy on Taiwan was important not only because it prevented the reunification of the island with the rest of China, but also because it initiated a long period during which the USA attempted to isolate the People's Republic of China from contact with the non-Communist world. A strict trade embargo was enforced, US citizens were rarely allowed to visit mainland China, and the USA used its influence at the United Nations to maintain the Nationalists there as representatives of China, thereby excluding the People's Republic. Many other states, taking their lead from the USA, continued to recognize the Nationalist government on Taiwan. They included Japan, which chose to sign the peace treaty concluding the hostilities of the Second World War with the Nationalists, ignoring the government of the Chinese mainland.

Mainland China was therefore isolated from most of its important neighbours around the Pacific Ocean, and was driven to rely almost entirely on assistance from the Soviet bloc. Though the Sino-Soviet entente lasted only for the first decade after the founding of the People's Republic, it had a profound influence on the internal development of China and on its foreign relations. Only within the last two or three decades has the People's Republic of China begun to assume its proper place in the world and stabilize its internal development. The dropping of US opposition allowed the People's Republic at last to replace the Nationalists at the United Nations in 1971. President Nixon visited Beijing in 1972, and in 1979 Deng Xiaoping signed an agreement with President Carter normalizing US–Chinese relations. A treaty of peace and friendship was signed with Japan in 1978.

The significance of these moves has not been lost on the Nationalist government on Taiwan. Though the USA would still take a dim view of any military action by the mainland against the Nationalists, and has continued to supply military equipment to Taiwan despite protests from the People's Republic, the extent of support for the Nationalist Chinese has been greatly reduced. Pressure has increased for a settlement between the two Chinese factions, and in the long run an agreement is likely to be reached. The mainland government has already declared its willingness to allow the economic system on Taiwan to continue unchanged for a long period after reunification, and even to allow local control of armed forces. There have now begun to be direct talks between official government organizations from the two sides and strong business links across the Taiwan Straits have developed. Large numbers of Taiwanese tourists visit China every year. Progress has not been entirely smooth, however. Taiwan has recently shown more desire to maintain its independence. Mainland Chinese naval manoeuvres and test firings of missiles close to Taiwan seem to have been intended to intimidate, but have only brought about a deepening of distrust.

Current Policies and the Future

As early as January 1975 Zhou Enlai announced the 'four modern-izations' (of agriculture, industry, science and technology, and defence), despite opposition from the ultra-leftist Gang of Four and their supporters, who then held control of the Party and government. His death a year later seemed to seal the fate of such policies, but a few months later Mao also was dead and the Gang, which included Mao's widow Jiang Qing, were unable to maintain their position. Their fall from power led to drastic revision of the policies pursued not only during the ten years since the beginning of the Cultural Revolution in 1966, but even before then. The Gang were publicly tried as criminals for their activities whilst in power, a clear indication that new policies were going to be very different.

DENG XIAOPING

The man who emerged as leader of the pragmatic faction which has held power since the fall of the Gang of Four was Deng Xiaoping. He in fact never held the highest posts in the government of the People's Republic, but this cannot be taken as a direct reflection of his actual position. When the new Party Chairman, Hua Guofeng (b. 1920), began to build up a personality cult similar to that of Chairman Mao, he was very soon demoted. Deng had a strong, often paramount, influence on all major political appointments in China after 1977. This is not to say, however, that he was able to grasp absolute authority. There is a delicate balance of power in China which rarely allows any one person to achieve such a position (this was so even in the imperial past). The person at the top may hold absolute power, but must be careful not to wield it in such a way as to alienate too many of his supporters, for without their support he becomes vulnerable to attacks by rivals. Thus everyone in the Chinese government system is constantly aware of the insecurity of his or her position. At lower levels of government this is demonstrated by the great reluctance of officials to take any action which might at some time lay them open to criticism. Only entirely routine matters for which there is established precedent can easily be transacted. At higher levels it is shown by the great care with which every action is taken.

Deng Xiaoping had to tread extremely carefully in promoting his new policies and in appointing his own adherents to office. Had he upset too many Party members at the same time, he might have found himself under attack and suffered again the fate which befell him twice during the period from the beginning of the Cultural Revolution to the downfall of the Gang of Four, when he was dismissed from office. It is said that only the personal protection of Zhou Enlai saved him from suffering even more severely during the Cultural Revolution; otherwise, like Liu Shaoqi, he might not have escaped with his life. Deng learnt the hard way the dangers of holding high office in China and manoeuvred very cautiously after his last reinstatement. He had to, for many of the old hard-line supporters of Mao Zedong remained alive and active until very recently. Deng was unable to retire to a less active role himself, despite his great age, until he had managed to push virtually all of the old hard-liners into retirement or non-executive positions. He managed to outlive virtually all of them.

They have increasingly been replaced with younger men who have been groomed to continue Deng's policies after his own death. But not everything has gone smoothly. Hu Yaobang (1915–89) had to be dismissed from his post as Party Secretary, either because he aroused too much opposition from hardliners in the Party or because he tried to go too far, too fast for Deng himself. His successor, Zhao Ziyang (b. 1918), was also too liberal for Deng's liking and was disgraced when he took a soft line towards the demonstrators in Beijing in 1989. Much-publicized intentions to replace aged office-holders with younger men have commonly resulted only in the substitution of people aged about sixty for people aged about seventy. But it is in fact often not the age difference which is important, but the attitudes of those concerned. Deng Xiaoping tried to impart a new style to the government of China, one less bound by caution. Many of the new appointees seem more willing to take initiatives than their predecessors; they are normally also, of course, supporters of Deng's line. Deng was able to weaken the radical Maoist section of the Party so much that it seems unlikely that it could now ever displace his successors in the leadership.

PRESENT POLICIES

The present policies of the government of the People's Republic of China therefore seem likely to continue very much along current lines for some time to come. They have completely reversed many of the policies pursued since the mid-1950s, and are working great changes in the Chinese economy and in Chinese society. One of their most important features is the shift from stress on collective economic activity to the encouragement of individual initiative. Economic development is now being put first, and Communism second, in the government's goals.

Outside the purely economic field, there have been radical changes such as the introduction of a comprehensive legal code. For the first time since 1949 lawyers are operating in China. Much attention has been paid to improving social order, with effective campaigns in the major cities against such things as spitting on the streets (a long-established Chinese custom with serious drawbacks for public health). In the past such campaigns had often occurred, but never with such marked and lasting effect. It has also been very noticeable in recent years that the chaotic traffic situation on city streets, with cyclists all over the place and the constant clamour of bells and horns, has been dramatically improved, at least in many of the larger cities.

But despite the dramatic nature of the changes in economic policies in China since 1976, there is no likelihood of major political changes following quickly. The Chinese Communist Party intends to remain in control of the government of China. The pressure from Chinese intellectuals for greater freedom and democracy, which culminated in the demonstrations in Beijing and other cities in May and June 1989, was never very likely to meet with any success. The ferocity of the final suppression of the demonstrations surprised and dismayed most Chinese and foreign observers alike, but no one who understood China at all well really expected that the demands of the demonstrators would be met. Interesting in this connection is the attitude of the Chinese government towards British moves to increase democratic representation in Hong Kong, which was hostile. The old structure of Hong Kong's government system, which allowed no elected representatives on the Executive and Legislative Councils, was considered very satisfactory by the government of the People's Republic.

Hong Kong has a very different legal and economic system from the People's Republic, but this does not necessarily mean that there will be serious difficulties in incorporating it into the rest of the country. Hong Kong could still have a settled and prosperous future, if the government of the People's Republic will allow it. There is room for regional diversity in China, which is not a new phenomenon there. The problem of Hong Kong is a problem of confidence, for without faith in the future prospects of the colony its prosperity will inevitably be destroyed. The events of June 1989 have not altered the basic question about Hong Kong's future, which is whether or not the Communist Chinese government will respect the letter and the spirit of the Sino-British agreement on the return of the colony to Chinese rule. What *have* changed are expectations about the likely answer to this question. Reports in Western media tend to be over-pessimistic, however. A more balanced East Asian view was taken by the semi-retired leader of Singapore, Lee Kuan-yew: when asked what would happen to Hong Kong after 1997, he replied '1998'. Thus far, his assessment seems about right.

The basic structure of government on Taiwan is very much along the same lines as on the mainland. There is even some collectivization of agriculture, in accordance with the original socialist principles of Sun Yat-sen. Sun is still revered as a great hero by both Communists and Nationalists alike. The reunification of Taiwan with mainland China would probably pose few economic or administrative problems if the Taiwanese could be persuaded to trust the Beijing government.

The return of Hong Kong to the jurisdiction of the mainland has improved the overall economic prospects of China. Despite the general economic weakness which has recently afflicted East and South-east Asia, China and Hong Kong have suffered less than their neighbours, largely because the economy of mainland China is still comparatively self-contained and because Hong Kong's overseas trade links are not solely regional. Hong Kong has in recent years tended to become again what it had originally been intended to be: a gateway to trade with China. That, no doubt, is where its future lies. It is strongly in the interests of the Chinese government to maintain the economic prosperity of Hong Kong. Thus far, the Chinese leadership seems to have appreciated this. It is to be hoped that it will continue to do so. Similarly, Taiwan would be a complete province already industrialized and modernized to the kind of standard now being sought for the whole of China. It would be a catalyst to similar development of other parts of China, particularly neighbouring Fujian.

THE FUTURE

China is a huge country with enormous resources. There are vast reserves of coal, and large oilfields both on- and off-shore, as well as many other mineral resources. There is great scope for hydro-electric generation in some parts of the country. The economy has developed considerably since 1949 and is now modernizing very rapidly. At last China is beginning to achieve the status of a major world economic power. The pace of progress during the last decade or so has been astonishing. If it continues successfully in the coming years, China will almost certainly become the world's largest economy during the next decade.

There are, however, many problems still to be overcome. Population has reached levels which threaten further improvements in standards of living. Rapid industrialization is bringing terrible problems of pollution. Deforestation has left China not only with severely reduced timber resources but also with many adverse effects on climate and soil. Rapid erosion of soil from bare hillsides has caused difficulties because of

The skyline of Central District, Hong Kong, with water traffic
on Victoria harbour in the foreground

silt-deposition behind dams and on riverbeds; combined with rapid
run-off of water from deforested slopes, this has again brought the
danger of severe flooding, which had been greatly reduced by
river-control projects in the 1950s and 1960s. China is suffering a net
loss of agricultural land because of soil erosion, desertification, alkalini-
zation and similar problems, many of them connected with loss of forest
cover. These problems are being confronted but will require radical
solutions.

In a country which is still predominantly agricultural, with 80 per
cent of the population living in the countryside and depending basically
on agriculture for their livelihood, such problems are fundamental to
long-term prospects. China will continue to have an agriculture-based
economy for several decades, and with its limited industrial capacity will
not be able to afford to import food on a large scale. If food production
is drastically outstripped by population increase, the country will
become severely impoverished and starvation will result. Despite great
success in increasing agricultural production and limiting the effects of
natural disasters, famines have occurred within recent times, and even
within the last twenty years. If famine were to become widespread in
many regions of China for several consecutive years, unrest would be
inevitable and in the most extreme situation could lead to disintegration
of central authority. The current leadership is aware of the problems
caused by the rapid growth of population, and is very sensibly taking

strong measures to try at least to slow the rate of growth. Given that China has a very young population, with ever-increasing life-expectancy, even the strict application of the one-child-per-couple policy would take many years to bring population growth to an end. At the moment the regulations are strictly enforced only in urban areas, many peasants continuing to have two or even three children, despite sanctions imposed upon them.

The political unrest now beginning to become serious in China will also have to be resolved in the long term by means other than forcible repression. The young have very different ideals from their elders who remember China before 1949. As the elderly leadership of the Chinese Communist Party fades into senility or dies, the resistance to political change will lessen. Though it must not be imagined that any far-reaching changes can happen quickly in a land as large and as conservative as China, they are already beginning to happen and will surely gather pace. The next few decades will be critical, but whatever occurs the Chinese people will no doubt win through. Through all the great upheavals of their long history they have maintained their national identity and distinctiveness of culture, and there is no reason to suppose that they will not continue to do so.

The Chinese Language and Chinese Characters

Chinese belongs to the Sino-Tibetan group of languages, which also includes Tibetan, Burmese and a number of languages spoken by ethnic minorities in south-west China and south-east Asia. It is quite remotely related to the other languages of the group, however, belonging to a distinct sub-group of its own. It is not related to Japanese, Korean or Mongolian (although it has contributed many loan-words to the first two of these languages). The similarity between written Chinese and Japanese is a result of the borrowing of the Chinese system of writing for the Japanese language. As the Chinese were the only literate race in the Far East for many centuries, their script had a profound influence on many of their neighbours.

To speak of Chinese as a single language is really a simplification. It is well known that many dialects of Chinese exist: Cantonese is one example. Some of these so-called dialects are in fact so different from the standard Chinese language that they really deserve to be considered languages in their own right. Speakers of Shanghainese, Cantonese and Mandarin cannot understand one another. In Fujian province there is a whole group of dialects that are so distinct even from each other that many of them are not mutually comprehensible. Although it is true that all written Chinese can be understood by any person literate in the language, this is to a great extent because written Chinese is not identical with any form of spoken Chinese and often does not reflect the usage of the spoken Chinese dialects. In fact, until this century written Chinese was based on the Chinese language as spoken many centuries ago and made no sense to anyone when read aloud. This situation was comparable to the use of Latin as the language of learning in Europe until a few centuries ago, long after it had ceased to be the spoken language of any race or nation. The use of Classical Chinese as the normal written language was not finally abandoned until the 1920s. Many Classical Chinese phrases and grammatical conventions have found their way into modern written Chinese and even into the spoken language.

Chinese as written today is based on the standard spoken language which has for some time been accepted as the common tongue of all educated Chinese.

251

As it was formerly used by all Chinese officials or mandarins, it came to be called Mandarin. It was derived from the usual spoken dialects of northern and western China, the Mandarin group of dialects, with major differences of pronunciation and grammar smoothed out. After the republican revolution of 1911 it came to be called Guo Yu (the National Language), and is often still referred to as such in Taiwan. On the mainland it was renamed Putonghua (literally Common Speech, but usually translated Modern Standard Chinese). It has not remained unchanged during the last hundred years. Current Modern Standard Chinese is very closely based on the Beijing dialect of Mandarin as spoken by educated people.

This all sounds very complicated, and in fact it is, but with the spread of education in China and the use of Modern Standard Chinese in radio and television broadcasts and in films, the standard language has come to be understood and spoken very widely. It is in any case only the south-eastern provinces that have very distinct languages of their own. The native tongue of the great majority of Chinese is some form of Mandarin (though it has to be said that even the various dialects of Mandarin are often scarcely mutually intelligible). For the sake of simplicity, all spoken usages referred to below will be those of Modern Standard Chinese unless otherwise indicated.

It is often thought that Chinese must be a very difficult language for Westerners to learn. This is not really true. Certainly there are some hard initial obstacles, but after these have been overcome learning to speak Chinese becomes quite easy. The initial hurdles are (1) the total unfamiliarity of Chinese (there are no recognizable words in it, as there are, for native English speakers, in French or German, for example); (2) certain sounds which have to be pronounced which do not exist in any European language; and (3) the system of tones. Because of these obstacles, it is extremely difficult for anyone to teach themselves Chinese unless they are living in an area where they are able to listen to native speakers. Many foreigners resident in China for long periods manage to learn only a very small amount of the Chinese language.

The things that make Chinese easy are the very limited number of different sounds which now exist in it and its very simple grammatical structure. Only just over 400 different basic syllables exist in Modern Standard Chinese, some of which are used very rarely. This number can be multiplied by four because each syllable can be pronounced with four different tones, but it still represents a very limited number of sounds. Evidence from dialects and from old dictionaries which indicated pronunciations shows that there used to be many more possible syllables and that pronunciation has become less and less complex with the passage of time.

Chinese does not have clusters of consonants. Sounds such as the 'str' in English 'string' do not exist in Chinese. The most complex Chinese syllables consist of an initial consonant, a semi-vowel and a vowel (which may or may not be nasalized). Formerly some Chinese syllables also had terminal consonants, but although these still exist in some dialects they have all disappeared from Modern Standard Chinese. (See pp. 6–8 for more information about Chinese sounds.)

Perhaps the most difficult aspect of Chinese pronunciation for most foreigners is its use of tones. Every syllable can be pronounced with one of four different inflections of the voice. The differences between these four tones are important and change the meaning of the syllable. The first tone is high and level, the pitch of the voice neither rising nor falling. The second tone is a rising tone, the pitch of the voice starting moderately high and then going up (rather like the inflection of voice used to indicate a question in English). The third tone begins quite low, drops further and then rises. The fourth tone starts high and falls rapidly. These tones can be indicated in transliterating Chinese by adding marks above the main vowel of the syllable. Thus, ma (first tone) means 'mother', má (second tone) means 'hemp', ma (third tone) means 'horse' and mà (fourth tone) means 'to curse'. It would be possible to say in Chinese 'mama mà ma' ('mother curses horses').

The grammar is exceptionally uncomplicated. The basic sentence structure is subject–verb–object. Nouns have no case-endings. This is quite similar to English grammar. In English the difference of meaning between 'the dog bit the man' and 'the man bit the dog' is expressed entirely by the order of the words. The same is true in Chinese. Chinese is even simpler than English, however, as it has no articles ('the' or 'a'). Nor do Chinese verbs have tenses; time is expressed by additional words: translated absolutely literally, Chinese would say 'I go yesterday, I go now, I go again tomorrow'. Verbs do not change their endings to agree with their subject. In fact, each Chinese word is immutable: Chinese words do not change to indicate plural, case, tense or anything else. Things which in other languages are indicated by altering a word are indicated in Chinese by the addition of other words. Very often, however, it is not necessary to be so specific in Chinese as it is in other languages. In English and most other languages, singular or plural have to be expressed: one must say either 'a horse' or 'horses'. This is not necessary in Chinese: 'ma' means any number of horses from one upwards. Precision is increased by using additional words: 'yi pi ma' ('one horse, a horse'), 'ji pi ma' ('a few horses') and so on.

There are a few words which are placed after verbs, effectively forming suffixes, to express such things as completion of action or having at some time experienced an action (as in 'have you ever been to China?'). The usage of these can seem strange and difficult to comprehend to foreigners learning Chinese. In order to become really fluent in Chinese, it is in fact necessary to learn to think differently, because the Chinese language functions in ways different from those of most foreign languages. In this sense, acquiring a thorough command of Chinese can be considered rather difficult.

What is indisputably difficult about Chinese is the way that it is written.

Chinese does not use an alphabetic script. Fundamentally, each Chinese word is represented by a sign or character specific to that word alone. Thus, instead of having to learn twenty or thirty letters of an alphabet, Chinese who want to become literate have to learn several thousand characters. It is necessary to know about 3,000 in order to read everyday Chinese texts; a well-educated Chinese might easily know 6,000 characters. In the whole of Chinese literature, from the earliest times to the present day, more than 60,000 different characters have been used! New characters are no longer being created. If new words are required they are made up from combinations of existing characters. In fact, many words in modern Chinese consist of two or more characters. This became necessary to avoid ambiguity as the number of different sounds in spoken Chinese reduced: characters which originally had different pronunciations came to sound the same and had to be combined with other characters in order to distinguish their meanings. Thus, the syllable 'shi' pronounced with the first tone can mean either 'teacher', 'louse', 'poem' or 'lion'. These are distinct words, each written with a different character (see Fig. 1), but in spoken Chinese it is necessary to make clear their differences by combining them with other words: thus the normal word for 'teacher' in spoken Chinese is 'laoshi'. 'Lao' means 'old' and is a term of respect. 'Louse' and 'lion' are both combined with the common noun suffix 'zi' to become 'shizi', but context is unlikely to allow confusion between them.

Figure 1. Homophones

师	虱	诗	狮
Teacher	Louse	Poem	Lion

These four characters are entirely different in meaning but are pronounced exactly the same

The way in which new concepts can be expressed using combinations of existing Chinese characters works in much the same way that words for new inventions and discoveries can be made up from Latin and Greek elements in English. 'Telephone' is an example: in Chinese the word 'dian' ('electricity') is combined with 'hua' ('speech') to make 'dianhua' (literally, 'electric speech'). In the same way, 'dianying' ('electric shadows') means 'film (movie)'.

Chinese characters are often believed to be pictographs, that is, a form of writing derived from pictorial representations. Actually only a small percentage of characters is (or rather, originally was) genuinely pictorial (see Fig. 2). There are also characters that are ideographs, derived from drawings which expressed an idea or concept (see Fig. 3). The great majority of characters are, however, made up of combinations of other characters, used either because of an association of meaning or because of similarity in sound. Most characters consist of a combination of two other characters, one used to give a general indication of meaning and one used to indicate the sound (see Fig. 4). Unfortunately both the form of characters and their pronunciation have changed greatly over the many centuries since they were first created, so that today it is usually impossible to gain any very useful idea of either their sound or their meaning from how they are written. Learning characters is hard work, not only for foreigners but also for Chinese schoolchildren, but they are part of Chinese culture, a legacy from its past. Many characters have been simplified in recent times to make them a little easier to learn. The more drastic step of replacing them altogether with an alphabetic script has been proposed but seems very unlikely to happen in the foreseeable future.

Figure 2. Pictographs

Modern form   Ancient form

The character for moon, pronounced 'yue'.

The character for mouth, pronounced 'kou'.

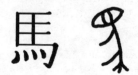

The character for horse, pronounced 'ma'.

Figure 3. Ideographs

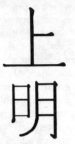

This character, a line with something above it, means 'above' (pronounced 'shang').

This character means 'bright': it depicts the sun (on the left) and the moon (pronounced 'ming').

Figure 4. A compound character

 + =

nü
woman
(rough
indication of
meaning)

ma
horse
(phonetic)

ma
mother

Chronology of Major Events

BC

c. 1.5–0.5 million	*Homo erectus* living in China near Beijing, Lantian, Yuanmou and other sites
c. 80000	Appearance of modern man, *Homo sapiens*, in China
c. 7000	Beginnings of agriculture and of the Neolithic period
c. 2550	Reign of the Yellow Emperor (legendary)
c. 2300	Reign of Yao (legendary)
c. 2200	Reign of Shun (legendary)
c. 2140	Yu the Great controls the great flood (legendary)
c. 2100	Beginning of the Xia dynasty (historicity uncertain)
c. 2100	Beginning of the Chinese Bronze Age
c. 1600	Tang the Accomplished overthrows the last Xia king and establishes the Shang dynasty
c. 1300	Earliest Shang inscriptions on oracle bones
c. 1100	Reign of King Wen of Zhou
c. 1050	The forces of King Wu of Zhou defeat those of the last Shang king in the Battle of Muye: end of the Shang dynasty
c. 900	Emergence of horse nomadism in the steppes north of China
841	Earliest certain date in Chinese history
c. 820	Zhou China attacked by the Xianyun (probably mounted warriors from the north)
771	King You of Zhou killed in attack on the royal capital by rebellious vassals and barbarians
770	First year of the reign of King Ping of Zhou, enthroned in the eastern Zhou capital near modern Luoyang; beginning of Spring and Autumn period
c. 650	Chinese begin to cast iron
552 or 551	Birth of Confucius
479	Death of Confucius
463	Beginning of Warring States period
c. 450	Long defensive wall built on the borders of the state of Qi

256	Zhou kingdom finally annihilated by the state of Qin
221	King Zheng of Qin completes the conquest of all the Chinese states and declares himself First Emperor of the Qin dynasty
214	Completion of the first Great Wall of China
210	Death of the First Emperor of Qin
209	Outbreak of uprisings against the Qin dynasty
206	Han dynasty established
c. 140	Confucianism becomes the dominant state philosophy
138–126	Zhang Qian travels from China to Bactria and Sogdiana
c. 90	Sima Qian finishes the first complete history of China

AD

9–23	Reign of Wang Mang, only emperor of the Xin dynasty; all land declared state property
c. 65	Buddhism reaches China
105	Cai Lun brings paper to the attention of the emperor
184	Rebellion of the Yellow Turbans begins
220	Final collapse of the Han dynasty; China splits into three states
c. 250	Tea-drinking begins to spread through China
c. 399–414	Fa Xian travels from China to India
589	Sui dynasty reunites China
605	Completion of the first Grand Canal, linking the Yangtze with the Yellow River
610	Grand Canal extended south to the Qiantang River
c. 629–45	Xuan Zhuang's journey from China to India
641	A Chinese princess marries the King of Tibet
668	Chinese subjugate Korea
690–701	Reign of the Empress Wu
694	Buddhism ceases to be treated as a foreign religion
751	Battle of the Talas River; Chinese power in Central Asia destroyed by the armies of Islam
755–7	Rebellion of An Lushan
758	Muslims from Arabia and the Persian Gulf burn and loot Guangzhou
763	Tibetans invade China and briefly occupy Chang'an
843	Large quantities of Buddhist church property seized by the government
868	Earliest surviving dated printed book produced in China
875	Outbreak of rebellion of Huang Chao
906	Tang dynasty collapses; China again divided

c. 901	Paper money first used in China
919	Gunpowder begins to be used in China
932–53	Printing of the complete texts of the Confucian Classics
975	China reunited during the reign of the first emperor of the Song dynasty
1044	Description of the magnetic compass in a Chinese text
1069	Reforms of Wang Anshi
1126	The Song capital, Kaifeng, falls to Jurched invaders, who establish the Jin dynasty in north China
1161–5	Song armed forces repulse Jin attacks
1194	Major flood and change of course of the Yellow River
1234	The Mongols complete the conquest of north China and destroy the Jin Dynasty
1271–97	Marco Polo in China
1279	Khubilai Khan completes the conquest of south China
c. 1290	The Grand Canal is rebuilt and extended
1294	John of Montecorvino establishes a permanent Christian mission in Beijing
1368	The Ming dynasty is founded with its capital at Nanjing
1403–33	Voyages by large Chinese junks to India and East Africa
c. 1412	Rebuilding of the Great Wall
1421	The Ming court moves to Beijing
1449	The Mongols invade China and seize the sixth Ming emperor
1514	Portuguese ships reach the China coast
1535	The Portuguese first begin to use Macao
1581	Tax reform: the land tax and poll tax are combined under the 'single whip system'.
1592	The Japanese invade Korea
1598	Chinese forces push the Japanese out of Korea
1601	Matteo Ricci, Jesuit missionary, establishes himself in Beijing
1629	Manchus loot Beijing
1629–45	Rebellion of Li Zicheng
c. 1640	The first tea is brought to Europe
1644	Li Zicheng seizes Beijing and overthrows the Ming dynasty; Wu Sangui invites the Manchus through the Great Wall to help drive Li Zicheng out of Beijing; the Manchus establish themselves in China, moving their capital to Beijing
1683	The Manchus take Taiwan, completing their conquest of China
1689	The Treaty of Nerchinsk partially settles the border between Russia and Manchuria

1720	The Manchus incorporate Tibet into the Qing empire
1729	An imperial edict forbids the selling and use of opium
1790–1	Qing forces subjugate Nepal
1793–4	First British embassy to China, led by Lord Macartney
1793–1804	White Lotus rebellion
1816	Second British embassy to China, led by Lord Amherst
1834	The British East India Company's monopoly of the China trade is abolished
1836–9	The opium trade at Guangzhou is suppressed by the Chinese
1839–42	First Opium War
1842	Treaty of Nanjing: Hong Kong Island ceded to Britain, Shanghai opened as a 'treaty port'
1851–64	Taiping rebellion
1853	Taiping rebels take Nanjing
1853–68	Nian rebellion
1855	The Yellow River floods and changes its course; the northern section of the Grand Canal loses its water and falls into disuse
1855–73	Muslim rebellion in Yunnan
1857–60	*Arrow* War or Second Opium War
1860	British and French forces enter Beijing and destroy the Yuan Ming Yuan summer palace
c. 1862	The Empress Dowager Ci Xi becomes the dominant force at the Qing court
1862–78	Muslim rebellion in north-west China
1863	Robert Hart becomes inspector-general of the Chinese Customs service
1879	Japan annexes the Ryukyu Islands
1894–5	Sino-Japanese War
1895	Treaty of Shimonoseki: Taiwan is ceded to Japan
1897	The Germans seize Jiaozhou Bay and Qingdao and force the Chinese to grant a lease
1898	Russia obtains a lease on Port Arthur and Dalian
1898	Britain obtains leases on Weihaiwei and the New Territories of Hong Kong
1898	The 'Hundred Days of Reform'
1898–1900	The Boxer uprising
1900	Siege of the Foreign Legations; Western troops occupy Beijing
1904–5	Russo-Japanese War; Japan takes over Russian interests in Manchuria
1908	Death of the Empress Dowager Ci Xi; accession of the last

	emperor, Pu Yi
1911	The Nationalist Revolution overthrows the Qing dynasty
1912	Yuan Shikai becomes first president of the Chinese Republic
1914	Outbreak of First World War; Japan attacks German concessions in the Far East and takes Qingdao
1915	Yuan Shikai accepts Japan's 'Twenty-one Demands'
1916	Yuan Shikai abandons plans to become emperor and dies soon afterwards
1917	Brief restoration of the last Qing emperor; China enters the First World War against Germany
1919	The May Fourth Movement: Chinese students demonstrate against the Versailles settlement
1921	First general meeting of the Chinese Communist Party
1922	Japan returns Qingdao to Chinese control
1925	Sun Yat-sen dies; Chiang Kai-shek becomes leader of the Chinese Nationalists
1926–8	The Northern Expedition succeeds in establishing Nationalist control over much of China
1930	Britain returns Weihaiwei to China
1931	Japan seizes much of Manchuria
1933	The League of Nations condemns Japanese aggression in China: Japan walks out of the League
1934	Pu Yi becomes emperor of the Japanese puppet state of Manchukuo
1934–5	The Long March
1936	The Xi'an Incident; the Chinese Nationalists and Communists form a united front against Japan
1937	Outbreak of war between China and Japan
1941	US volunteer fliers form the 'Flying Tigers' in Kunming
1945	The USSR attacks the Japanese in Manchuria; Japan surrenders
1946	Resumption of civil war between the Nationalists and Communists
1949	Foundation of the People's Republic of China
1950	US Seventh Fleet sent to the Taiwan Straits to prevent a Communist invasion of the island; China sends troops into Korea
1951	The People's Liberation Army takes control of Tibet
1953	End of the Korean War
1957	'Hundred Flowers' campaign
1957–9	Anti-rightist campaign
1958	The Great Leap Forward; People's Communes established
1960	Split between China and the Soviet Union

1962	China defeats India in a war over the border of Tibet
1964	China explodes its first atomic bomb
1966	Outbreak of the Great Proletarian Cultural Revolution
1971	Death of Lin Biao; the People's Republic of China replaces Taiwan at the United Nations
1972	President Nixon visits China
1975	Zhou Enlai announces the 'Four Modernizations'
1976	Death of Zhou Enlai; death of Mao Zedong
1977	The 'Gang of Four' are arrested
1979	The USA recognizes the People's Republic of China
1981	First Special Economic Zones established
1989	Suppression of the democracy movement in Beijing
1993	Exchange rate of the Chinese yuan allowed to float
1995	Chen Yun, last of Deng Xiaoping's major Maoist opponents, dies
1996	US President Clinton, after his election for a second term, agrees to exchange state visits with Jiang Zemin
1997	Deng Xiaoping dies on 19 February aged ninety-two; Hong Kong is handed back to the People's Republic of China by Britain; Jiang Zemin pays an official visit to the USA, during which he obliquely admits that the use of military force to suppress demonstrations in 1989 was an error
1998	Li Peng retires as Premier at the end of his term of office and is replaced by Zhu Rongji; US President Clinton visits China
1999	Almost 2,500 people are killed by an earthquake in Taiwan; Jiang Zemin visits the UK and other Western countries; Portugal returns Macao to China
2000	Chen Shuibian is elected the first non-Guomindang President of Taiwan; elections to the Legislative Council in Hong Kong attract only a 43.6% turn-out, with the Democratic Party receiving only 34.7% of the vote; Cheng Kejie, a vice-chairman of the Standing Committee of the National People's Congress, is executed for corruption; the USA grants China permanent normal trade relations, opening the way for China to become a full member of the World Trade Organization
2001	A US Navy EP-3 'spy-plane' collides with a Chinese fighter and lands on Hainan Island, triggering a crisis in China/US relations; Beijing is selected as the venue for the 2008 Olympic Games; China finally becomes a full member of the World Trade Organization
2002	Tung Chee-hwa is re-elected Chief Executive of the Hong Kong government unopposed

List of Dynasties and Selected Rulers

Note: the personal names of Chinese rulers were rarely used after they ascended the throne. For the Shang and Zhou dynasties, the names shown below are the formal ones taken by kings on their accession. For the Qin dynasty, the personal titles used by the rulers are given. After the Qin dynasty, reigning emperors were normally referred to only as 'Imperial Highness' or something similar and had no personal titles during their lifetimes. After their deaths, they were given posthumous titles: these are the titles shown below for rulers from the Han to the Yuan dynasties. (Wang Mang is an exception: this was his personal name). Personal names of rulers of the Han, Sui and Tang dynasties appear in parentheses. Mongol titles or names are given in parentheses for rulers of the Yuan dynasty. For the Ming and Qing dynasties it has become the usual practice to refer to emperors not by any personal title or name but by the title of their reign-period (which was used in the Chinese system of dates): for these two dynasties, therefore, titles of reign-periods are given. Strictly, it is incorrect to refer to, say, 'the Emperor Qianlong' as 'Qianlong' is not the emperor's personal name or title. 'The Qianlong Emperor' is preferable.

Xia *existence not proven, probably c. 2100–c. 1600 BC*

Shang *c.1600–c.1050 BC*
King Zhou *last Shang king, killed in c. 1050 BC*

Zhou *c. 1050–256 BC*

WESTERN ZHOU *c. 1050–771 BC*
King Wen *reigned before the overthrow of the Shang dynasty*
King Wu *succeeded King Wen, destroyed the Shang dynasty*

EASTERN ZHOU 770–256 *BC*
Spring and Autumn period 770–464 *BC*
King Ping 770–20 *BC*
Warring States period *463–222 BC*

Qin 221–206 *BC*
Qin Shi Huangdi *221–10 BC*
Er Shi Huangdi *209–7BC*

Han 206 *BC–AD* 220

WESTERN HAN 206 *BC–AD* 9
Gao Di (Liu Bang) *206–195 BC*
Wu Di (Liu Che) *140–87 BC*

XIN *AD* 9–23
Wang Mang *AD* 9–23

EASTERN HAN *AD* 25–220
Guang Wu Di (Liu Xiu) *25–57*

The Three Kingdoms 220–80

WEI (in north China) *220–65*

SHU HAN (in Sichuan) *221–63*

WU (in south-east China) *222–80*

Jin 265–420

WESTERN JIN *265–317*
(in north China and Sichuan 265–80, then in control of all China until 304, after which much of the north was lost to the Huns)

EASTERN JIN (in southern China) *317–420*

The Sixteen Kingdoms (in parts of northern China) *304–439*

The Northern and Southern Dynasties *420–589*

THE SOUTHERN DYNASTIES:
Song *420–79*
Qi *479–502*
Liang *502–57*
Chen *557–89*

THE NORTHERN DYNASTIES:
Northern Wei *386–34*
Eastern Wei *534–50*
Northern Qi *550–77*
Western Wei *535–56*
Northern Zhou *557–81*

Sui *581–618*
(founded in the north in 581, controlled all China after 589)
Wen Di (Yang Jian) *581–604*

Tang *618–907*
Tai Zong (Li Shimin) *627–49*
Gao Zong (Li Zhi) *650–83*
Empress Wu *684–704*
Xuan Zong *712–55*

The Five Dynasties *907–60*

LATER LIANG *907–23*

LATER TANG *923–36*

LATER JIN *936–47*

LATER HAN *947–50*

LATER ZHOU *951–60*

Song *960–1279*

NORTHERN SONG *960–1127*
Tai Zong *976–97*

Zhen Zong *998–1022*
Ren Zong *1023–57*
Wei Zong *1101–25*

SOUTHERN SONG *1127–1279*
Gao Zong *1127–62*
Li Zong *1225–64*

Liao (in part of north China) *907–1125*

Jin (in part of north China) *1115–1234*

Yuan *1206–1368*
(destroyed the Jin in 1234, the southern Song in 1279)
Tai Zu (Chenghiz Khan) *1206–27*
Shi Zu (Khubilai Khan) *1260–94*
Cheng Zong (Timur) *1295–1307*

Ming *1368–1644*
Hongwu *1368–98*
Jianwen *1399–1402*
Yongle *1403–24*
Hongxi *1425*
Xuande *1426–35*
Zhengtong *1436–49*★
Jingtai *1450–6*
Tianshun *1457–64*★
Chenghua *1465–87*
Hongzhi *1488–1505*
Zhengde *1506–21*
Jiajing *1522–66*
Longqing *1567–72*
Wanli *1573–1619*
Taichang *1620*
Tianqi *1621–7*
Chongzhen *1628–44*

★The same emperor ruled during both these reign-periods: he had been carried off by the Mongols and was replaced on the throne by a brother, but was later able to return and rule again.

Qing *1616–1911*
(founded in Manchuria in 1616, conquered Beijing in 1644)
Tianming *1616–26*
Tiancong *1627–35*★
Chongde *1636–43*★
Shunzhi *1644–61*
Kangxi *1662–1722*
Yongzheng *1723–35*
Qianlong *1736–95*
Jiaqing *1796–1820*
Daoguang *1821–50*
Xianfeng *1851–61*
Tongzhi *1862–74*
Guangxu *1875–1908*
Xuangtong *1909–11*

★The same emperor ruled during both these reign-periods: until the Ming dynasty, it had been common for reign-periods to change during the course of a single reign, but after 1368 such changes became exceptional.

The Republic of China *1912–49* (still in existence in Taiwan)

Presidents and Heads of State
Sun Yat-sen (Sun Yixian, Sun Zhongshan) *1912*
Yuan Shikai *1912–16*
Li Yuanhong *1916–17*
Feng Guozhang *1917–18*★
Xu Shichang *1918–22*★
Li Yuanhong *1922–3*★
Cao Kun *1923–4*★
Duan Qirui *1924–6*★
Sun Yat-sen *1921–5*★
Wang Jingwei *1925–7*★
Hu Hanmin *1927–8*
Chiang Kai-shek (Jiang Jieshi) *1928–75*
Jiang Jingguo *1978–88*
Li Denghui *1988–2000*
Chen Shuibian *2000–*

★From 1917 until 1927 there were two rival governments in China, one in the north, enjoying international recognition, and one in the south, backed by the Chinese Nationalist Party. The southern government was led until his death in 1925 by Sun Yat-sen, though he did not take the title of president until 1921.

From 1926 the northern government was totally dominated by the warlord Zhang Zuolin and had no chief executive. It collapsed in 1927. Zhang Zuolin fled from Beijing the following year shortly before it was occupied by Nationalist forces.

THE PEOPLE'S REPUBLIC OF CHINA *1949–*

Heads of State / Presidents
Mao Zedong *1949–59*
Liu Shaoqi *1959–68*★
Dong Biwu *1968–75*★
Li Xiannian *1983–8*★
Yang Shangkun *1988–93*
Jiang Zemin *1993–*

★Liu Shaoqi was unconstitutionally removed from office during the Cultural Revolution – legally he remained head of state until his death in 1969. After his death his deputy, Dong Biwu, became acting head of state. The post was not officially filled again during the period of the Cultural Revolution and was abolished by the constitution promulgated in 1975, its powers being transferred to the general secretary of the Chinese Communist Party. The current constitution, adopted in December 1982, created a presidency: Li Xiannian became the first president in June 1983.

Premiers
Zhou Enlai *1949–76*
Hua Guofeng *1976–80*
Zhao Ziyang *1980–87*
Li Peng *1987–98*
Zhu Rongji *1998–*

Party Chairmen / General Secretaries
Mao Zedong *1949–76*
Hua Guofeng *1976–81*
Hu Yaobang *1981–7*
Zhao Ziyang *1987–9*
Jiang Zemin *1989–*

Further Reading

General

BARTKE, W. *Who's Who in the People's Republic of China*, 3rd. ed. (London, Saur 1991)

NEEDHAM, J. *Science and Civilisation in China*, 12 vols (Cambridge, Cambridge University Press 1954–84)

POPULATION CENSUS OFFICE OF THE STATE COUNCIL OF THE PEOPLE'S REPUBLIC OF CHINA AND THE INSTITUTE OF GEOGRAPHY OF THE CHINESE ACADEMY OF SCIENCES *The Population Atlas of China*, English ed. (Oxford, Oxford University Press 1987)

Culture and Society

BALAZS, E. *Chinese Civilization and Bureaucracy* (New Haven, Yale University Press 1964)

BLUNDEN, C. and ELVIN, M. *Cultural Atlas of China* (Oxford, Oxford University Press 1983)

DAWSON, R. *The Chinese Experience* (London, Weidenfeld & Nicolson 1978)

DAWSON, R. (ed.) *The Legacy of China* (Oxford, Oxford University Press 1964)

JOHNSTON, R. F. *Lion and Dragon in Northern China* (London, John Murray 1910; reprinted by Oxford University Press 1986)

Prehistory and Early History

BARNES, G. L. *The Rise of Civilization in East Asia*. (London, Thames & Hudson 1999)

BODDE, Dirk *China's First Unifier* (Leiden, Brill 1938)

CHANG, K. C. *The Archaeology of Ancient China* 4th. ed. (New Haven, Yale University Press 1986)

HO, PING-TI *The Cradle of the East* (Hong Kong, The Chinese University of Hong Kong 1975)

HSU, CHO-YUN *Ancient China in Transition* (Stanford, Stanford University Press 1965)

KEIGHTLEY, D. N. (ed.) *The Origins of Chinese Civilization* (Berkeley, University of California Press 1983)

The Pre-Modern Period

DAWSON, R. *Imperial China* (London, Hutchinson 1972)

GERNET, J. *Daily Life in China on the Eve of the Mongol Invasion* (London, Allen & Unwin 1962)

LOEWE, M. *Everyday Life in Early Imperial China* (London, Batsford 1968)

POLO, MARCO *The Description of the World*, trans. and annot. A. C. Moule and P. Pelliot (London, Routledge 1938)

Modern History

AISIN-GIORO PU YI *From Emperor to Citizen* (Oxford, Oxford University Press 1988)

CHANG, H. P. *Commissioner Lin and the Opium War* (Cambridge, Mass., Harvard University Press 1964)

CHEN, J. *Mao and the Chinese Revolution* (Oxford, Oxford University Press 1965)

CHESNEAUX, J. *Peasant Revolts in China, 1840–1949* (London, Thames & Hudson 1973)

FITZGERALD, C. P. *Communism takes China* (London, BPC 1971)

FLEMING, P. *The Siege at Peking* (Oxford, Oxford University Press 1983)

HSU, I. C. Y. *The Rise of Modern China* (Oxford, Oxford University Press 1970)

JOHNSTON, R. F. *Twilight in the Forbidden City* (London, Gollancz 1934; reprinted by Oxford University Press 1985)

MCALEAVY, H. *The Modern History of China* (London, Weidenfeld & Nicolson 1967)

MCALEAVY, H. *A Dream of Tartary* (London, Allen & Unwin 1963)

SNOW, E. *Red Star over China*, rev. and enlarged ed. (London, Gollancz 1968)

TENG, S. Y. *The Taiping Rebellion and the Western Powers* (Oxford, Oxford University Press 1971)

China since 1949

BONAVIA, D. *The Chinese* (London, Allen Lane 1981)

CLAYRE, A. *The Heart of the Dragon* (London, Collins/Harvill 1984)

HINTON, W. *Fanshen* (Harmondsworth, Penguin 1972)

HINTON, W. *Shenfan* (London, Secker & Warburg 1983)

HORN, J. S. *'Away with all pests . . . '* (London, Hamlyn 1969)
JENNER, D. *Letters from Peking* (Oxford, Oxford University Press 1967)

Philosophy and Religion

CONFUCIUS *The Analects* (Harmondsworth, Penguin 1979)
CREEL, H. G. *Chinese Thought from Confucius to Mao Tse-tung* (London, Eyre & Spottiswood 1954)
LAO TZU *Tao Te Ching* (Harmondsworth, Penguin 1963)
MENCIUS *[The Book of Mencius]* (Harmondsworth, Penguin 1970)
WALEY, A. *Three Ways of Thought in Ancient China* (London, Allen & Unwin 1939)

Literature and Art

CAO XUEQIN *The Story of the Stone*, 5 vols. (Harmondsworth, Penguin 1973–86)
JENNER, W. (ed.) *Modern Chinese Stories* (Oxford, Oxford University Press 1970)
LU XUN *Silent China* (Oxford, Oxford University Press 1973)
SICKMAN, L. and SOPER, A. *The Art and Architecture of China* (Harmondsworth, Penguin 1956)
SULLIVAN, M. *The Arts of China* (London, Thames & Hudson 1973)
SULLIVAN, M. *Symbols of Eternity: the art of landscape painting in China* (Oxford, Oxford University Press 1979)
ZHAO SHULI *Rhymes of Li Youcai and other stories* (Beijing, Foreign Languages Press 1950)

Relations with Minorities and Neighbouring Peoples

BELL, C. *Tibet: past and present* (Oxford, Oxford University Press 1924; reprinted by Asian Educational Services 1992)
CHEN, V. *Sino-Russian Relations in the Seventeenth Century* (Dordrecht, Nijhoff 1966)
GOULLART, P. *Forgotten Kingdom* (London, John Murray 1957)
HOPKIRK, P. *Trespassers on the Roof of the World* (Oxford, Oxford University Press 1983)
LATTIMORE, O. *Inner Asian Frontiers of China* 2nd. ed. (Oxford, Oxford University Press 1951)

LATTIMORE, O. *Studies in Frontier History* (Oxford, Oxford University Press 1962)

WU, A. K. *Turkistan Tumult* (London, Methuen 1940; reprinted by Oxford University Press 1984)

YOUNGHUSBAND, F. *India and Tibet* (London, John Murray 1910; reprinted by Oxford University Press 1985)

Historical Gazetteer

Numbers in bold refer to main text

Beijing The capital of all China since the reign of Khubilai Khan, except for a short time at the beginning of the Ming dynasty and for most of the period from the Nationalist Revolution of 1911 until 1949. The layout of the Mongol city is still largely preserved. Beijing is a planned city, all the main streets running north–south or east–west in a grid pattern. The city is increasingly looking like any modern city anywhere but is liberally scattered with ancient buildings, and a few areas, such as that north of the Bei Hai park, still maintain their ancient character. Remnants of the walls of the Mongol city can still be seen in the north-west suburbs along Xitucheng Road. The white dagoba of Miaoying Temple (often called White Pagoda Temple) also survives from the Mongol period, dating from 1271. All the other major ancient buildings in Beijing are of Ming and Qing date. The former imperial palace, the Forbidden City, was completely rebuilt in the early 1400s, with much renovation and rebuilding during the Qing dynasty. It is staggering in its scale and requires much longer than the half-day al-lowed to most tour groups to be fully appreciated. Immediately to its south is the huge Tianan Men Square, with the Great Hall of the People and the main museums of Beijing facing each other across its northern end. At its southern end are the mausoleum housing the body of Mao Zedong, and the Zheng Yang Gate or Qian Men.

The Temple of Heaven, with its round buildings and blue roofs, is mainly Ming in date and is both unusual and very striking. Emperors came here to offer prayers and sacrifices so that heaven might bless the crops and provide good harvests. The lesser-known Temples of the Earth, the Sun and the Moon are much less impressive, but the Temple of the Earth in the north of the city is well-preserved and worth a short visit. There is a good restaurant in one of its old buildings. Not far away to the south are the Yong He Gong, former residence of the crown prince who became the Yongzheng Emperor in 1723. After his accession it was turned into a Tibetan Buddhist temple. The huge lacquered wooden statue of the Bodhisattva Guanyin in its most northerly hall, carved from a single tree-trunk, is a very fine work of art. Just across the road and down a side-street is the Temple of Confucius, with some fine old halls and gate buildings in very early style. An ancient cypress to the left of the main hall is said to have 'rooted out evil' by dropping a branch on a corrupt official of the Ming dynasty!

Most of the old city walls of Beijing were demolished after 1949, but a few remnants have recently been restored. One short section with a gate tower is at Dong Bian Men, just east of the main Beijing railway station. A little way north of here, near the Jian Guo Men interchange, is the old astronomical observatory, originally constructed in 1442, with various instruments dating from the Ming and Qing dynasties.

The Yi He Yuan Summer Palace lies on the north-western edge of the city. Most of its buildings were completely reconstructed in the late 19th century after they had been destroyed by the Anglo-French invasion force in 1860. On the north side of the Hill of Great Longevity, Wan Shou Shan, stands the Many Treasures Pagoda, Duo Bao Ta, decorated with glazed tiles of several colours and hung with bells which chime in the wind. As it could not be burned, it survived the destruction of 1860 more or less intact and is a relic of the late 18th century. The stone hull of the famous marble boat at the edge of Kunming Lake near the western end of the hill also dates from the 18th century, though the superstructure was entirely rebuilt after 1860. Apartments can be seen in the palace where the Empress Dowager Ci Xi kept the Guangxu Emperor in detention.

The most famous sites outside the city are the *Ming Tombs* and the *Great Wall*. The tombs of thirteen emperors of the Ming dynasty are situated at various points around the edge of a valley where the Yan Shan mountains rise up from the North China Plain. The earliest and largest is that of the third Ming Emperor (Yongle reign-period, 1403–24). The tomb is called the Chang Ling. From the walls around its tomb-mound most of the other tombs can be seen, including the Ding Ling, tomb of the thirteenth emperor, the only one which has so far been excavated. It is possible to descend into the underground tomb chamber of the Ding Ling, but there is little to be seen there now as the excavated objects are displayed in side halls at the tomb and in the main hall at the Chang Ling.

It is usual to combine a visit to the Ming Tombs with a visit to the Badaling section of Great Wall nearby to make a one-day excursion. A lengthy section of the Wall at Badaling has been restored and it is an impressive sight, snaking its way up and down the mountains and along ridges. This section, like all those usually visited today, dates from the last rebuilding during the Ming dynasty. Slightly further from the city, but near enough also to be combined with a visit to the Ming Tombs in a single day, is the Mutianyu section of Wall; there are usually far fewer tourists at this section. A stiff climb up stone steps leads from the parking area

The Putuo Zong Sheng Temple, or 'Little Potala', at Chengde

to the Wall itself, but this can be avoided by using a cable-car. A fairly short section of Wall has been fully restored here and it is reasonably easy to walk as far as the unrestored portions. The hills at Mutianyu are more heavily wooded than those near Badaling.

A long way north of Beijing city is one of the most spectacular sections of Great Wall at Simatai. Visiting the Wall here is a full day excursion from the city on its own. Quite a lengthy walk leads from the parking area to the Wall itself, which runs up a very steep hillside from a deep river valley (where there is now a small reservoir). At the crest of the hill the Wall follows the edge of a high cliff which drops sheer behind it for hundreds of feet. Restoration is still going on here. Only a few short sections of the Wall have been restored; much of it is in poor condition and heavily overgrown. It is quite obvious to anyone who has walked long stretches of the Wall that the much-repeated story about it being visible from the moon is just a myth. **20, 54, 77, 84, 97, 110, 120, 125, 129, 132, 133, 136, 139, 160, 172, 187, 205, 213**

Chengde (Hebei)   Formerly often known by its Manchu name of Jehol, this is the site of a large Summer Palace built when the Qing dynasty was at its zenith. Work began in 1703 and major construction continued until 1790. It was neglected after 1820, however, as it gained a reputation as an unlucky place after the Jiaqing Emperor was struck by lightning and died there in that year. The imperial court ceased to use it from then until 1860, when it became a refuge for the emperor and his retinue after the Anglo-French invaders occupied Beijing. The Xianfeng Emperor remained at Chengde until his death in August 1861, the last time any emperor resided there. Subsequently the eastern palace complex was destroyed by fire; only its stone foundations can be seen today. The main palace area has been restored and includes some fine buildings, particularly the main ceremonial and audience hall built entirely with *nanmu* wood from south-west China. A large area of lakes and pavilions behind the palace has been restored to something like its original glory, but most of the rest of the walled park has suffered badly from long neglect.

Outside of the palace proper are a number of very fine temples, several of which have now been restored. At least one has a small community of monks in residence, adherents of the Tibetan form of Buddhism, many of them from Inner Mongolia. The Pu Ning Si (Temple of Universal Peace) is in a mixed Sino-Tibetan style of architecture and contains a huge wooden statue of a many-armed Guanyin. It was built in 1755 to celebrate the subjugation of the Mongols of Junggaria. Several smaller temples lie to the south of the Pu Ning Si. The most interesting is the Pu Le Si (Temple of Universal Happiness), dating from 1766, with its round main hall reminiscent of buildings at the Temple of Heaven in Beijing. The carved and gilded ceiling of this hall is superb. Beneath it is a large wooden mandala housing a metal statue of the tantric Buddhist deity Shamvara embracing his consort Vajravarahi.

West of the Pu Ning Si are two very large temples mainly in Tibetan style. The biggest was modelled on the Potala in Lhasa and was constructed between 1767 and 1771. The buildings within the red wall at the highest level of the temple were de-stroyed by fire at some time in the past and have been completely rebuilt recently. The other was modelled on the Trashilhunpo lamasery in Xigaze and dates from 1780. It was used to house the Banqen Lama when he came to congratulate the Qianlong Emperor on his seventieth birthday. The gilded roof of its central hall, with huge dragons mounted on its angles, is quite magnificent. From the terraces of these temples and from parts of the park it is possible to see some of the extraordinary rock formations around Chengde, particularly the famous Club Rock which rises from a ridge to the east. The temples and palace buildings at Chengde constitute one of the largest surviving assemblages of traditional Chinese architecture outside Beijing. **148, 160, 161, 168, 183**

Chengdu (Sichuan) This is now a very dirty city which has little to recommend it except as a starting point for visits to Tibet and other parts of the lovely province of Sichuan of which it is the capital. The zoo has several pandas. The River-viewing Pavilion Park is worth a visit for those interested in bamboo – about 100 different kinds are cultivated there. A short drive north of the city is the Bao Guang Si (Divine Light Temple) with a fine stone pagoda said to date from the late Tang dynasty. It also has a hall with 500 statues of Arhats, constructed in 1851. Rather further away, to the north-west, is the ancient Dujiangyan irrigation system, first built in the 3rd century BC and still in use. It diverts water from the Min River to irrigate the Sichuan Basin around Chengdu. **73**

Chongqing (Sichuan) A very polluted city, though it has improved a little recently as its industries have been converted to using electricity from hydro-electric power stations instead of burning coal. Until recently within Sichuan, it is now a municipality of provincial rank. It stands at the confluence of the Jialing and Yangtze Rivers, and is usually visited by those boarding or leaving the river-boats which sail through the Yangtze Gorges. There are pandas in its zoo and it has some fascinating markets – this is an excellent place to buy Sichuan pepper. There is a noticeable absence of bicycles in Chongqing because it is so hilly. A few areas of old housing still cling to the slopes here and there and are worth looking at. The Nationalist government made Chongqing its capital after the Japanese invaded eastern China and took Nanjing. It was out of reach of Japanese armies but was heavily bombed from the air. Old air-raid shelters tunnelled into the hillsides can still be seen in many places and are sometimes in use as workshops or cafés.

A short distance outside the city are the Northern and Southern Hot Springs, set in pleasant parks. The countryside around Chongqing is interesting and attractive and it is worthwhile to drive out into it and explore a village or two. **184**

Datong (Shanxi) Situated in a major coal-mining area, Datong is a grimy, industrial city. It is only just south of the Great Wall and has a very dry climate with cold winters. Though it is not on the main tourist routes, it possesses not only some extremely fine old temples but also a superb set of Buddhist cave-temples of very early date and so is well worth a visit. One of the states established in north China by invaders from north of the Wall during the period of disunity after the fall of the Han dynasty established its capital here from AD 386 until 494. Virtually all the major work on the Yungang caves just outside Datong was done during this period of the Northern Wei dynasty. The caves are one of the three or four finest examples of Buddhist cave-temples in all China.

The Upper and Lower Hua Yan Temples stand in the west of the city itself. They were first built during the Liao dynasty in 1122 and largely rebuilt in 1140 after a fire. The main hall of the temples is a very fine and rare surviving example of Chinese architecture of this period. It contains three wooden statues of Buddhas carved in 1427; the walls are decorated with Qing dynasty murals. Another building, used for storing Buddhist scriptures, dates from 1038 and is an even rarer example of architecture of that time. It contains a superb set of clay sculptures of Buddhas, bodhisattvas, disciples and so on made during the Liao dynasty.

The main buildings of the Shan Hua Temple in the south of the city are also early, dating from the Jin dynasty. The main halls were erected in the years 1128–43, and a tall pavilion to the west dates from 1154. The three statues of Buddhas in one of the halls, though restored during the Qing dynasty, preserve much of their original Jin style.

Datong also boasts the earliest sur-viving Nine Dragon Wall in China, which was erected in 1392 in front of the residence of one of the sons of the first Ming emperor. It is famous among railway enthusiasts for its loco-motive factory, the last in China to build steam engines. Production ceased at the end of 1989 and now diesel and electric locomotives are built there, but it still carries out repairs on the decreasing number of steam engines that remain in use on the Chinese railway system. **95**

Dunhuang (Gansu) This little oasis town isolated in the desert in northern Gansu would attract scant notice were it not for the superb series of Buddhist cave-temples in a cliff nearby. There are hundreds of caves, many of them decorated from floor to ceiling with murals and statues, and dating from as early as the 4th century AD until as late as the Yuan dynasty. This is the finest collection of Buddhist art anywhere in China. Unfortunately many of the caves are now rarely on view, but even so there is plenty to fill at least a half-day's visit. Try to see some of the very early caves and a few dating from the Tang dynasty. Cave 96 contains a very large seated Buddha originally modelled in the 7th century. Cave 17, a small cavern in a side wall of Cave 16, is famous as the cave in which was discovered a large cache of ancient documents, all dating from before AD 997. Many of these were acquired by Western archaeologists and are now in London and Paris. They in-clude the world's oldest surviving printed book, a copy of the *Diamond Sutra* dated equivalent to AD 868

(now in the British Library).

Set amid huge sand-dunes on the edge of the Dunhuang oasis is a small lake of fresh water, the Crescent Moon Lake, which has survived among the dunes for millennia with-out ever being swallowed by the sands. For a small fee it is possible to take a ride on a Bactrian camel (two-humped) to view the lake, which attracts large numbers of tourists in the high season. Just west of the present town are the remains of the old town of Dunhuang. Here the ancient Silk Road between China and countries to the west divided into two, one route passing to the north of the great Taklimakan Desert and one to the south. The White Horse Pagoda which stands in the south of the old town dates from the Later Qin dy-nasty (*c.* AD 400). **95, 99**

Emei Shan (Sichuan) The best known of the four holy Buddhist mountains in China. This is the west-ern one, sacred to the Bodhisattva Samantabhadra (in Chinese Puxian), who is said to have stopped here while flying past on his magic elephant. At one of the many temples on the mountain there is a small pool where the elephant is supposed to have bathed to refresh itself on the journey. The pool would scarcely contain a large pig, but according to the legend it mystically grew to accommodate the elephant! At the Wan Nian Si (Temple of the Myriad Ages) there is an ancient bronze statue of the Bod-hisattva seated on his elephant. Cast in AD 980, it weighs more than 60 tons.

There is now a road which reaches to the Lei Dong Ping (Thunder Cave

Terrace) high up the mountain, and a cable-car from near the end of this road to the summit ridge. It is thus easy to reach the summit, more than 10,000 feet high. Most tourists now take this easy route up and down, perhaps with a night on the top of the mountain to be able to see the sunrise and have time to look at the large, almost brand-new, temple on the ridge. For those with the time and the interest, and a fair degree of fitness, it is worth making at least the descent on foot. Allow two or three days to walk all the way down. Temples provide accommodation on the way. The paths up the mountain follow different routes from the motorable road and are usually fairly quiet now. The vegetation of Mount Emei is extremely fine, with luxuriant forests of differing composition according to altitude. There are several species of rhododendrons on the upper slopes and Dove Trees (*Davidia*) on the mid-levels. There is also a good chance of seeing some of the monkeys that live on the mountain (Tibetan macaques). They are quite used to people and will come to be fed (and pick pockets!); it is useless to try to give them a few peanuts at a time – they will ignore those offered and snatch the whole bag! It is also easy to see small squirrels in the trees and birds of many kinds are abundant. **92**

Guangzhou (Guangdong) Still perhaps better known in the West as Canton, this was the main port for trade between China and Europe from the 16th century until 1842. Although it has since been surpassed by Shanghai, it remains a major port

and commercial centre, benefiting from its proximity to Hong Kong. Many Western-style buildings can still be seen on Shamian Island in the Pearl River, site of British and French concessions from 1861 until 1949. Guangzhou was an important port long before Europeans reached the China coast. A mosque in the city still has a minaret which was erected during the Tang dynasty, at a time when Arab and Persian ships were regular visitors.

Guangzhou was the scene of fighting during the Opium Wars and was a centre of revolutionary activity during the last years of the Qing dynasty (Sun Yat-sen came from a nearby town). During the troubled period after the 1911 revolution the city served as the Republican capital from time to time. It was occupied by the Japanese from 1938 until 1945.

There are few surviving ancient buildings. The Liu Rong Si (Temple of the Six Banyan Trees) has a pagoda built during the Song dynasty, in 1097. The temple is usually crowded with devotees making offerings to Buddha and burning incense. The Guang Xiao Si (Temple of Illustrious Piety) is one of the oldest complexes of buildings in the far south of China. Two small iron pagodas in its grounds were cast in the 10th century. Its halls are mainly of the late Ming and early Qing dynastic periods. The Guangzhou Museum is housed in a five-storey building in the Yue Xiu Park which was originally erected in 1380 but has undergone much rebuilding and restoration since. The Chen Family Ancestral Temple is a highly ornate complex of buildings constructed in the 1890s.

The Sun Yat-sen Memorial Hall is a good example of the mixed Chinese and Western style of architecture that developed during the 1920s. It was erected in 1929–31, shortly after Dr Sun's death. Scattered around the city are several other monuments of various sorts to heroes of uprisings and revolutions.

The Orchid Garden in the north of the city is an attractive haven from the general noise and bustle; a cup of orchid tea in one of its pavilions can be a very welcome refreshment. On a very much larger scale are the South China Botanic Gardens in the north-east suburbs, where a great variety of hot-climate plants from China and other parts of the world are grown.

The north Chinese have a saying about the Cantonese diet: 'They eat everything with legs except a table and everything with wings except an aeroplane.' There are some extraordinary things on sale in the food markets. Only those with strong stomachs should venture to take a look. If you fancy trying snake or other exotic food there are restaurants which specialize in serving such items.

An hour or so's drive from Guangzhou takes you to Foshan, where there are ceramic and handicrafts factories and a large Daoist temple originally built in the Song dynasty, rebuilt in 1372 and extensively renovated several times thereafter. It is decorated with highly ornate tilework and includes an old stage for performances of Chinese opera. **15,** **20, 33, 134, 146, 150, 152, 159, 162, 175, 180, 237, 239**

Guilin (Guangxi Zhuang Autonomous Region) It is the amazing scenery around this town which has made it famous. It stands on the banks of the Li River in a humid, sub-tropical region of lakes, rivers and rice-paddy out of which rise extraordinary crags and pinnacles of heavily-eroded limestone. Many millions of years ago the area was beneath the sea and innumerable tiny sea-creatures left deep deposits of their limy shells and skeletons. These deposits compacted and hardened into rock, which was later uplifted and heavily eroded by water. Seeping through cracks in the soluble limestone, the water slowly created ever-wider fissures, eventually creating the landscape seen today. It also opened up tunnels and caverns inside the rock, some of them of staggering proportions.

The highlight of any visit to Guilin is a journey by boat down the river as far as Yangshuo, a small but increasingly prosperous town some 50 miles (80 km) away. The river meanders among the crags, many of which have fanciful Chinese names derived from their supposed likeness to various creatures and objects. Here and there are small villages, where local ferries cross the river and fishermen hang their nets to dry. The famous fishing cormorants can often be seen resting and sunning themselves on bamboo punts pulled partly up onto the shore. They are usually used to fish at night. Raised in captivity, they are tame and allow their owners to place a cord around their necks to prevent them swallowing large fish. Other common sights along the river are water-buffaloes, sometimes seen in quite deep water grazing on water-weed. Birds and butterflies are usually numerous over and near the water. Lunch on the boat may include local specialities, perhaps freshwater shrimps purchased from fishermen on their punts as the boat passes downstream. Menus in Guilin can be rather startling – local specialities include soft-shelled terrapin, snake and pangolin. I was once offered a special menu which included all these as well as 'things from the mountains' – I did not have the courage to find out exactly what 'things' they were!

Yangshuo now seems to rely principally on the tourist trade for its livelihood. The street by the river is lined with stalls selling every kind of souvenir and curio. T-shirts are usually very cheap here but bargaining is essential. Beware of 'antiques' – they are virtually all fakes. A walk away from the river into the town quickly leaves the tourist area behind. There is an interesting local market with all kinds of produce, including Chinese herbal medicines. If you have time, take a ramble out of town into the countryside beyond – almost everything to be seen is interesting.

Guilin also has its markets, both for tourists and for locals. The night-markets near the river are the worst tourist-traps. There is an interesting but rather pitiful bird-market on the street above the river during the day. There is a still a passion for keeping cage-birds in China, particularly among elderly men. It is believed that keeping birds in small cages encourages them to sing more, so the cages are usually much too small. But at least the birds are taken out for 'walks' in their prisons and can often be seen hung on the branches of trees in parks while their owners chat or play cards or Chinese chess.

Major landmarks within the town of Guilin include Elephant Rock, which does indeed resemble an elephant drinking water from the river. A number of hills, often with caves in them, can be climbed to gain views over the town and the river. The best known are Fubo Hill and Die Cai Shan. The Qi Xing (Seven Star) Park includes the extraordinary Camel Rock, which really does look like a camel. Just outside the town is the Lu Di (Reed Flute) Cave, an enormous cavern with wonderful formations of stalagmites and stalactites, impressive despite the numbers of visitors and the garish coloured lights used to illuminate them. There is an interesting Neolithic site with a small museum at the Zengpi Cave, south of the town. There are also remnants of a Ming dynasty palace in the town and of tombs of Ming princes to the east. **28 *Gyangze*** (Tibet Autonomous Region) One of the four most important towns in Tibet, situated at an altitude of more than 13,000 feet, to the south-west of Lhasa. The town is dominated by the Zong, a fortification built on a crag rising several hundred feet above the floor of the river valley in which Gyangze lies. In 1904, during the Younghusband expedition, this fort was stormed by British troops (see under Lhasa). Immediately adjacent to the Zong is a large Tibetan monastery originally founded in 1390. It consists of several halls; the most striking building is the Paiknor Chorten, a large pagoda containing numerous rooms decorated with statues and wall paintings of Tibetan Buddhist deities.

Hainan Island   Now elevated to provincial status, this was formerly part of Guangdong province. It is China's tropical paradise, with sandy beaches backed by palm trees. There are virtually no historic monuments here, though there are ethnic minorities in the interior whose customs and lifestyle are of interest. The tropical flora and fauna are also fascinating, though they are under considerable pressure as the island is being rapidly developed.

Hangzhou (Zhejiang)   One of the most attractive cities in China, Hangzhou is the provincial capital. It lies on the north bank of the Qiantang River and the shore of the West Lake, surrounded by green hills and waterways. The southern end of the Grand Canal is here. It was the capital of the Southern Song dynasty and was at that time the largest city in the world. Marco Polo saw it after the Mongols had finally overthrown the Song, when its glories had undoubtedly faded somewhat, but still lauded its 'pre-eminence to all others in the world, in point of grandeur and beauty'.

The lake is divided by causeways, the longest being that constructed in 1089 at the orders of Su Dongpo, renowned as a poet and at that time the prefect of Hangzhou. There are several parks and pavilions on its shores and on islands. On a hill to the north lies the Bao Chu Pagoda, originally built early in the Song dynasty but rebuilt several times, most recently in 1933. On the north-western shore stands the Temple of Yue Fei, a general whose remains were interred here in 1163; he had successfully led Song forces against those of the Jin dynasty, pushing them back towards the Yellow River, but was betrayed at the height of his success and murdered in prison. He had gained a high reputation among the people, however, and was later elevated to the rank of a god. As early as 1221 a temple was erected on the site of his grave, but most of the buildings to be seen today are from the Qing dynasty.

South of the lake, on the bank of the Qiantang River, stands the Liu He (Six Harmonies) Pagoda. First erected in 970, it was burned in 1121 and rebuilt in 1153. The brick core of the pagoda has survived from this time, though the wooden galleries around it are much later, having being most recently rebuilt in 1899.

Perhaps the most impressive buildings in and around Hangzhou are at the Ling Yin (Soul's Retreat) Temple in a valley a little way west of the lake. This is one of the most important Buddhist temples in China, much visited by pilgrims as well as tourists. It is of very ancient origins, but the current buildings are 19th-century. Some of the statues are probably older and there are two small stone pagodas in front of the main hall which date from the 10th century. On the stone cliffs opposite are numerous carvings and grottoes dating from the 10th–14th centuries.

The Hangzhou area is famous for its tea, especially the renowned Long Jing (Dragon Well) tea. It is possible to visit tea-plantations and see how the leaves are processed. This is also a centre of silk production and one can visit factories to see how the silk is spun and woven. **19, 97, 100, 118, 119, 127**

Harbin (Heilongjiang) The provincial capital of the most northerly of the three Manchurian provinces. It originated as a railway town on the junction of the Russian-built railways to Vladivostok and Port Arthur (the original Trans-Siberian Railway ran across Chinese territory here). There are many surviving Russian buildings, including former Orthodox churches. There is also a memorial to the Russians who died fighting the Japanese in Manchuria in 1945. Harbin is really only worth visiting in winter, when temperatures drop a very long way below freezing and the Sungari River, on which the city stands, freezes solid enough for lorries to be driven across it. Blocks of ice are cut from the river and taken to the parks, where they are carved into statues and built into pavilions, often lit by electric lights inside the ice. These can be a wonderful spectacle at night but make sure you take plenty of very warm clothing! **165**

Heng Shan (Shanxi and Hunan) A good example of the problems involved in romanizing Chinese characters: there are *two* sacred mountains in China called Heng Shan. The characters are different, but when romanized the distinction disappears. Both these mountains are among the five sacred peaks of the directions (east, south, west, north and centre). One is the northern sacred peak, the other the southern.

The northern Heng Shan is in Shanxi province, to the south-east of Datong. The main summit is more than 6,500 feet high. There are about a dozen surviving temples and other places of interest on the mountain, of which the most interesting is the Xuan Kong Si (Temple Hanging in the Air). It is built on the face of a cliff, using caves for the rear of the halls, with wooden verandahs and galleries fastened to the rock. The foundation of the temple dates back to the 6th century, though the surviving buildings are mainly from the Qing dynasty.

The southern Heng Shan is in central Hunan province and is much lower, no more than about 4,000 feet high. It is also much more accessible, with a motorable road reaching more or less to the summit. As the climate is warm and moist the vegetation is luxuriant, and a large botanic garden has been established here. On the mountain and its foothills stand numerous temples and other buildings, mainly from the Qing dynasty. The main Temple to the Southern Sacred Peak is a fine large complex of buildings, some of which still preserve Ming and Song dynasty architectural styles. **92**

Hua Shan (Shaanxi) The western sacred peak, a little way to the east of Xi'an. This is a precipitous mountain, with some very dangerous paths; its main peak is more than 8,000 feet high. The scenery is spectacular and a number of temples and pavilions are scattered about the mountain, including Daoist temples. **92**

Huang Shan (Anhui) This mountain area ranks with Guilin as some of the most renowned scenery in China. The highest peaks rise to just over 6,000 feet. The hard rock of the area has been naturally sculpted into amazing shapes, with lofty pinnacles and sharp ridges rising from the forests that clothe most of the slopes. The flora is very fine and many different kinds of birds can be seen here, especially during migration periods. There are waterfalls and hot springs. Scattered around the area, from the foot of the range to high up among the peaks, are several hotels and guest-houses of varying standards. Huang Shan is now reasonably easily accessible, with its own airport, and attracts large numbers of tourists.

Jiu Hua Shan (Anhui) This is the southern holy Buddhist mountain of China and is one of the most active centres of Chinese Buddhism today. Numerous temples with large numbers of monks are scattered around the slopes. The mountain has several peaks, the highest rising to rather more than 4,000 feet. There are many streams, waterfalls, caves and curious rock formations among the bamboo groves and forests on the hillsides. **92**

Kashgar (Xinjiang Uighur AR) In the far west of China, this is a very interesting Muslim town inhabited mainly by Uighurs, a Turkic people. It was an important point on the old Silk Road, where the northern and southern routes around the Taklimakan Desert met. There are a couple of large old Muslim tombs and a large mosque in the town, as well as the remains of ancient abandoned cities in the desert outside it. The most interesting sight of Kashgar, however, is the Sunday Bazaar. People of several different ethnic groups (Uighurs, Uzbeks, Kazakhs, Kirgiz) come from miles around to buy and sell. The trading in horses, donkeys, sheep and camels is especially interesting to watch, but the bazaar is very large and a vast range of merchandise is on sale. **99, 100, 130, 160**

Kunming (Yunnan) The chief city of the far south-western province of China. Sited at an altitude of almost 6,000 feet not very far north of the tropics, it enjoys one of the best climates in all China. Early in the year (January to March) the camellias for which it is famous come into bloom. There is a good collection of these beautiful flowering shrubs at the Botanic Gardens north of the city near the Black Dragon Pool. Several large old camellia trees grow in the grounds around the Pool itself, which is fed by a spring of clear water. There are also ancient camellias at the Golden Temple, a Daoist temple founded during the Ming dynasty and rebuilt in the early Qing in 1671; one of the trees there is said to have been planted in the early 1600s. The main hall of the temple itself is made entirely of bronze weighing more than 200 tons. West of the city is the Qiongzhu Si (Bamboo Temple) with its set of 500 clay figures of Arhats modelled in the 1880s. To the south is a large lake, the

Dian Chi, surrounded by hills. On its western side cliffs rise steeply above the shore. Cut into this cliff is a gallery with niches for figures of deities. Called the Long Men (Dragon Gate), work on this began in 1781 and was completed in 1853. Along the road leading to the Dragon Gate are a number of temples and pavilions, including two large Buddhist temples, the Huating Si and the Taihua Si. A forested area around the temples contains a good variety of vegetation, including rhododendrons, camellias and daphnes.

A moderate drive to the south-east of Kunming is the extraordinary Lunan Stone Forest. It is possible to visit it in one day from Kunming, but it is worth spending a night there. The local people belong to one of the ethnic minorities, the Sani, a branch of the Yi. The Forest itself is an area of limestone, heavily eroded into pinnacles and screens of bizarre shape. **185, 211**

Lanzhou (Gansu) Situated on the banks of the Yellow River, this large industrial city has little to recommend it except for an excellent museum. It is the home of the famous bronze 'flying horse', though unfortunately this is often absent, on loan to exhibitions elsewhere. There are also superb collections of Neolithic pottery painted with swirling patterns and of ancient artefacts from the eastern end of the Silk Road, including fragments of books written on strips of bamboo, 2,000 years old. A Han dynasty bronze army of warriors in chariots (much less than life-size) is also on display. On a hill above the Yellow

River stands the White Pagoda. Its base dates from the Mongol period and its upper part is Ming. **15, 83**

Leshan (Sichuan) Situated at the confluence of the Min and Dadu Rivers, the major sight of Leshan is the Great Buddha carved out of the solid rock of a cliff rising above the Min. At well over 200 feet high, this is the largest image of Buddha in China and is said to be the largest seated Buddha in the world. It took some 90 years to carve, in the years 713–803 during the Tang dynasty. A pagoda on top of the cliff nearby was built during the Song dynasty, with later repairs and restoration.

Lhasa (Tibet AR) The capital of Tibet is situated on the bank of a river among mountains at an altitude of 12,000 feet on the high Tibetan plateau. At one time one of the most inaccessible places in the world, there are now regular flights to the nearby airport from Chengdu in Sichuan and from Kathmandu in Nepal. Visitors arriving by air from these much lower places can expect to feel the altitude keenly for some days. There has been much new building going on in Lhasa recently and the character of the city is changing. It is still dominated by the Potala, however. Perched on a rocky prominence well above the rest of the city, this palace of the Dalai Lama contains a multitude of rooms. Many are shrines containing a great number and variety of religious statues and other images, but one side of the structure consists of residential quarters for the Dalai Lama and his entourage, unoccupied during his current exile. There are good views over the city and its surroundings from the top of the Potala.

The Jokhang is one of Tibet's holiest shrines, dating from the mid-7th century. It is a highly-ornate structure containing long rows of prayer-wheels, where traditional butter-lamps burn in their thousands in front of the many holy images. One of the most precious relics is a gold statue of Sakyamuni brought to Tibet by a Chinese princess who married the Tibetan king in AD 641. The gilded roof-ornaments of the temple look splendid, gleaming in the strong sunshine which usually bathes Lhasa. In front of the temple there are usually many Tibetan pilgrims performing prostrations and a market is held in the street which runs round it.

Three major lamaseries stand in and around Lhasa. To the west is Drepung, founded in 1416. Once the largest lamasery in Tibet, with 10,000 monks, it now houses about 500. On the northern edge of the city is Sera, founded in 1419. Ganden, a little way to the east, was almost totally destroyed during the Cultural Revolution and has to date been only partially rebuilt. Drepung and Sera are large and magnificent complexes of buildings full of treasures of Tibetan religious art.

During the second half of the 19th century a sort of competition developed among European travellers to see who could manage to reach Lhasa. One of the most persistent was the Russian Nikolai Przevalski, who made four journeys into Tibet in the hope of reaching the fabled city. The first time he ran out of supplies well short of his destination, and on another occasion illness forced him to turn back. In 1879 he was stopped by Tibetan officials and soldiers about a week's march north of Lhasa and told that he must go no further, an order with which he could only comply. In 1890 Prince Henri d'Orléans and Gabriel Bonvalot reached a point much closer to the city before they also were stopped and turned away. The great explorer of Central Asia, Sven Hedin, made an attempt in 1901 but was likewise foiled by the Tibetans. Not until 1904 did any Westerner succeed in reaching the holy city, and then it was a fully-equipped British military expedition which arrived there, escorting Francis Younghusband, a political officer in the British Indian service, who had come to negotiate a treaty with the Tibetans on the Sikkim–Tibet frontier and on trade between Tibet and India. A number of battles were fought along the route from Sikkim through the Chumbi valley to Gyangze and then on to Lhasa, including one engagement just below the summit of the 16,500-foot Karo La pass. This was probably the highest-altitude land battle ever fought. Strangely, Anglo-Tibetan relations seem to have improved dramatically after this short war, for in 1910, when a Chinese army entered Lhasa, the Dalai Lama fled to India. **226, 229, 230**

Luoyang (Henan) This city ranks with Xi'an as one of the ancient capital cities of China. During the Zhou dynasty there was a city in the area which was at first a subsidiary capital but became the main capital after 771 BC. There was also a capital city here during the Han and Tang dynasties as well as during several lesser dynasties. The city today is scarcely any larger than it was during the Sui dynasty, 1,400 years ago. What is believed to be the oldest Buddhist temple in China stands to the east. The Bai Ma Si (White Horse Temple) was founded in AD 68, though the existing buildings are much later; the oldest structure still to be seen there is a pagoda first built in 1175.

The most important site near Luoyang lies just south of the city on the banks of the River Yi. At Long Men is a fine collection of Buddhist cave-temples and niches cut into the cliffs above the river. The earliest date from AD 493 after the capital of the Northern Wei dynasty was moved to Luoyang from Datong. New ones continued to be cut until late in the Tang dynasty. Though much damage was caused later, principally by the removal of statues (or parts of statues) by collectors during the 19th century, there is still much very fine sculpture to be seen. **53, 54, 86, 96, 97, 105, 107, 109, 110**

Nanjing (Jiangsu) Another of the former capital cities of China – the name in fact means 'Southern Capital' – it first became the centre of government of all China at the beginning of the Ming dynasty, but had previously been the capital of several southern states during periods of disunity. After several centuries during which the seat of government was in Beijing, Nanjing again came to prominence during the Republican period when the Nationalists estab-lished their government here until 1938, when the city fell to the Japanese. It suffered severely at their hands, thousands of civilians being slaughtered and many buildings destroyed. At the time Nanjing had scarcely recovered from its sufferings 80 years earlier during the Taiping Rebellion, when the whole area around it was devastated by years of fighting and many tens of thousands died. Most of the important ancient buildings in the vicinity were destroyed at this time, usually by fire, so that today the only really old structures of note here are those built of stone.

Nanjing stands on the south bank of the Yangtze River, and one of the recent structures usually shown off to visitors is the Yangtze River Bridge. Spanning the river was a considerable feat as it is a mile wide; moreover, plenty of clearance had to be left under the bridge for the sizeable ships which sail as far upriver as Wuhan. Construction began in the 1950s under Russian supervision, but after the Sino-Soviet split in 1960 the Russian engineers left, taking the plans with them. Chinese guides sometimes point out the bases of piers near the completed bridge, saying that they were all the Soviets had managed to construct before they left. The Chinese continued work unaided and completed the bridge in 1968. It is a two-tier bridge, with railway tracks on the lower deck and a road above. It is possible to ascend one of the towers at the city end of the structure, from the top of which there are good views across the Yangtze.

Considerable parts of Nanjing city wall survive and some have recently been restored. The Zhonghua Gate in the south of the city is a massive structure with several layers of defences; it was built early in the Ming dynasty. The Drum Tower near the centre of the city was first built in the Ming dynasty, but the wooden upper part was destroyed during the Taiping Rebellion and the existing structure is of late Qing date. There is also an excellent museum where a Han-dynasty jade burial suit is on display.

The other major things to see here are all outside the city proper, among the hills to the east. The largest and most tiring place to visit is the Mausoleum of Sun Yat-sen, with its 392 steps. It was completed in 1929; Dr Sun's body was then moved from Beijing to be interred here. On a hot, humid day the climb to the top of the long flight of steps is scarcely worthwhile. Nearby is a much older tomb, that of the first emperor of the Ming dynasty. Little remains of the complex of buildings that would originally have stood in front of the tomb mound, but the avenue of pairs of stone figures leading to it should not be missed. These are of course slightly older than those at the Ming Tombs near Beijing.

Also in the same area is the Ling Gu Si (Soul Valley Temple). Only one old building survives here, the Wu Liang Dian (Beamless Hall) which is

A general carved in stone stands beside the avenue leading to the tomb of the first Ming emperor outside Nanjing

entirely of brick and therefore could not burn. It was built in the 1380s. The rest of the temple was burned down during the Taiping Rebellion and what can be seen now is all recent; the pagoda was built in 1929. Some distance to the north-east of the city is the Qixia Temple. As at the Ling Gu Si, the wooden halls are no earlier than late Qing. There is a cliff carved with images of Buddhist deities here, some of which date back to the 6th century, but they are almost all in very poor condition. **114, 118, 128, 131, 132, 136, 152, 154, 156, 158, 162, 177, 180, 182, 213, 242**

Putuo Shan (Zhejiang) The eastern holy Buddhist mountain is an island of the Zhoushan (Chusan) group, off the coast of Zhejiang province just south of the Yangtze estuary; its highest point is a little more than 600 feet above sea level. It is said that the first temple was founded here by a Japanese monk in 916. The island is devoted particularly to the veneration of the Bodhisattva Guanyin. Many pilgrims still flock here to make offerings at the many shrines. There are several fine temples, with a number of early Qing halls. **92**

Qingdao (Shandong) A port city on the south coast of the Shandong peninsula. Qingdao was a small place of little significance until after 1897, when it became a German concession. The Germans had noticed the large bay on which it stands and wanted it as a naval base; to this day, a large part of Qingdao consists of western-style buildings erected by the Germans. It is also the site of one of China's best breweries, producing Tsingtao Beer.

The Germans did not hold the city for long, for when the First World War broke out in 1914 the Japanese attacked the German Far Eastern possessions and quickly seized Qingdao. It remained in their hands until 1922 when they were finally persuaded to return it to China.

There are some fine beaches around Qingdao, but they can be very crowded during the summer. The crowds thin in the autumn but the water remains warm well into October and swimming then is very enjoyable. Beware of sharks, though, for when the official season ends on 1 October the shark-nets are taken in – even though there are more sharks inshore in the autumn! Sometimes small ones can be seen in shallow water near the pier, a curious affair with a Chinese-style pavilion at its end. Looking back to the city from here the spires of the Catholic cathedral are very obvious; it is still in active use but is not normally open except during services. There are several pleasant parks, the largest being Zhongshan Park where there is a small botanic garden. The Badaguan district has several very interesting old German buildings. The markets, which are generally clean and well managed, offer a range of shellfish and other marine products, as well as fruits and vegetables from inland.

To the east of the city are the Laoshan hills, a limestone range reaching a height of more than 3,700 feet. The scenery is very attractive, with the hills rising from the sea, and there are several Daoist temples scattered around the slopes. The famous

Laoshan Mineral Water comes from nearby springs; it is the quality of this water which helps to make the local beer so good. **165, 171, 181**

Qufu (Shandong)   During the Zhou dynasty this town was the capital of the state of Lu, a rather small state which would have been of no great note had it not been for the fact that Confucius was born there. When he died in 479 BC he was buried just north of the town. After the acceptance of his teachings as the state philosophy of China increasingly large and majestic buildings were erected at Qufu in his honour. The surviving Kong Miao (Temple of Confucius) and the adjacent Kong Family Mansion, where his direct descendants resided, are one of the largest assemblages of traditional architecture still to be seen in China today. His tomb and those of many of his descendants lie in a large area of attractive woodland enclosed by a wall. There are some fine stone obelisks and statues in the tomb area.

Most of the extant buildings of the Kong Miao and the Mansion are of Ming and Qing date. The main hall of the Temple as seen today dates from 1724; its main outer pillars are of stone carved with writhing dragons. In front of it stands the small square Apricot Altar, where Confucius is said to have taught his disciples. Slightly further to the south is the Kui Wen Ge, the library of the temple, which was built in 1018, repaired in 1191 and underwent considerable alterations in 1500.

The main railway from Shanghai to Beijing passes a little way to the west of Qufu. When it was built strong objections were made to this noisy, Western contrivance disturbing the sacred ground of Qufu, so it was diverted in a loop through the neighbouring town of Yanzhou. Visitors today must either leave the train at Yanzhou and drive into Qufu or make a longer drive from Ji'nan to the north, where there is an airport. **62, 204**

Shanghai   A big, bustling, dirty city which has recently begun to regain some of the cosmopolitan glamour of its pre-revolutionary days. It owes its importance to its location close to the mouth of the Yangtze as an international trading port with easy access to the interior of China. Before the days of large-scale foreign trade it was little more than a fishing village, but after it was opened to Western shipping as a result of the First Opium War it rapidly developed into a major city. It remains a largely 19th and early 20th-century metropolis, most of its centre still being dominated by Western-style buildings erected prior to 1937. The view of the Bund from the Huangpu River still looks much more like some great European or American port than somewhere in China. The vast new development going on across the river from the Bund, in modern international style, will not alter this impression.

But once you have walked along the Bund and perhaps taken a drink in the bar at the Peace (formerly Cathay) Hotel, with its jazz band, what is there to do in Shanghai? There is plenty of life to see here; the Nanjing Road with its shops full of all kinds of goods, crammed with shoppers (like Oxford Street before Christmas, but all year round); the shipping on the river; the bars at night and the parks during the day. The children's playground in People's Park (formerly the race-course) is worth seeing: Westerners usually find Chinese children delightfully cute (strangely, Chinese feel the same about Western kids!). On a Sunday, try looking for English corner in the Park; native speakers are rapidly surrounded by pressing crowds of those eager to practise their linguistic skills, from 10-year-olds to grey-headed old men who learnt their English in the days of the foreign concessions.

In the old Chinese city stands the Yu Yuan garden. Just outside it an ancient tea-house in the middle of a large square pool is reached by a zig-zag bridge (which prevents the passage of evil spirits, which can only travel in straight lines!). Many kinds of Chinese teas can be tasted here, drunk from traditional Chinese cups and tea-pots. If you can manage to squeeze in, it is a good place to take a short rest and refresh yourself. The garden itself, which originated in the Ming dynasty, is delightful, with its elaborate rock-work, waters full of large goldfish and carp, pavilions, trees and flowers. Look for the dragons along the tops of the garden walls. After viewing the garden, try not to get lost in the maze of streets outside. There are some interesting shops here, particularly those selling traditional Chinese medicines and handicrafts. Mixed with them are those selling more modern goods, such as jeans and other

Western-style clothes. This is a cheap place to stock up the wardrobe.

The gem of Shanghai for the historically-minded is the museum. Recently moved to a new building so that its displays could be enlarged, it has superb collections of ancient bronzes, pottery and paintings. It merits at least a full half-day's browsing.

The Jade Buddha Temple is not very old (late 19th century) but is worth seeing if only because there always seems to be something going on there. Monks chant almost continuously in some of the back rooms of the temple (though they do not like to be disturbed by crowds of tourists) and quite often there is some other service going on in one of the larger front halls. The smoke of incense drifts around the courtyards. The Jade Buddhas themselves (there are two) were brought from Burma in 1869 and moved to the present temple in 1918. On the southern edge of the city stands the Longhua Temple, an ancient foundation but now consisting mainly of late Qing buildings. The pagoda, however, is largely as built in 977, only the wooden galleries having been renewed more recently. It has a slight but noticeable tilt. **33, 152, 157, 158, 160, 162, 177, 183, 185, 201, 205, 211**

Shanhaiguan (Hebei) The Pass between the Mountains and the Sea is the eastern end of the Ming dynasty Great Wall. The Wall runs inland from the Lao Long Tou (Old Dragon's Head) on the shore to a walled city with an impressive east gate (the 'No. 1 Pass Under Heaven')

and then inland to the mountains. At the Jiaoshan hill it climbs steeply up the rocky slopes and runs away westwards across the Yanshan range. There is an interesting small museum in the town. Not far away are the port city of Qinhuangdao and the beach resort of Beidaihe. **138, 139**

Shaoshan (Hunan) A village famous as the birthplace of Mao Zedong. During the years when his personal cult was at its height, a special railway was built to carry the many thousands who came to see the house where he spent his youth. After the end of the Cultural Revolution the stream of visitors reduced to a trickle, but now quite large numbers are coming again as there has recently been something of a revival of the cult of Mao. Pictures of him are considered lucky and can often be seen hanging from the rear-view mirrors of cars. It is said that some people really think he was a god. Their reasoning is that he ordered the destruction of the old gods during the Cultural Revolution, when images were smashed and temples destroyed or put to secular use, yet he lived to a ripe old age. As he was therefore clearly more powerful than the old gods he must himself have been divine!

It is curious to visit Shaoshan now and see the stalls lining the road leading to his former home, with private traders competing to sell souvenirs. During his lifetime such capitalist enterprise was absolutely banned: 'capitalist roaders' suffered severely during the Cultural Revolution. China is full of such contradictions. Apart from the Mao family house there is also a fascinating museum filled with Maoist memorabilia, including a huge collection of Mao badges from all over China. Nearby is a villa in an attractive setting in the hills which was built at Mao's suggestion in 1960–2 and used by him when he visited Shaoshan.

Song Shan (Henan) The central sacred peak, between Luoyang and Zhengzhou; at its summit the mountain rises to about 4,600 feet. One of the oldest surviving pagodas in China, dating from AD 520, stands in the grounds of the Song Yue Temple at its foot. There are also Han dynasty gate towers, a Yuan dynasty observatory tower and a number of old temple buildings in the area. The famous Shao Lin Temple, where Chinese martial arts were developed, is in this area. The Zhong Yue Miao (Temple of the Central Sacred Peak) is a large complex of buildings mainly in Qing dynasty style. In front of it stand four cast iron statues dating from 1064. **92**

Suzhou (Jiangsu) An attractive town of waterways, gardens and pagodas, situated in the heart of the great rice-producing area of China and with a flourishing silk industry. Large parts of the centre of the town still preserve their ancient appearance. A good way to arrive is by boat along the Grand Canal; the most southerly section of this great waterway, first dug in AD 610, passes the west side of the town. There are several fine old gardens: one of the smallest but most attractive is the Wang Shi Yuan (Garden of the Master of the Nets). Both the Zhuo Zheng Yuan and the Liu

Yuan are much larger and are divided into several main sections. All of Suzhou's gardens are fine examples of traditional Chinese garden design, with large areas of water, elaborate and extensive use of curiously-shaped rocks (mostly water-worn limestone), winding paths and ornate buildings.

North-west of the town is Tiger Hill, on top of which stands a pagoda built in 961. Only its brick core remains, the wooden outer structures having been lost long ago. It has a distinct lean as a result of an earthquake 400 years ago. There is also a pair of brick pagodas in the town which were erected in the 980s. The North Temple Pagoda, not far from the railway station, is built mainly of wood but is in very good condition; it is essentially a Southern Song dynasty structure. Near the southwestern corner of the old town stands the Rui Guang Pagoda, another Southern Song building. Nearby is a surviving section of the old town wall, with a gate and a water-gate.

It is possible to visit silk-spinning factories in Suzhou to see how the cocoons are processed into silk thread. Silk embroidery of a very high standard of workmanship can also be seen. There are usually plenty of opportunities to buy silk cloth and garments as every factory and workshop has a sales department.

Tai Shan (Shandong) The eastern sacred peak and the most important of all holy mountains in China. At one time there were temples to the god of Tai Shan all over the country. It probably owes its national status to its strong association with Confucius as it stands close to his native town (see under *Qufu* above) and he is said to have personally ascended to its peak. Emperors used to come to make offerings to the god of the mountain and some even climbed to its peak. It is not a very high mountain, attaining only some 5,000 feet, but rises abruptly from the low North China Plain to much greater altitude than any nearby hills; it is particularly impressive when viewed from the south. All over the mountain are temples, pavilions and inscriptions carved in stone. There are also some fine old trees on the mountain, which supports an interesting, if not exceptionally rich, flora. It is now possible to drive about half-way up and then take a cable-car to the summit ridge. The ascent on foot involves climbing some extremely steep flights of stone steps, but for the fit it is worth making the effort at least to make the journey in one direction on foot, as there are things worth seeing along the path. For serious walkers with enough time there are a number of paths around the mountain in addition to the main routes.

The Dai Miao (Temple to the God of Tai Shan) in Tai'an at the foot of the mountain is a most impressive assemblage of ancient architecture. The main hall is truly magnificent: it was erected in 1009; on its inner walls is a large mural depicting the god of the mountain making a tour of inspection, which may date back to the Song dynasty. In the rear courtyard of the temple stand a bronze pavilion cast in 1615 and the lower three storeys of a cast-iron pagoda made in 1533. There are also several very ancient trees in the temple, some of which are said to be 2,000 years old.

Walking north from the temple a road leads directly to the main path up the mountain. Near the beginning of the path stand stone arches draped with vast old wisteria vines and the Hong Men (Red Gate), of uncertain date of foundation but known to have been rebuilt in 1626. The path passes a number of other buildings and shrines as it climbs through a forest of cypresses. At the end of a side path is a large inscription carved in the rock of a valley during the 6th century; it is the text of a Buddhist sutra. Shortly afterwards a fairly stiff climb leads to the Zhong Tian Men (Half-way Gate to Heaven), which can also be reached by road via a different route. Nearby is the lower end of the cableway. From this point the path becomes much steeper and in the heat of summer it is a great relief to reach the Nan Tian Men (South Gate to Heaven) which stands at a low point on the summit ridge. A short way further on stands the Bi Xia Ci (Azure Cloud Temple), a Daoist temple founded in about 1015 and enlarged during the Ming and Qing dynasties. Some of its halls are roofed with iron tiles. Another temple encloses the highest point of the mountain. The Chinese like to watch the sunrise from the summit, but at most times of year it is not exceptionally spectacular. **92**

Taiyuan (Shanxi) An ancient city, now heavily industrialized, it is the provincial capital. The site of most interest here is the Jin Ci (Jin Memorial Temple) to the south-west of the city. The main hall, the Sheng Mu Dian (Hall of the Holy Mother), though repaired during the Ming and Qing dynasties, remains largely as built in 1102. It contains more than 40 clay statues, all but two of which are original Song dynasty sculptures. To the right of this hall is an ancient cypress said to have survived from the Zhou dynasty. Close by are springs which are the main sources of the Jin River; a pool fed by one of them is spanned by a stone bridge originating from the Song dynasty. Four iron statues stand a short distance in front of this, beyond another old hall; the earliest of them was cast in 1089, two others just a few years later, though one needed a new head during the Ming dynasty. (The fourth is a replacement cast in 1913.) A number of other old buildings, several of them built in the Ming dynasty, make up the rest of this fine large complex of ancient architecture.

There are several old Buddhist temples in and around Taiyuan. Right in the city, close to the railway station, is the Chongshan Temple. Though much of it was rebuilt after a fire in 1864, a hall containing a fine statue of Guanyin with many arms survived. Both the hall and the statue date from early in the Ming dynasty. Nearby is the provincial museum, partly housed in an old Daoist temple. **172**

Tianjin A major communications centre serving as the port for Beijing. There is little of historical interest to see in the city itself, although it is worth looking at the Western-style buildings in the former concession areas. Tianjin suffered damage at the time of the Tangshan earthquake in 1976, the worst earthquake in China in recent times. **17, 20, 33, 59, 151, 157, 159, 160, 164, 169, 170, 172, 173, 187, 205**

Turpan (Xinjiang Uighur AR) An oasis settlement in the deserts of Xinjiang, Turpan is unusual in actually lying below sea level. The bottom of the Turpan Depression is in fact the second lowest point on the land surface of the earth, about 500 feet below sea level (only the Dead Sea is lower). In order to avoid a long descent into the basin and climb out of it, the railway which serves Turpan runs some distance to the north of the town.

The majority of the population are Turkic Uighurs. Their religion is Islam; one of the sights of Turpan is the 18th-century Imin Minaret at a mosque on the edge of the town. Before the expansion of Islam into Central Asia, however, this area was predominantly Buddhist, and there are remains of Buddhist cave-temples in the area. They are mostly in bad condition, as a result of being defaced by Muslims, who disapprove of representations of the human figure, and of removal of statues and murals by foreign archaeologists early this century. The Bezeklik Caves still have some murals worth seeing; they are situated in a valley near the Flaming Mountains, so called from their reddish colour and the fact that they shimmer as if burning in the heat-haze of summer. Turpan becomes extremely hot at this season, temperatures often rising above 40° C (104° F). There is scarcely ever any

rain here – it is said that if rain does fall it evaporates before it hits the ground! The existence of the settlement and the growing of crops to feed it are made possible by an ancient system of underground irrigation, drawing water from the streams which run down from the Tian Shan mountains to the north. This system, called *karez*, allows the cultivation of a variety of crops, including the grapes for which Turpan is famous. Most of the grapes are dried to become raisins; the drying houses are a common sight in the area, square or rectangular sheds or towers built with bricks laid with gaps between them. There is an interesting bazaar in the town of Turpan, though it scarcely rivals the one at Kashgar.

There are two ancient abandoned cities near modern Turpan – Jiaohe on the western edge of the town and Gaochang farther away to the east. Both faded in importance as a result of problems with water-supply and were finally destroyed in fighting in the 14th century. Near Gaochang are the Astana Tombs, a number of excavated burials where the bodies were preserved by desiccation. Most of the contents of the tombs have been removed to museums (principally in Urumqi), but murals and other things of interest remain. **11, 31, 99, 102**

Urumqi (Xinjiang Uighur AR) The regional capital of Xinjiang stands at an altitude of about 3,000 feet in a wide gap in the Tian Shan range. The great snow-capped peak of Mount Bogda towers above it a short way to the north-east: on clear days the mountain is easily visible from the northern side of the city. Urumqi itself is not very attractive, but it has a museum with some very interesting displays, both of artefacts associated with the local ethnic minorities and of finds from sites along the old Silk Road. There are also several mosques in the city.

The main attractions of Urumqi are outside the city proper, however. A couple of hours' drive to the north and east, across desert and semi-desert and through oasis settlements, leads to a short, stiff climb up a winding road into the mountains near Mount Bogda. At about 6,000 feet altitude the road ends near the Tian Chi (Heavenly Lake). In summer nomadic Kazakhs bring their flocks and herds up here to graze on the alpine pastures. There are also fine stands of spruce fir on the mountain slopes; in early summer the area is awash with flowers. There is accommodation near the lake and for those with enough time it is worth spending a few nights up here. Driving in the opposite direction from the city leads to another mountainous area. The Kazakhs also graze their camels, sheep, horses and cattle on the extensive pastures in the Nan Shan, but further on, in the Baiyanggou valley, the pasture gives way to forest and steep rocky slopes. The road ends at a waterfall. There is some fairly basic accommodation in this area and those who like walking in the mountains would enjoy spending some time here and exploring on foot. **227**

Wuhan (Hubei) A huge industrial conurbation on the Yangtze River in the centre of China. There is little to attract tourists to come here, except that the logistics of cruising through the Yangtze Gorges make it more or less impossible to avoid the city. It is, in fact, a good place to disembark from a river-boat after cruising downstream from Chongqing.

The one thing in Wuhan that is really outstanding, almost worth making a special visit to the city to see, is the Provincial Museum near the East Lake. The museum houses a display of artefacts from the tomb of Marquis Yi of Zeng. The marquis was buried in about 420 BC, during the Warring States period. There are some lovely pieces of lacquer-ware and a gold vessel which is the largest yet found dating from this period. The really outstanding objects are the bronzes, however. They include a set of 65 bells, one dated in an inscription to 433 BC. The museum has a replica set of bells which can be played for visitors – ingeniously, each bell can give two different notes, depending on where it is struck. One old temple still survives in Wuhan, the Guiyuan Buddhist Temple in the south-eastern section of the city. The buildings seen today are of late Qing date. One of its main attractions is a Hall of 500 Arhats. **33, 156, 176**

Wutai Shan (Shanxi) The northern holy Buddhist mountain is situated in the north of Shanxi province, some distance from any major city; access to the area is unfortunately not very convenient. This is one of the highest mountains in north China, rising to just over 10,000 feet. It has been a centre of Buddhism since the very earliest transmission of the religion to

China almost 2,000 years ago. Today more than 40 temples stand on and near the mountain. Among their buildings are the earliest surviving wooden halls in China: at the Nan Chan Temple stands a hall built in AD 782; a much larger Tang dynasty hall, built in 857, is among the buildings of the Fo Guang Temple. There are also many fine buildings from later periods, such as the hall dedicated to Manjusri (in Chinese, Wen Shu) at the Fo Guang Temple, built in 1137. For anyone with a serious interest in ancient Chinese architecture, the numerous old temple buildings on this mountain are a compelling attraction. There are also many fine old statues and other devotional art in the temples. At the Luo Hou Temple is an interesting mechanical lotus flower, which opens when turned to reveal carved images of Buddhas within. **92**

Wuxi (Jiangsu) Not very far from Suzhou, and with similar attractions to that town, though less old buildings survive here. One of the finest attractions is the Jichang Garden, one of the most famous old gardens in southern China. Its main area is taken up mainly by a large pool full of huge carp. Surrounded by rocks, trees and simple pavilions, this is one of the loveliest pieces of garden art still to be seen in China. The garden stands at the edge of the Xihui Park on the western side of the town, close to the Grand Canal.

Further to the south-west is the great Tai Hu lake, one of China's largest bodies of fresh water. Surrounded by hills and dotted with islands, it is a picturesque area enlivened by the activities of local fishermen.

Xiamen (Fujian) Formerly known as Amoy, this major port on China's south-east coast is today developing and modernizing very rapidly, and has been designated a Special Economic Zone. Its main area of interest is the island of Gulangyu, which was settled by foreign merchants during the late 19th and early 20th centuries, when the port was an important centre of the tea trade. Most of the buildings on the island are survivals from this time, in Western style. Playing the piano was popularized by the foreigners and music students still come here to study the instrument. A wander along the quiet old streets, devoid of vehicles, can be a very enjoyable and interesting experience. Here and there are restaurants, with bowls and tanks full of live delicacies: crabs, lobsters and a variety of shellfish. There are attractive parks and gardens and some lovely beaches (though the water in the harbour area does not look very clean). Huge old banyan trees overhang the streets and paths, long roots descending from the branches towards the ground.

South-east of the city stands the Nan Putuo Temple. Though most of its buildings appear to be quite recent, it is a very active centre of Buddhism with a long history. A restaurant attached to it serves famous vegetarian food. Behind the temple rises the Wulao Hill. If it is not too hot and humid, it is worth walking up to see the shrines among its rocks. There are fine views over Xiamen and its harbour from the hillside. **146, 152**

Xi'an (Shaanxi) This city must attract more Western tourists than any other in China, except perhaps Beijing, for it is here that the world-famous Terracotta Army can be seen. Xi'an was a major city when Beijing was just a small regional centre, and the area around it is full of major archaeological sites. In its vicinity stood the early Zhou dynasty capital cities and it continued to be used as the capital for a large part of the next 2,000 years. At the height of its glory under the Tang dynasty the city of Chang'an, as it was then called, covered a much larger area than modern Xi'an.

In 246 BC King Zheng became the ruler of the state of Qin in the north-west of China. Shortly afterwards, work began on the construction of his tomb. As the conqueror of all the other Chinese states of the period, the man who took the title of First Emperor wanted an exceptionally splendid burial. The Chinese records speak of a tomb chamber made in the image of the world as then known in China, with a vaulted ceiling encrusted with jewels to represent the stars and a floor with rivers and seas of mercury. The site of the tomb was known throughout later history, but whether its contents were really as described remained unknown. Even today the actual tomb chamber has still not been opened. But about 20 years ago peasants digging a well in a village about a mile from the tomb-mound stumbled upon some broken statues of fired clay. Subsequent excavations revealed a great army of warrior figures, parading in columns, guardians of the First Emperor after his death. This Terracotta Army is quite staggering in its scale and the

modelling of the soldiers. It was a startling discovery because there is no mention of such an army in the historical accounts of the tomb (no doubt it is only a minor part of the grave goods buried with the emperor), and also because no comparable sculptures of similar date have ever been found elsewhere in China. Since 1979, when the first pit containing the Army was opened to public view, the displays at the site have been expanded to include two other pits full of soldiers and two bronze chariots, less than life-size, that were discovered in a small excavation on the west side of the tomb-mound. There must be much more here still to be unearthed.

There is a new museum in Xi'an which has excellent displays of objects from the many sites in the area, from the Stone Age onwards. The old museum is in the former Confucian Temple in the city, which still houses the famous Forest of Stelae, a large collection of inscribed stone slabs dating from the Han to the Qing dynasties. The collection of stelae here began during the Song dynasty, so that this is one of the world's oldest museums. Among the most famous stone tablets are those inscribed with the complete texts of all the Confucian Classics, made during the Tang dynasty. Another museum on the eastern side of the city displays finds from the Neolithic village of Banpo, and part of the site, preserved as excavated. This was an extremely important excavation which provided very significant material relating to the Neolithic period in China, at a time

The Great Wild Goose pagoda in Xi'an, built during the Tang dynasty as a repository for Buddhist scriptures brought from India

when it was still very poorly known. The site was used over a very long period of about 2,000 years and therefore helped establish temporal relationships in the development of Neolithic artefacts in northern China.

The Ming dynasty city wall still survives and has been extensively renovated. It is the best city wall still to be seen in China, the great majority having been demolished during last century. The Bell and Drum Towers from the same period stand near the centre of the walled city. Not far from the Drum Tower is the Great Mosque, one of the largest in China. Its buildings are mainly in Chinese style, with decoration that shows strong Islamic influence.

There are two large pagodas built during the Tang dynasty in the city. The better-known is the Great Wild Goose Pagoda, originally built in the 7th century to house sutras brought back from India by the famous monk Xuan Zhuang. The Little Wild Goose Pagoda is very different in style and lacks part of its top because of damage by an earthquake in 1555.

In the hills to the south of Xi'an are several interesting old Buddhist temples, perhaps the most important being the Xing Jiao Si, where the tomb pagoda of Xuan Zhuang can be seen. North-west of the city are several royal tombs of the Han and Tang dynasties. Some have been excavated; as they are some distance from the city they are only visited by tourists who are able to stay for several days in Xi'an. When the road to the new airport was being built a large army of warrior figures was unearthed, associated with a tomb dating from the Han dynasty. At present these are not on display, but can be expected to be exhibited in the near future. Though they are smaller than life-size, they are said to be almost as spectacular as the Terracotta Army. 20, 41, 50, 51, 53, 54, 55, 70, 77, 78, 79, 96, 103, 136, 173, 184, 194, 221

Xigaze (Tibet AR) The second most important settlement in Tibet. The vast Trashilhunpo lamasery stands on the west side of the town. This is the seat of the Banqen Lama, second only in importance to the Dalai Lama in Tibetan Buddhism. The last incarnation of the Banqen died some years ago and his new incarnation has caused dispute. An imposing new building has recently been erected at the lamasery to house his funerary pagoda. Because the last Banqen Lama remained in China and co-operated with the Chinese Communist government, the Trashilhunpo was given favourable treatment and is clearly more prosperous than other lamaseries in Tibet. It was founded in 1447 but has been enlarged and rebuilt several times since then. One of its most notable treasures is a huge bronze statue of Buddha, almost 90 feet high. Some of the roofs of the most important halls are cov-

ered with gold. Two palaces for the Banqen stand on the edge of Xigaze but they are both of recent date. The older, the Gonqogling, dates partly from the early 19th century and is now a park.

About 14 miles away is another, much smaller, lamasery at Xalu, belonging to a different sect of Tibetan Buddhism from the Trashilhunpo and the major lamaseries at Lhasa. It was founded in 1087 and as now seen dates at least partly from 1333.

Xishuangbanna (Yunnan) In the far south-west of China, close to the borders with Burma and Laos, is a tropical area of cultivated valleys and forest-covered hills inhabited by some of the many minority peoples of Yunnan province. The chief town of the region is Jinghong on the banks of the Mekong River (called the Lancang Jiang in Chinese). Most people here belong to the Dai ethnic group, readily distinguishable from local Chinese by their dress and appearance. The women especially tend to stick to their traditional costumes of a long skirt held at the waist by a silver belt, a short tunic fastened at one side and very long hair wound into a bun on top of the head. Many traditional Dai houses stand around the edges of the town and there are also several small temples. The Dai are Hinayana Buddhists. The market is fascinating, all kinds of strange fruits and vegetables being on sale. Sometimes it attracts people of other minorities from outside the town, such as Jinuo and Hani.

Outside of Jinghong itself there is an increased possibility of coming across such people. There are also several pagodas in a style more Burmese than Chinese. The best of these is the White Pagoda near Damenglong. There is a tropical botanical garden south-east of Jinghong near Menglun. **224**

Yangtze Gorges (Hubei and Sichuan) The Three Gorges of the Yangtze River are situated in western Hubei and eastern Sichuan. Travel through them by boat usually takes about 3–5 days. Chongqing is usually the upriver end of the trip, the other being either Yichang or Wuhan. In addition to the scenery of the Gorges, there are a number of interesting places to stop along the route. In many ways it is more interesting to make the journey upstream, thus passing from the more accessible east of China westwards into Sichuan, but it is more comfortable to travel downstream, as the engines need to work less hard and so are quieter and cause less vibration. As a choice has to be made, this account will begin at the upstream end of the journey (with apologies to those going the other way).

After sailing from Chongqing, the landscape is at first only moderately hilly, with many villages and much cultivation along the banks. After just over 100 miles the boat reaches Fengdu on the north bank. Here on the slopes of a hill stands an extraordinary Buddhist temple commonly known as the Gui Cheng (City of Ghosts), where the torments of the Buddhist hell are graphically depicted in sculpture. From this point on the banks become increasingly hilly, rising to greater and greater heights. A little way beyond Fengdu and also on

the north bank is Shibaozhai, where an unusual storeyed building rises up the side of a rocky outcrop. Climbing the stairways inside this pagoda-like construction, which was built around the turn of the 19th century, leads to the flat top of the outcrop, where stands a small temple. The little town below, with its narrow streets and old wooden buildings, is very picturesque. Leaving Shibaozhai, the next major settlement, again on the north bank, is Wan Xian. Many boats stop here, though there is little to see except a small museum and a silk factory. After another 75 miles or so the first of the gorges proper is reached. Immediately before it is the town of Fengjie and a temple on top of a hill, called the Bai Di Cheng (City of the White Emperor). There are excellent views from the top of this hill along the Yangtze to the gorge and up a tributary which flows in from the north. This is the Qutang Gorge, the shortest of the Three Gorges but in many ways the most spectacular. Approaching it on the river only steep mountains can be seen. The boat is almost in the gorge before a way through becomes apparent. Sheer cliffs rise above the river, especially on the south bank. The old towpaths, once used by large teams of men who hauled junks upstream against the strong current with massive hawsers, can be seen cut into the cliffs. Square holes cut in the cliffs used to hold wooden beams on which plank walkways were fixed.

After the Qutang Gorge the boat soon arrives at Wushan, which is only just over 20 miles below Fengjie. At this point the Daning River, a sizeable tributary, flows into the Yangtze from the north. It has its own series of gorges, often called the Lesser Three Gorges, which can be visited in small river-boats with powerful engines (if the river is in spate it may become too dangerous to make this excursion). The scenery is in many ways more spectacular than that along the Yangtze itself, as the gorges are very narrow and extremely precipitous. The furthest one is especially beautiful as its sides are clothed with green bamboo and scrub, where monkeys can sometimes be seen. On the cliffs in these gorges, as well as those of the Qutang Gorge, remains of ancient cliff burials can be seen, with wooden coffins wedged into openings in the rock-face.

Leaving Wushan the boat passes into the Wu Gorges, where the Yangtze is compressed to a width of a hundred yards or less while mountains tower 3,000 feet above the water on both banks. There are twelve famous peaks here, each with its own name:

the Goddess Peak is the best known, with a column of rock near its summit shaped like a standing figure. After leaving the Wu Gorges the town of Badong is passed on the south bank and then Zigui on the north. On the hillside above Zigui stands a memorial temple to the famous poet of the Warring States period, Qu Yuan. Continuing downstream the Xiling Gorges are entered, the longest series of gorges with some of the loveliest scenery. The Huang Ling Temple is passed on the south bank. This principally commemorates the legendary emperor Yu the Great, who is supposed to have relieved a great flood by opening ways for the water to flow to the sea. Its main hall was built in 1618. Shortly after this the river widens considerably above the Gezhouba Dam at Yichang. The voyage may end here, or it is possible to sail on downriver to Wuhan, but below the dam the scenery is much less interesting, with only low hills or flat plains on either bank. **19, 110**

Index

Abahai 138

Agriculture 20, 23ff, 28f, 30, 31, 70, 81, 126, 140f, 195, 196, 207f, 209, 217, 221, 249f; crops 23ff, 28f, 30, 31, 38ff, 64, 84f, 121; emergence of 37f; Shang dynasty 49

Albazin 145

Altay Mountains 21, 22, 30

Altun Mountains 21, 30

Amur River 21, 138, 145, 160

An Lushan 106ff, 228

An Qing the Parthian 86

Annam 110, 116, 124, 131, 149, 163

Anti-Rightist Movement 190f, 216

Anyang 47, 48

Archaeology 35ff, 45ff, 79

Architecture 24, 26f, 82f, 116, 119

Art 82, 95, 116, 127, 128

Arrow War (Second Opium War) 159ff, 168, 237

Astronomy 135, 139

Atom bomb, Chinese 190

Autonomous Regions 205, 220ff

Ba, state 73

Bacson culture 38

Bactria 84, 99

Banner organization 137, 142

Baojia 116, 143, 208

Beijing 1, 6, 8, 17, 20, 54, 59, 110, 119f, 121, 125ff, 131ff, 135, 136, 138, 139, 148, 157, 159, 161, 164, 167, 172, 178, 187, 201, 204, 205, 206, 213, 218, 229, 240; foreign legations at 160, 161, 172f; health care 211; Man 36; occupation of (1860) 160, 168; occupation of (1900–1) 173; Russian mission at 145, 148; taken by Communists 187; University 191; warlord government in 180, 182

Bodhisattvas 87, 92, 214

Bohai, Gulf of 15, 16, 20, 32, 49, 164

Boxer uprising 171ff, 175

Britain 135, 149ff, 156, 158, 159ff, 164, 169, 176, 181, 186, 229f, 235ff, 247

Bronze Age 44f

Bronze vessels 48f; casting techniques 48; inscriptions on 52

Buddhism 86 ff, 91f, 95, 100, 103, 104, 105f, 114, 125, 214, 224; arrival in China 85f, 98; Hinayana 87, 224; Mahayana 87f; persecution of 86, 108f; Tibetan 125, 223, 226, 228f

Bureaucracy 70, 104, 111, 113f, 116, 123f, 141ff, 170, 205

Cai, state 60

Canals 17, 19f, 82, 97, 119, 143 *see also* Grand Canal

Cao, state 60

Central States 61, 75

Chang'an 20, 96, 97, 99, 101, 103, 105, 106, 107, 108, 109, 228

Changbai Shan 32
Chen, state 60
Chen Yi 242
Cheng, King 52, 54
Chengde (Jehol) 148, 160, 161, 168, 183
Chenghiz Khan 119ff, 124
Chiang Kai-shek 180, 182ff, 189, 236, 242, 243
China Proper 20, 27, 36, 37, 74, 104, 111, 127, 138, 154, 220; defined 10
Chinese Communist Party 182ff, 188, 191ff, 204f, 206f, 216, 244, 246f, 250
Chinese language 4ff, 75, 77, 251ff; classical 181, 251; dialects 6, 8, 50, 201f, 251f; learnt by Europeans 135, 148
Chinese names 8; Imperial 132
Chinese script 5, 52, 75, 77, 251ff; early 42; transliteration of 5ff
Chinoiserie 1f
Chongqing 184
Christianity 125, 135, 155, 156, 170, 171ff, 214; Nestorian 108, 125
Chu, state: (Zhou dynasty) 59, 60, 65, 68f, 72f, 74, 75, 83, 93; (Ten Kingdoms) 110
Ci An, Empress Dowager 168
Ci Xi, Empress Dowager 167ff, 171, 174
Civil War 187, 239
Climate 22ff
Clinton, President 199
Coal 32, 113, 116, 191, 248
Communes 188f, 191, 192
Confucianism 63, 66f, 71, 80f, 87, 90f, 104, 114, 119, 125, 156, 158, 170, 214
Confucius 1, 61ff, 65, 66f, 80, 89f, 167
Crossbow 78, 98
Cultural Revolution 36, 193f, 206, 214, 216, 232, 233, 245
Customs, Imperial Maritime 162

Dadu 125
Dai ethnic minority 224

Dalai Lama 228, 229, 230, 232
Dalian 165
Dao De Jing 68, 69
Daoism 67ff, 81, 85, 87, 88f, 91, 125, 214
Datong 95
Demonstrations 196; in Beijing (1989) 198f, 236, 246, 247f; in Lhasa 232; of 4 May (1919) 181
Deng Xiaoping 192, 193, 194, 196, 198f, 235, 236, 244, 245f
Documents, early historical 45f
Dongting, Lake 15, 19, 110
Dorgon 139
Dunhuang 95, 99
Dutch 135, 241

East India Company 146, 147, 150f
Economy 93, 150, 189, 190, 191f, 199f, 208, 215, 219, 242, 247; development of 116, 118, 197, 199, 247, 248ff; decline of 136; Hong Kong 236, 247f; reform of 167, 194, 196
Education 82, 114, 166, 167, 199, 215f, 228, 242
Electrical power 32f, 191, 242, 248
Embassies to China: British (Amherst embassy) 148; British (Macartney embassy) 20, 148; Portuguese 134
Emei Shan (Mt. Emei) 92
Encirclement campaigns 183
Eunuchs 106, 132f, 136
Ever-victorious Army 157, 161
Everest, Mt. 11
Ewenki ethnic minority 223
Examinations 81, 104, 111, 114, 124, 127, 134, 154, 167, 216

Ferghana 84, 99
Festivals 216ff
First World War 181, 239
Flying Tigers 185
Four modernizations 194, 244
France 157, 159ff, 163, 164, 165, 170, 176, 181

Funerals 212f
Fuzhou 152

Gang of Four 196, 214, 218, 235, 244f, 246
Gansu Corridor 83, 84, 99, 102, 108
Germany 165, 171, 172, 173, 181, 183, 185, 187
Gobi Desert 23, 83, 101, 103
Gong, Prince 161, 163
Gongga Shan 14
Gongshu Pan 65
Gordon, Charles 157, 161
Grand Canal 17, 20, 97, 126f
Great Hinggan Mountains 30, 32
Great Leap Forward 191f
Great Wall 77f, 79, 83, 84, 93, 94, 97, 101, 103, 128, 129f, 138, 183
Guangxu Emperor 168f
Guangzhou 15, 20, 33, 134, 162, 175, 237, 239; attacked by British 152, 159; Bay 165; burned by Muslims 100; defence of 162; Nationalist capital 180; seized by rebels109; Western trade at 134, 146f, 148, 150ff, 159
Guanyin 86f, 214
Gunpowder 99, 114, 116f, 123
Guomindang *see* Nationalist Party

Hami 100, 102
Han Chinese 9f, 24, 27, 121, 204, 220, 221, 223, 228, 232, 233; attitudes to minorities 225, 233f
Han: dynasty 34, 80ff, 92f, 96, 98, 100, 101, 110, 226; Southern, state 110; state 71, 73, 74; Wu Di 84
Han Fei Zi 71
Hangzhou 19, 97, 100, 118, 119, 127; Bay 38, 39
Harness 98
Hart, Robert 162
He Shen 149
Health care 211f, 227
Heavenly Kingdom of Great Peace 154, 156, 158, 160

Heavenly Peace, Gate of *see* Tianan men
Hemudu 38ff
Heng Shan 92
Hezhe ethnic minority 223
Himalaya 11, 14, 21
Hong Kong 152, 159, 160, 165, 176, 196, 235ff, 247f
Hong Xiuquan 156ff
Hongwu Emperor 132
Hu Yaobang 198, 246
Hua Guofeng 245
Hua Shan 92
Huai Nan Zi 88
Huai: Army 157; River 14, 17f, 19, 20, 23, 39, 46, 97, 118, 127, 136
Huang Chao 109
Hui: ethnic minority 221; King 66
Hunan Army 157
Hundred Days of Reform 167ff
Hundred Flowers campaign 190
Huns (Xiongnu) 83f, 94, 98

Ili: region 163; River 22
Industry 33, 116, 162f, 164, 191f, 194, 196, 242, 249f
Iron 116, 163, 191f; cast 98; first use of 64
Islam 100, 125, 158, 172, 214, 221, 222, 233

Japan 103, 135, 136, 163ff, 167, 173, 179, 180f, 184ff, 194, 216, 225, 238, 239, 242, 243; defeats Russia 174; occupies Manchuria 183, 232; Sun Yat-sen in 176, 179; surrender of (1945) 187, 189
Jehol *see* Chengde
Jesuits 135f, 138, 139, 145, 160
Ji'nan 15, 16, 138, 207, 214, 219
Jiang Qing 193, 196, 245
Jiang Zemin 200
Jin: dynasty 94, 117ff, 121, 137, 138; Later, dynasty 110; Marquis of 59; state (Zhou dynasty) 59f; Western, dynasty 86

Jiuhua Shan 92
Journey to the West 103
Junggarian Basin 21, 22
Jurched 117f, 137

Kaifeng 109, 113, 117, 118, 120
Kang Youwei 167, 169, 170
Kangxi Emperor 140, 141, 144, 146
Karakorum 125, 129
Kashgar 99, 100, 130, 160
Kazakhs 221, 232
Ketou (kowtow) 148
Ketteler, Baron von 172
Khitan 103, 110ff, 114f, 116, 117,121f, 129
Khrushchev 192
Khubilai Khan 1, 20, 122, 124ff, 223, 228
Kirgiz 108, 221, 232
Korea 97, 102f, 113, 124, 136, 138, 163f, 181, 225
Korean War 2, 189f, 242f
Koreans 223, 225
Kowloon 160, 196, 235, 237, 238
Kunlun Mountains 21, 30
Kunming 185, 211

Lanzhou 15, 83
Lao Zi 68
Law courts 142
League of Nations 183
Legalism 69ff, 78, 80
Lhasa 226, 229, 230
Li ethnic minority 223
Li Guangli 84
Li Hongzhang 157, 158, 161, 162, 163, 165, 168
Li Shimin 104
Li Si 71, 73, 78
Li Zicheng 136f, 139
Liang, state 66
Liao: dynasty 110, 114, 117, 122; River 20, 145
Liaodong peninsula 32, 59, 164f, 181
Liberated areas 187
Lin Biao 193, 194
Lin Zexu 151, 152, 162

Liu Bang 79ff, 83
Liu Shaoqi 192, 193, 246
Liu Ying 85
Liuqiu Islands *see* Ryukyu Islands
Loess 15, 40
Long March 183, 191, 194
Longshan: culture 38ff; site 40, 42
Lop Nor 99
Loulan 99
Lü Buwei 72, 73
Lu Jia 80
Lu, state 60, 62, 63, 66
Lu Xun 5
Lun Yu 63
Luoyang 53, 54, 86, 96, 97, 105, 107, 109, 110
Lushan Conference 192

Macao 20, 135
Macartney, Lord 3, 20, 148, 149
Magnetic compass 98, 116f
Manchuria 10, 21, 26, 27, 110, 117, 129, 137ff, 142, 143, 184; climate 11, 31f; definition of 9; industries 33; Japanese influence in 33, 165, 181, 182; Japanese puppet state 183, 232; occupied by USSR 187, 189; river systems 20f; Russian influence in 165; taken by Chinese Communists 187
Manchus 137ff, 223, 226, 229, 230
Mao Zedong 183, 187, 189, 190f, 204, 207, 216, 235, 245, 246
May Fourth Movement 181
Mencius 66f
Miao ethnic minority 224, 233
Middle Kingdom 61
Min, state 110
Ming: dynasty 128ff, 138, 139, 140, 146, 163, 175, 229, 241; Tombs 133, 213
Missionaries 2, 86, 87, 125, 135, 145, 158, 160, 166, 170ff; attacks on 159, 165, 170ff, 230; Protestant 155, 156
Mo Zi 64ff, 67

Money 64, 75, 116; paper 116, 119; standardization of 77
Mongol conquests 103, 119ff, 228
Mongolian (People's) Republic 21, 188, 225, 226, 231, 232f; origins 182
Mongoloid race 36f
Mongols 119ff, 129f, 133, 135, 136, 137, 138, 139, 143, 144, 221, 222f, 229, 232f, 241
Mountains, sacred 92
Mukden *see* Shenyang
Muslims *see* Islam

Nanjing 114, 118, 128f, 131, 132, 136, 152, 158, 162, 213, 242; capital of Republic 177, 180, 182f; capital of Taiping rebels 154, 156; retaken by Qing forces 157
Nanzhao 103, 110, 124
Nationalist Party (Guomindang) 179, 182, 188, 194
Neolithic period 37ff
New Territories 165, 235, 238
Nian rebellion 158
Ningbo 146, 147, 152
Nixon, President 194, 244
Nomads 55, 73, 77, 121, 130, 221
North China Plain 15, 17, 24
Nurhaci 137f

Oilfields 32, 248
Opium 150ff; War 151ff, 159, 161, 237; War, Second *see Arrow* War
Oracle bones 46, 49, 50, 52
Ordos 15, 77
Oroqen ethnic minority 223

Pamirs 21, 99, 102
Paper 98, 117
Pearl Harbor 186
Pearl River 15, 20, 146
Peng Dehuai 192f
Penghu Islands 241, 242
People's Liberation Army *see* Red Army, Chinese

People's Republic of China 2, 6, 27, 30, 204ff, 215, 220, 227f, 235, 243f, 245ff; foundation of 33, 187, 194, 217
Pigtails 139, 156, 230
Ping: King 55; Southern, state 110, 112
Pinyin 6ff
Polo, Marco 1, 100, 117, 119, 124, 126
Population 33, 117, 141, 249; control 208, 209f, 233, 250
Port Arthur 165, 189
Portuguese 134f, 145f, 150
Pottery 127: exports 100, 147; Neolithic 38ff
Poyang, Lake 15, 19
Prehistory 34ff
Printing 98, 110, 116f
Putuo Shan 92
Puyi 174, 180, 183

Qaidam Depression 30
Qara-Khitai 117
Qi, state 59f, 61, 74
Qianlong Emperor 144, 148, 149, 150
Qilian Mountains 30, 83
Qin: dynasty 34, 70ff, 80, 81, 83, 97; Shi Huangdi 74, 75, 78f; state 55, 59f, 93
Qing dynasty 138ff, 223, 229, 230, 235, 238, 241
Qingdao 165, 171, 181
Qinghai Lake 29
Qinghai-Tibet plateau 14, 18f, 27, 83, 99, 102; climate 29f
Qinling Mountains 14, 23
Qufu 62, 204

Railways 163, 176, 217f; destroyed by Boxers 172; Trans-Siberian 165
Red: Army, Chinese (People's Liberation Army) 183, 187; Guards 193, 194; River 27

Religion 63, 108, 156, 210, 213f;
     primitive Chinese 89ff, 214; Shang
     dynasty 47 *see also* Buddhism,
     Christianity, Confucianism,
     Daoism, Islam
Republic of China 176ff, 236
Republican movement 175f
Revive China Society 175
Ricci, Matteo 135
Russia 1, 21, 135, 145, 148, 156, 159,
     160, 163, 165, 182, 229; influence
     in Mongolia 188, 226; influence in
     Xinjiang 226f; October
     Revolution 181, 222; relations
     with Japan 174 *see also* USSR
Russian ethnic minority 222
Russo-Japanese War 174, 180f
Ryukyu (Liuqiu) Islands 163, 181,
     225

Salar ethnic minority 221
Sea voyages 100, 126, 130f, 133
Second World War 184, 239, 242,
     243
Self-strengthening 162f, 164, 166
Shang dynasty 34, 45ff, 51, 75;
     overthrown by Zhou 51, 58;
     religious beliefs 46f, 49,
     53
Shang Yang 70f
Shanghai 1, 33, 152, 157, 158, 160,
     162, 177, 183, 185, 201, 205,
     211
Shanhaiguan 138, 139
Shao, Duke of 54
She ethnic minority 81, 223
Shen Nong 44
Shenzhen 196f, 238
Shenyang (Mukden) 33, 137f, 139,
     210
Shu: region 81f; state (Zhou dynasty)
     73; state (Ten Kingdoms) 110,
     112; state (Three Kingdoms) 93f
Shun, mythical ruler 45
Shunzhi Emperor 139f
Sichuan Basin 14, 19, 73, 93, 112, 201

Silk 122, 127, 146; exports 84, 100,
     108, 147; industry 98; production
     24, 26; Road 83, 84, 85, 98ff, 102
Sino-Japanese War: (1894–5) 163ff,
     167, 169, 170, 175, 180, 238, 241f;
     (1937–45) 184ff, 239, 243
Society of Worshippers of God 156
Song: dynasty 111ff, 128, 228, 241;
     Shan 92; state 60, 65
Soviet Union *see* USSR
Spain 135, 146, 185, 241
Special Economic Zones 196
Spring and Autumn period 57, 58ff
Stirrup 98
Sui dynasty 91, 95ff
Sun Yat-sen (Song Zhongshan) 175ff,
     182, 248
Sungari River 21, 145

Tai Shan (Mt. Tai) 92
Taiping rebellion 147, 154ff, 160,
     162, 175, 188
Taiwan 235–6, 240ff
Taiyuan 172
Tajik ethnic minority 222
Taklimakan Desert 11, 22
Talas River, Battle of 100, 103
Tang dynasty 20, 91f, 97ff, 133, 221,
     228; Southern 110, 112f
Tanguts 114
Tarim: Basin 11, 21, 22, 84, 99, 100,
     103; River 22
Taxation 77, 106, 109, 115, 118, 122,
     123f, 136, 137, 141, 143f
Tea 3, 26, 83, 146, 147
Terracotta Army 79
Tian Shan Mountains 21, 22, 30, 99
Tianan Men (Gate of Heavenly
     Peace) 181, 187; Square 196, 198f,
     216, 236, 240
Tianjin 17, 20, 33, 59, 151, 157, 159,
     160, 164, 169, 170, 172, 173, 187, 205
Tibetans 50, 100, 102, 103, 107, 108,
     109, 114, 124, 143, 182, 188, 220,
     221, 224, 225, 226, 228ff, 233f
Timur Leng 130

Tokharians 84
Tongzhi Emperor 168
Trade 1, 3, 64, 77, 83, 84, 98ff, 108, 109, 113, 116, 118, 123, 134f, 145ff, 148, 150, 196, 199, 243; balance 101, 147, 150; routes across Central Asia 72, 84; sea routes 84, 100
Treaties 159, 170; Convention of Beijing 237; Convention of Chuanbi 237; of Nanjing 2, 152, 237; of Nerchinsk 145; of Shimonoseki 164; of Tianjin 2; with USSR 189
Tujia ethnic minority 81
Turks 97, 101, 103, 108, 109, 130, 221
Turpan 99, 102; Depression 11, 31
Tuyuhun 102
Twenty-one Demands 179, 181

Uighurs 9, 107f, 221
Ulaan Baatar 160
United Front 184, 185
United Nations 2, 190, 194, 243, 244
Urumqi 227
USA 2, 11, 158, 159, 165, 185, 186, 187, 189f, 194, 243f; Chinese students in 163, 216; Sun Yat-sen in 176
USSR 189f, 192f, 197, 226, 233; declares war on Japan 187
Ussuri River 21, 160
Uzbeks 221

Versailles Conference 181, 239

Wang Anshi 115f
Wang Jingwei 185
Wang Mang 92, 93
Ward, Frederick 157
Warring States period 57, 69, 72ff, 75, 93
Wei: Northern, dynasty 86, 95; River 16, 17, 37, 40, 46, 50, 54, 97; state (Zhou dynasty) 60, 70f, 73, 74, 90; state (Three Kingdoms) 93f

Weights and measures 75, 143; standardised 77
Weihaiwei 165
Wen, King 51
West River 20; tributaries of 27
Wheelbarrow 98
White Lotus Sect 149
Women, status of 210f
Wu 91
Wu: Empress 104f; King 51, 52; state (Zhou dynasty) 60; state (Three Kingdoms) 93f
Wu Sangui 139
Wuhan 33, 156, 176
Wutai Shan 92
Wuyue, state 110

Xi Xia 114f, 116, 119, 124
Xi'an 20, 41, 50, 51, 53, 54, 55, 77, 96, 103, 136, 173, 184, 221; incident 184, 194
Xia dynasty 34, 45f, 48, 49
Xiamen 146, 152
Xianbi 94
Xianfeng Emperor 160, 168
Xianyang 77
Xin dynasty 92
Xiongnu *see* Huns
Xuan Zhuang 103
Xuan Zong 105ff
Xuantong Emperor 174
Xun Zi 71, 90

Yan: Prince of 131f; state 54, 59, 73, 74
Yan'an 183, 184, 185
Yang Guifei 106f
Yang Zhu 67
Yangshao: culture 40ff; site 41
Yangtze Gorges 19, 110
Yangtze River 14f, 17, 18f, 20, 26, 37, 39, 54, 57, 60, 73, 81, 83, 93, 96, 110, 112f, 118, 127, 128, 136, 147, 152, 154, 156, 157, 163, 183; crossed by Communists (1949) 187; names of 19; tributaries of 27

Yangzhou 97
Yao: mythical ruler 45; ethnic
    minority 224
Yarlung Zangbo River 21
Yehe Nara *see* Ci Xi
Yelü Chucai 122
Yellow Emperor 45
Yellow River 14, 15ff, 20, 31, 37, 40,
    46, 54, 77, 83, 93, 97, 109, 118,
    158; brides of 90, 91; changes of
    course 17, 119, 171; delta 16, 32;
    floods 15, 17f, 119, 128, 171
Yi ethnic minority 224
Yi He Yuan (Summer Palace) 169
Yihe quan 171
Yongle Emperor 132f
Yongzheng Emperor 144
You, King 55
Yu the Great 45
Yuan dynasty 127f, 137, 223
Yuan Ming Yuan 160
Yuan Shikai 169, 171, 178f, 181
Yue 38, 39, 220
Yuezhi 83f
Yugur ethnic minority 221
Yungang caves 95
Yunnan-Guizhou plateau 14, 20;
    climate 27ff
Yuntaishan 146
Yuxian 171ff

Zeng Guofan 157, 158
Zhang Qian 84

Zhangzhou 146
Zhao, state 73, 74
Zhao Erfeng 230
Zhao Gao 78
Zhao Shuli 210
Zhao Ziyang 246
Zheng: King 73, 74; state 60
Zheng Chenggong 241
Zheng He 132f
Zhengzhou, archaeology 47
Zhi Chan the Yuezhi 86
Zhong Yuan (Central Plains) 50;
    Neolithic culture 40, 42ff
Zhongdu 121, 125
Zhou, Duke of 52f, 54
Zhou dynasty 45, 50ff, 75, 89, 96;
    area of control 54; destruction of
    57; Eastern 57ff, 59, 80;
    government system 51f, 58f; royal
    domain 51, 55, 60, 73; Western
    57, 58, 59
Zhou Enlai 184, 190, 194f, 244,
    246
Zhu De 183
Zhu Xi 119
Zhu Yuanzhang 128f
Zhuang ethnic minority 220
Zhuang Zhou (Zhuang Zi) 68, 88
Zhuang Zi 68f, 88
Zhu Shuofo the Indian 86
Zongli Yamen 161f
Zou, state 66
Zunyi conference 191